Fast Boats
and Flying Boats
A Biography of Hubert Scott-Paine

Fast Boats

A N D

Flying Boats

A biography of Hubert Scott-Paine
Solent Marine and Aviation Pioneer

ADRIAN RANCE

Published by Ensign Publications
2 Redcar Street
Southampton SO1 5LL
England U.K.

in association with Southampton City Museums
Devised by David Graves
Edited by Michael Burns

British Library Cataloguing in Publication Data
Rance, Adrian
Fast boats and flying boats,
1. Aeronautical engineering. Scott – Paine,
Hubert, 1891–1954
I. Title
629.13′0092′4

ISBN 1–85455–026–8

Half-title page:
Hubert Scott-Paine photographed in 1937

Contents

Acknowledgements

In 1979, I was Curator in charge of the Maritime Museum, Southampton, when Miss Jenny Lane of Southampton arranged for a number of ship models to be donated to the Museum by John Scott-Paine of Greenwich, Connecticut. The models were of craft designed by Hubert Scott-Paine and built by the British Power Boat Company. They were brought to Southampton from Greenwich via New York on the *Queen Elizabeth 2*, courtsey of Captain D. Ridley. I would like to acknowledge my indebtedness to Jenny Lane who introduced me to the story of Hubert Scott-Paine and who arranged for me to meet Bill Sheaff who had been chauffeur to Scott-Paine and who had corresponded with him between 1939 and his death in 1954. Bill Sheaff died a few months after I met him but he set me on a trial of enquiry which has lasted ten years, during which many individuals have helped me to reconstruct the remarkable story of Hubert Scott-Paine. I would like to acknowledge the help that they have given me and to thank them for their interest, time and courteous consideration of my often ill-informed enquiries.

Members of the Scott-Paine family have given me invaluable help and encouragement, including John Scott-Paine who spoke to me over three days when I visited Canada in 1981, Mrs Rosanne Wells (née Scott-Paine), Mrs Elizabeth Ridgway (née Scott-Paine) and Mr Russell Ridgway, and Mrs Joyce Zissu (née Scott-Paine). Joyce Zissu and her husband Leonard afforded me the hospitality of their home at Ancramdale, New York State, and gave me free access to the extensive collection of family papers in their possession. I would like thank all the members of the family that I have met or corresponded with over the last few years.

Most of the documentary archive of the British Power Boat Company was destroyed in 1945, but several individuals have kept documents and archives which have been made available to me. The main collection is that kept at Ancramdale. In addition, Richard Barker, son of Stuart Barker, General Manager of the British Power Boat Company and godson of Hubert Scott-Paine, has made available the correspondence between his father and Scott-Paine between 1939 and 1945. Mrs Edna Stowell has given me access to the papers of her father, Bill Sheaff, and I would also like to thank, Mr Alf Palmer, Mr Graham Cooksey, Mr W. Bundy and the late Kenneth St John Beaumont who showed me papers and collections of photographs in their ownership.

I have made tape-recorded interviews with several ex-employees of Scott-Paine, including George Selman, Chief Naval Architect to the British Power Boat Company from 1936 to 1945, who designed the most successful air sea rescue craft and motor gun boats of World War Two and who was largely responsible for the design that formed the basis of the American PT Boat. I would like to thank him and the following who talked to me about their time with Scott-Paine: Len Parfitt, Edward Carmen, Harry Banks, Bill Wilson, 'Nanny' White, George Hall, Graham Cooksey, Len Cox, Vic Stride and Kenneth St John Beaumont.

During the course of my research I have corresponded with many whose knowledge had been put at my disposal in a most generous manner. I would like to make particular mention of Geoffrey Hudson whose extensive knowledge of the coastal craft of World War Two has made it possible to reconstruct details of craft produced by Scott-Paine at Hythe and in Canada. His help, which has entailed considerable correspondence, has been invaluable and has made possible the appendices at the end of this book. The Supermarine section of this book has likewise been considerably improved through the help of Philip Jarrett who has made a special study of Noel Pemberton Billing.

I would also like to thank all of the following whose help has likewise been invaluable: Mr D. Anderson, Peter R. Ayling, John Bagley, Harry Banks, the late Kenneth St John Beaumont, Mr G. Blay, Mrs P.A. Brazier, Prof. W. Brice, Mr W. Bundy, Mr Ted Carmen, Mr Childs, Mr J. Crammer, Mr David Cobb, Mr John Coleman, Mrs J. Cooper, Mr Len Cox, Mr Kevin Desmond, Dr A.P. McGowan, Mr Peter Dewrance, Captain Peter Dickens DSO, MBE, DSC, Mr Maldwin Drummond, Cdr Christopher Dryer, Mr W.D. Ewell, Mr and Mrs Forrester, Mr John Frost, Mr C.W. Gardner, the late Mr Jack Garside, E.W.H. Gifford, Mr George Hall, Mr Harris, Mr John de la Haye, Mrs Hampton, C.W. Headland, Mr A.S. Heal, Mr High, the late Mr Reg Holley, Mr R.E. Howes, Mrs C. Hichens, Mr Trevor Hughes, Mr Ron Forrest, Cdr D.E.J. Hunt DSC, Mr Ken Hunter, Mr David Glenn, Mr Jack Garside. Mr R.G. Kemp, Mr. John Lambert, Mr C. Matheson, Mr A.F. MacLeary, Mr Peter Magnus, DSC, VRD, Sqn Ldr R.J.M. Manson, Mr Peter Madsen, Mr M.A. Marsden, Mr E.B. Morgan, Mr Leonard Munn, Mr Grahame Nicholls, Mr J.M. Newberry, Mr Alf Palmer, Mr Leonard Parfitt, Mr Kieren Phelan, Mr John Price DSC, Mr John Pritchard, Mr T. Quelch, Mr J. Read, Mr M. Richardson, Mrs H.P. Scott, Mr Al Ross II, Mr A.W. Rowell, Mr Philip Simons, Mr John Smale, Mr L.R. Smith, Mrs G.D. Smith, Mr Vic Stride, Mr G. Taylor, the late Cdr Peter Thornycroft, Mr G. Thomas, Mrs Gordon Thomas, Mr Derek Thomas, Mr Jeremy Wilson, Mr Bill Wilson, Col. G.H. Wotton, Mr A.O. Van Raalte and Mr J.S. Young.

In conclusion, I would like to thank my colleagues at the Southampton City Museums for their patient help over the years of this project, particularly Nigel Overton and Simone Clark whose knowledge of the Maritime Museum and its collections is extensive, and Mrs Jill Neale who has indefatigably tracked down past employees of the British Power Boat Company, has transcribed the many hours of tape recording, and who has been a constant source of encouragement.

CHAPTER 1
How Many? How Much?

Many years of patient endeavour were about to come to fruition as Hubert Scott-Paine climbed the steps of the White House. It was Tuesday, October 3rd, 1939, and he had been invited to meet the President of the United States of America, Franklin D. Roosevelt. The invitation had been made by Charles Edison, Acting Secretary of the United States Navy, for Scott-Paine was the inventor of a unique warship that the Navy Department wished to add to the arsenal of weapons with which to fight the war in the Pacific that it was sure would be forced upon the United States. The outcome of the meeting was to be of considerable significance to America in a war that most peace-loving people thought would never happen.

The powerful personality of the famous British boat designer, who had travelled to America on a secret mission for the Third Sea Lord of the British Admiralty, dominated the meeting in the White House. President Roosevelt faced Scott-Paine across the room, and welcomed the Englishman with a warm enthusiasm. Senior members of the Navy Staff were there, together with representatives of one of America's most famous ship building companies, the Electric Boat Company. Those present included Henry Sutphen, President of Elco, Irwin Chase, the company's Chief Designer and Harry Spier, Vice-President of the Elco Submarine Company.

The meeting had been called to authorise the development of an entirely new arm of the United States Navy, the PT Boat Squadrons. Roosevelt had taken a personal interest in the development of fast, torpedo carrying motor boats for some time, and the previous year he had been given authority by Congress to spend fifteen million dollars at his own discretion on the construction of experimental craft. Five million dollars of this allocation remained unspent, and Charles Edison had told the President that this should be committed to the construction of

twenty-three boats of an outstanding design developed by the Englishman, Hubert Scott-Paine. In March of that year, Roosevelt had personally authorised Elco to purchase one of Scott-Paine's revolutionary boats, following a visit to England by Henry Sutphen and Irwin Chase in February 1939 to look at various developments of motor torpedo boats. Sutphen and Chase had seen a new 70 ft boat designed and built by Scott-Paine. They were soon convinced that this was better than anything that had been built either in Europe or America. Within weeks, construction had started on a boat ordered by Henry Sutphen at Scott-Paine's yard at Hythe, near Southampton. The work had continued at a record-breaking pace amidst the greatest secrecy during the summer months of 1939, as war clouds gathered over Europe. Early in September, Edison had been able to report to the President that the boat, by then designated PT (Patrol Torpedo) 9, had been shipped across the Atlantic just four days before the fateful German invasion of Poland.

The conference at the White House rapidly approved Charles Edison's plans and, despite the anticipated outcry from American boat builders, it was decided that the first PT Boat Squadrons were to be equipped with Scott-Paine designed torpedo boats. The President scribbled on the margin of the Secretary of the Navy's letter the words 'How Many? How Much?'. At that moment the American PT boat was born, and it was Scott-Paine boats that were to achieve immortality in countless dramatic actions in all theatres of war, particularly in the Pacific war against the Japanese.[1]

Scott-Paine was well known to the American public as the 'Red Fox of Hythe'. A reference to his red hair, he had acquired this name during his brilliant and skilful challenge for the Harmsworth International Motor Boat Trophy in 1933. The American hero, Gar Wood, the 'Grey Fox of Algonac', had retained the trophy but Scott-Paine was still widely remembered as a brilliant motor boat designer and racer. He was forty-nine years old when he boarded the liner *Aquitania* on the outbreak of World War Two on his mission that was to be of such importance to the Allies on both sides of the Atlantic. He carried with him a considerable personal fortune that he pledged to the cause of defeating the Nazi enemy, a fortune made in a career dedicated to the pursuit of speed in the air and on water.

Scott-Paine was no newcomer to such risks: he had risked all he had built up on previous occasions during his long campaign to persuade conservative naval authorities on each side of the Atlantic to adopt the motor torpedo boat, which he had designed and developed at his own expense. The British Admiralty had reluctantly accepted the motor torpedo boat at the insistence of the far-sighted Third Sea Lord, Sir Reginald Henderson, but the 'establishment's' lack of foresight subsequently failed to ensure a source of supply for the high-powered engines to drive the new mosquitoes of the British Navy. Scott-Paine's mission for the Third Sea Lord was to establish a source of supply for the engines that were necessary to power the motor torpedo boats, the motor gun boats and the air sea rescue boats that were to be needed in the narrow seas around the British Isles.

In August of the previous year the British Magazine *Courier* had described Scott-Paine as:

Icarus, with a mechanical basis. He threw himself, body and soul, into the science of pure speed . . . he is the rarest of all men, the thinking man of action. He wanted to ride on a rocket so he made one. Then, with the object of revolutionary war at sea, he evolved a new weapon; the Power Boat. He is a great man; a master of men and money who used both to achieve a definite end; who guarded his men, and flung his money to the wash and the winds behind his racing engines— technician, man of thought, innovator, destined to the generations yet unborn.[2]

Hubert Scott-Paine was born at Shoreham, on the south coast of England on March 11th, 1890 to Henry Paine and Rosannah née Scott who owned a successful ironmongery and ship chandlery business in the port. Henry Paine died when Hubert was a young boy and the children were brought up by their mother at Dolphin Chambers, a large family house by the Hard. Hubert's mother was a Roman Catholic with great strength of character. Throughout his life Hubert was to retain both his Catholic faith and a devotion for his mother who passed onto her son the force of her charm and personality. The

second eldest member of the family was his sister, Katie. Hubert was the youngest of four children. His elder brothers, Victor and Philip, both shared with him an aptitude for mechanical inventions. All three brothers were to become closely involved in aviation; Hubert was to become associated with an eccentric aviation pioneer, Noel Pemberton Billing; Philip was to become an airman in the Great War, although he was to spend some years as a prisoner of war; and Victor was to become public relations manager to Vickers Supermarine.

As the family grew up in Shoreham, Hubert, later known as Scotty to his closer friends, developed his expertise as a mechanic. He became a regular visitor to the nearby Shoreham aerodrome where he got to know the aviation pioneers and their machines. At an early age he built a 'monocar' with his brothers, a single-seater machine with motorcycle wheels and belt driven by a JAP motorcycle engine. Another early experiment undertaken with Philip was to take the JAP engine out of the home made car and to fit it into a canoe—with erratic results. Later, he was to admit in a contribution as an adult to his old school magazine that he had much preferred to be mucking about with a spanner and oil rag than doing what he called his 'paper work' at the Shoreham Grammar School.

In later life, Scotty enjoyed talking about his early mechanical adventures with friends and colleagues. His chauffeur in later years, Bill Sheaff, recalled how Scott-Paine would tell him about his young days as they drove on long journies across the country. One such adventure involved the annual 'Winton Carnival', a local water regatta at Shoreham. Scotty entered a Canadian canoe that he had acquired. Finding it unstable and liable to roll over, he lashed a framework constructed from orange boxes to the outside to stabilise the boat. It worked and Scotty was later to look back at this episode and muse that it was this that set him thinking about the construction of boats and, later, flying boats.[3]

Scotty was about eighteen years old when Noel Pemberton Billing came to live in Shoreham, having made a large amount of money out of some dubious property speculation at nearby Lancing. Billing had purchased a bungalow on the Beach at Shoreham where the Scott-Paine family also had a wooden bungalow. Scotty first met his neighbour when he was at the Beach, delivering paraffin on his bicycle for the shop. Billing came rushing up, exclaiming, 'Hey Boy, can I borrow your bike? I want to get to the ferry quickly and I'm late for my train!' In those days there was no bridge linking the Beach with the mainland and Scotty lent him the bike to rush for the station. The two families became friends and the eighteen year old Scotty, became closely involved with Pemberton Billing, working as his assistant and general factotum.

The two men were alike in temperament. Both were fascinated by the developments in technology that had come in the wake of the internal combustion engine, and Billing, who saw himself as both entrepreneur and inventor, had associated for a short time in 1909 with aviation pioneers such as Gordon England and Howard Wright. Billing clearly valued his young protégé's abilities and aptitude for hard work and was to involve Scotty in his next venture, the buying and selling of steam yachts. Perhaps his family did not share Scotty's enthusiasm for his swashbuckling patron as he was to write in his diary: 'Joined Billing on Wednesday December 20th, 1911. Left home amidst much weeping for Southampton with my little hat and bag and stayed on until just before Christmas. I wonder.'[4]

During January 1912, Scotty was on board the yacht *Hildegarde* which was being delivered to the

Mediterranean. In April, he was travelling to Marseilles, via Paris, to take charge of the *Princess Alice* which Billing had purchased from the Prince of Monaco. One story that Scotty delighted in telling in later life was that on one occasion he was stuck in Marseilles with no money and no way of returning home so he entered a boxing ring at a fair and won enough money for his fare.

1912 saw Scotty travelling to ports in Britain, France, Spain and all over the Mediterranean as, what Pemberton Billing was later to describe, the 'chief of the little bodyguard of fellows'. He travelled the world assisting his 'governor' with his 'ship-running' in a spirit of carefree adventuring. Scott-Paine, with his red hair that earned him the occasional nickname of 'Ginger', was powerfully built and, with his seemingly boundless energy, soon learned from his sea-going education all about ships and their machinery.

By the beginning of 1913, Scotty was back in Southampton looking after Billing's yachts. He lived

Hubert Scott-Paine, probably in Billing's Napier-engined racing car, built by Scott-Paine at White's Yard, Southampton, 1913.

on board the *Princess Alice*, which was berthed at White's Yard on the River Itchen, spending his days managing the large steam yacht, a two-masted schooner of 500 tons, *Utopia*, a 225-ton schooner, *Moira*, a smaller yacht, *Clara*, and the *Hildegarde*. Pemberton Billing visited Southampton occasionally to provide Scotty with money to pay his hired hands who were employed from time to time as the yachts returned from, or were prepared for, charter. Much of Scotty's time was spent working on the machinery of the yachts, scrubbing decks, cleaning bilges or cleaning the accommodation for the next customer. Occasionally, the work took Scotty away and in April he was in Grimsby preparing *Clara*, re-named *Hiawatha*, for a government charter in the North Sea fisheries. He supervised a team of forty-eight men, caulking decks, fitting a new steam winch, dry-docking and preparing for a Lloyds survey of hull and machinery. Billing left Scotty in total charge of the project, not without its difficulties: 'Charlton's and Co have done work in my opinion very badly', Scotty wrote in his diary, 'However I was badly tied by Gov. previous arrangements & couldn't help it.' But his hard work, involving four days and nights without sleep, paid off, 'The Gov. was exceedingly pleased with all results & that's all I care about so hurrah!'

Finding crews for the yachts was not always easy and the powerfully-built Scotty was a familiar sight in the bars and pubs of the Southampton waterfront. On August 3rd, he was told that the crew of *Utopia* on charter for the Cowes Week had left the ship. 'Men hunting all day with Mr Billing,' he wrote, 'eventually got 'em & went to Cowes in Mr Smith's launch.' During the first week of September he had to rush to Le Havre to bring back *Utopia*, which was required for another charter. 'Unfortunately,' Scotty wrote upon his arrival on board the yacht, '6 of the crew's taken leave and I start my usual pub hunting for men. For five hours I searched Havre finding my "hands" in all sorts of wierd places. The worst being the engineer, who thinking I had come for his job, (laughter) had to be forcably [sic] walked for about 300 yards and finally carried into launch.' Scotty's physical strength was a considerable asset and he was a formidable opponent in the boxing ring. He would attend local boxing matches, recording in his diary one such occasion, 'went across to Pelican Hall and saw Boxing contest. Good show. Joined in general scrap at end of show & haven't I a face on me. Oh! My!???' Scotty enjoyed a scrap and on November 30th he noted: 'Went to Mills for tea, wrecked Spiritualist Church and turfed the huts in the Avenue and had a glory to be scrap, & certainly hurt some of their fellows.' He was not averse to

using his strength in controlling employees, 'had some trouble with Harry & beat him up, he's been asking for it for two days now.'

Scotty was a highly skilled mechanic and engineer and spent much of his time building a car around a 180 hp Napier engine for Billing. He had the use of a small garage at White's yard where he built and assembled the chassis, suspension, steering and other components. He designed the body for the car, and for other cars that Billing brought down for his attention, but the body work was actually fabricated by Hale and Pierce, a local firm. Scotty enjoyed sailing, taking out Billing's 6-metre yacht, *Fiddlesticks*, or, if that was not available, 'went for a sail in a little 4 tonner moored near *Alice*, don't know who it belongs to'. During the hot summer of 1913, he enjoyed the occasional boating party and picnic up the local Hamble and Beaulieu Rivers as a relief from his long hours of work on board ship. On June 29th, he wrote: 'had a crowd in a big launch & I joined the party. We all went up Beaulieu River, a most beautiful spot, passed Duck, Swan and many other birds and also met above all things, a seal.'

Both Scott-Paine and Billing had a long standing interest in aviation and this re-emerged during September 1913 in an episode that was to earn Billing notoriety in aviation circles. Fellow aviation enthusiast Frederick Handley Page had made a wager that Billing would not be able to learn to fly and obtain his Royal Aero Club Certificate within twenty-four hours of first sitting in an aeroplane. Billing accepted but, as no flying school would risk its own aircraft in such a venture, he had to purchase his own aircraft, a Henry Farman biplane powered by a Gnome engine. Scotty had some misgivings, although he was fascinated with the construction of aircraft; he noted his dislike of flying, 'Did my first flight in 1909, practically made up my mind to give it up.' Billing began his lessons on September 17th and before breakfast the same day had obtained his certificate at Brooklands and had won his wager. Scotty wrote in his diary, 'well done for. Made a World's Record of England. I'll be at it myself again unless I change my mind.'[5]

On September 22nd, Scotty took 'the big car' to Brooklands where he met Billing's instructor, Robert Barnwell, the aviator Jack Alcock (later of Atlantic fame) and a Mr P. M. Muller. With Jack Alcock's help, he dismantled the Henry Farman machine and a Parson's biplane which had been built as an experimental machine for Muller, and which Billing had just purchased. The following day, the engine and fuselage of the Henry Farman were packed in boxes and, with the main planes, were taken by cart to the railway station. Upon its arrival at Southampton West station, the dismantled aircraft were taken to Parson's works at Town Quay, and then to White's yard where Scotty started erecting the Farman machine with the help of Jack Alcock.

Billing came down to Southampton and discussed his aviation plans with Scott-Paine who drove out to the New Forest with his 'governor' to look at the site of a proposed aerodrome. The idea never materialised and on October 3rd, Scotty was at Shoreham Aerodrome where Billing had purchased a Radley England 'Hydro-Aeroplane' and 'enough spare gear to build 2 more machines'. With the help of his old friends at Shoreham, Scotty loaded the aircraft onto carts and then onto three 30-foot trucks at the railway station. Once in Southampton, he took them to White's Yard. Scotty, with his experience of ships and boats, sat down with Billing in the saloon of the *Princess Alice* and persuaded his 'governor' that the flying boat was the great hope of British aviation.

Artist's impression of the Supermarine Factory at Woolston, Southampton, 1914.

Scotty's vision was that the future of aviation lay in the development of aircraft that were in fact boats that could fly, rather than aeroplanes that could float. He was convinced that flying boats should be seen as the aerial counterpart of the submarine, and the name 'Supermarine' was coined as the two men drew out sketches of possible flying boats.

On October 28th, 1913, Billing registered an application for a patent in respect of a flying boat which had been designed by himself and Scotty so that if forced to alight on open water, it could shed its wings and proceed as a motor launch. The forward fuselage was envisaged as a bouyant capsule containing both pilot and engine held 'like a cigar in a cigar holder' in the remainder of the hull to which the wings and tail surfaces were attached. There was not enough space at White's yard for Scotty to build the Supermarine so Billing purchased a yard at Oakbank Yard at Woolston on the River Itchen, about a mile downstream from White's Yard. On November 13th, Scotty wrote in his diary, 'Painting etc on "Supermarine" on wharf'.

Scotty started to work all out on the new project. He erected a 15-foot 'gallows' on a car and carried out experiments on wind resistance: 'made a proper job of it, staying it with wire, turnbuckles etc. Experiments very satisfactory, doing speeds up to 60 mph.' Other experimental work included the design and construction of a 'height recorder' and in late November Scotty wrote: 'We shall try my new ideas re propellers, everyone thinks I'm mad but PB says its alright for me to try.' The Henry Farman and the Radley England aircraft were moved from White's yard to Oakbank Wharf where two new sheds, each with two floors, 200 feet long, were soon under construction at a final cost of £500. With his vision of the passenger-carrying flying boat at the front of his mind, Scotty also drew up plans for a covered aero dock at the factory, from which flying boats could carry passengers to local destinations such as the Isle of Wight.

On December 1st, 1913, Scotty was appointed manager of the new Supermarine factory and set about the construction of the first Supermarine, PB 1, and the erection of Billing's fledgling collection of aircraft. 'Pattison, Bob, Tommy Fleming & I start at our new Aeroplane Factory at Oakbank Wharf, Woolston', he wrote, 'started erecting Radley England Machine, got main planes on the two floats and starboard wing erected into place'.[6]

Word of what Scotty and his 'governor' were up to in Southampton soon reached the aviation world. On February 24th, 1914, Scotty met a reporter from *Flight*, the magazine dedicated to the new and growing world of aviation, at the Southampton West railway station. He introduced himself as 'Secretary and Head Mechanic' of the new aeroplane works as he drove the reporter across the town in an AC motorcar. He showed the visitor all over the buildings under construction, and that evening the reporter was entertained by Scott-Paine and Pemberton Billing on board the schooner *Utopia*, moored in the River Itchen near the factory. The reporter was to recall the visit twenty-six years later when the Woolston Works were turning out the most successful fighter aircraft of all time, the Supermarine Spitfire, just in time to defeat the German Air Force in its attempt to clear the way for Hitler's invasion of Britain. But that was in the future; all that was to be seen in the works was the frames and planking of the prototype PB 1 that was to be exhibited at the Aero, Motor Boat, Marine and Stationary Engine Exhibition that was to open at Olympia on March 16th. Scotty and Billing had a spirited discussion that evening on the yacht: 'And what schemes we discussed', wrote the reporter, 'What arguments we had! The boat that was building was unorthodox enough in all conscience, but it was nothing compared with the ''paper boats''.'[7]

Scott-Paine's ability to work several days and nights without a break was to become legendary, and the preparation of PB 1 for the Olympia Show was to be the first demonstration of his immense energy and organisational skills. Throughout his career these were to bring projects to fruition in timescales that repeatedly impressed and amazed competitors and customers alike. The hull of the cigar was completed on February 21st when a sweepstake was held on its weight. It was won by Carol Vasilesco, a Rumanian described by Scotty in his diary as 'the French draughtsman'. Scotty worked day after day, driving the joiners, boatbuilders, metalworkers, wiremen and other craftsmen to get the machine completed on time. On Sunday March 1st, a night shift was started and the following Sunday saw the first erection of PB 1 in the workshop. Two days later the temporary wiring was replaced and on the Wednesday the works lorry was prepared for the trip to London. On Sunday, March 15th, Scotty was at Olympia preparing the aircraft and stand with five men from Southampton, listed in his diary as Cook, Patterson, Tommy, Malcolm Ross and Vasilesco.

PB 1 attracted the admiration of many visitors to Olympia, including King George V and Winston

Noel Pemberton Billing with the Supermarine PB 1 at the Olympia Aero Show, March 1914.

Churchill. The distinctive shape of the flying boat also produced some entertaining comments; Billing's friend C. G. Grey, editor of *The Aeroplane*, found the cigar shape amusing, writing: 'There certainly was something of the comic in the tip-tilted nose and round goggly face of the egg-like engine casing'. Scotty, when asked by an inquisitive visitor the purpose of the nacelle which was designed to house a Gnome rotary engine, apparently exclaimed that it was where they kept the coffee.[8]

Scott-Paine manned the exhibition throughout the week, arriving back in Southampton with Vasilesco and PB 1 to find that Billing planned to attend the hydroplane meeting to be held at Monaco. Scotty was instructed to prepare two racing motor boats, *Vicuna IV* and *Frigidi* for the event, and to prepare to travel to the south of France as mechanic. The hydroplane meeting was to achieve fame as the event that saw the first British win in the long contest for the Jacques Schneider Trophy. However, Billing decided to leave Scotty behind in charge of the factory in view of the possibility of orders arising from their success at the Olympia Show. On April 2nd, Scotty took up his new position as General Manager.

The aviation world had now heard of the Pemberton Billing Works in Southampton. Scotty saw the opportunities ahead and that his appointment could be the beginning of career bringing him both fame and fortune. It was a small beginning but Scotty clearly saw what lay ahead for two days later he went to the post office in Southampton and opened an account with £7. "Oh Joy, my £7", he wrote in his diary. It was a modest beginning for a man who, less than ten years later, was to sell his share in the Supermarine works for £192,000.[9]

CHAPTER 2
A Question of Survival

Despite his loyalty to Billing, Scott-Paine was quick to realise that PB 1 would never actually fly. He knew that the hull construction was good, for it was based on the construction methods developed by the famous yacht designer, Linton Hope, but the engine and wing arrangement was unsatisfactory. On April 15th he noted in his diary: 'Work going on to PB 1, I'm afraid all this will be for nothing, of course, its no use telling PB but I am sure that it all spells pas bon'. PB1's first flight was set for Saturday, May 30th, and Scotty threw himself into a final effort of preparation and adjustment to the aircraft. Without sleep, he worked for ninety-six hours before the first flight, undertaking the final erection of the wings, the installation of the engine, the lining up of the chain guides and the fitting and fairing up of the propellers. At two o'clock on the afternoon, in front of a large crowd, which included Scott-Paine's mother and his sister Katie, PB 1 took to the waters of the River Itchen with Howard Pixton, test pilot to the aviation entrepreneur Tommy Sopwith, at the controls. The machine refused to lift off the water, and despite a later attempt with a different propeller and wing arrangement, the forerunner of the world famous Supermarine flying boats failed to fly. On July 28th, 1914, it was dismantled and placed in the work's lumber store.

For a while it looked as if Billing's Aviation Works would become just one more enthusiastic failure, and that Scott-Paine would become just another piece of detritus in Billing's colourful career. There was so little work for the factory that in May, 1914, Scott-Paine leased the recently completed large shed to the aviation pioneer, Tommy Sopwith, who required facilities to test his Sunbeam-engined Bat Boat, a flying boat that he had entered in the 1914 *Daily Mail* Round Britain Race. The Bat Boat arrived in Southampton on May 13th, and Scotty wryly noted, 'Won't that be fine, we shall see a machine that will

fly . . .'. However, Scotty managed to find some work and was able to employ forty-five men during the summer of 1914. The works constructed a number of motor launches, including a 27-foot launch for Prince Carl of Russia. Towards the end of May, the first firm order for flying boats arising from the Olympia show came when the German government ordered two machines of a type that were to be designated PB 7. The type, described as a flying lifeboat, was the first to incorporate the novel Supermarine 'slip-wing' principle. The hull was to be built as a cabin cruiser with a fully enclosed cabin for the pilot and passengers. The idea was that the rear half of the 34 foot hull, complete with wings, tail surfaces and propellers could be jettisoned in the event of the machine being forced down, enabling the vessel to proceed as an ordinary motor boat.[1] Work had started on PB 7 by the end of May.

Despite the order, Billing was running short of cash for the enterprise and Scotty was unable to pay his men their wages at the end of each week. On April 10th, the *Princess Alice* was towed off its mud berth and taken to Dry Dock No 3 in Southampton Docks to await inspection by Lord Inverclyde who was to buy her. Pemberton Billing recorded in his autobiography that the yacht was 'sacrificed on the altar of aviation' when it was sold to Lord Inverclyde for £13,000, but for Scotty the problem was that he had to find alternative lodgings.[2] He eventually found digs on board the *Lethie*, a yacht lent to him by a Mr Smith. 'I guess that this will be a very cosy home indeed', he wrote, 'she is so absolutely small after the *Alice* you know.'

Despite the difficulties at the factory, Scotty was in splendid form during the summer months that proceeded the outbreak of the Great War. He had met Alice Brenda Hockey, a girl who lived in Howard Road, Shirley, on the western side of the town, and had fallen in love. 'I've been thinking

The launch of PB 1, the first Supermarine flying
boat, into the River Itchen, May 30th, 1914.

about Brenda all evening', he wrote on April 19th,
'damn it, it worries some & beats me'. They had met
on the top of a tramcar some eighteen months
previously, but Brenda was engaged to another man.
A disappointed Scotty later wrote in his diary,
'Wrote Brenda but managed to tear it up I wonder if
she ever thinks of me? You fool! Oh! what she's
missed'. However, Brenda Hockey broke off her
engagement and on June 19th, Scotty took his future
wife to the Pageant in Southampton.

Scotty worked long hours at the factory, spending
days and weeks altering the ill-fated PB 1 for the
second, and again unsuccessful, attempt to get the
machine to fly. Engine installations were tried and
scrapped, and Scotty often worked all night, fitting
propellers, altering chain drives and experimenting
with numerous modifications. He also spent time
working on the old Henry Farman and Radley
aircraft. 'Oh My! Assembling our old Radley again,
My Aunt its funny I laugh to death, its never flown
yet, but its been carried miles', he noted.

The ebullient Scotty was becoming a figure in
Southampton, and amongst the men who earned
their living on the waterfront. On one occasion he
took a launch from the factory to view the torpedo

boat destroyer fleet moored near Royal Pier. He fell
overboard and 'walked round pier all dirty as hell
caused sensation'. Scotty loved a scrap and on one
occasion that summer someone shouted 'Ginger' at
him from the top of a tramcar whereupon Scotty
leapt on board, grabbed the offender and threw him
off into the street. 'Didn't hurt him much thought',
he wrote. On April 17th, he noted, 'Had hell on a
fight with two dockers & for a while things looked
rough, but I laid one out & nearly killed the other, so
I sang all the way home you see.' Bill Sheaff was later
to recall that Scotty recounted several occasions
when he went to the Bank Holiday fair on Southampton Common and fought bouts in the boxing ring.
(One of Scotty's prized trophies in later years was to
be a horseshoe presented to him by the heavy-weight
champion, Jo Beckett, on June 17th, 1919.)[3]

For some time Scott-Paine had been convinced
that the future of passenger carrying civil aviation lay
in the development of suitable flying boats, and
during June he was to start work on his first experimental passenger carrying machine. It was called the
PB 'Char-a-Banc' and appears to have been intended to provide a passenger service between Southampton and the Isle of Wight. Scotty proposed to

form a separate company to be known as the Aerial Marine Navigation Company to operate two flights a day from either Woolston or Town Quay. In the event, the machine was never completed, but it was the start of Scotty's long, and ultimately successful association with passenger flying boat services that were to link Southampton with the farthest corners of the Empire.[4]

Never one to miss a good bargain, Scott-Paine visited Hendon in June with Pemberton Billing, to purchase two Breguet machines, three Canton Unné engines and the entire stock in trade of a bankrupt outfit. The intention was to obtain engines for the PB 7 machines being built for the German government. Scotty then went up to the airfield with the works lorry, with 'three of the boys and two men'. The trip was an hilarious adventure: On the way to Hendon, Scotty's helpers pelted passers-by with fruit. On the return journey, a wheel came off at Marble Arch, and knocked a man over and a free fight ensued. A tyre burst near Staines and the group had to spend the night under a hedge and the next morning, the party, as Scotty noted in his diary 'took tube to be repaired, the new cover burst at Egham 1½ miles away, rode back and nearly killed the garage man, stole the new cover rode back, new tube not finished, had a bathe in Thames and good wash with Hudrana, got underway & altogether had tyre off 14 times, another burst & we carried on on the damaged tyre, saw haystack, went through gate and all slept in haystack 14 miles from Winchester'.[5]

Pemberton Billing visited the factory only occasionally. He spent much of his time at his Chambers at the Middle Temple where he was pursuing a short-lived ambition to study for the Bar, and from where he dispatched instructions and, at irregular intervals, cheques from which Scott-Paine could pay himself and the workforce. In July, Billing purchased a large house called Steep Hill Park at West End, near Southampton. On the Saturday morning of July 11th, Scotty was working in the factory supervising the erection of the centre cellule of PB 7 and preparing Billing's Vauxhall-engined, 21-foot launch, *Dyack*, for the Spithead Review the following week. Billing suddenly appeared at the factory with his wife and took Scotty to see the new house. Scotty was entranced: 'Oh such a beautiful fairyland', he wrote. The house stood in thirteen acres with views around for about twenty miles. There were lawns, terraces, meadows, orchards, gardens, stables and garages. Scotty saw before him a vision of what he would have for himself when he had made his fortune.

The enthusiasms, boyish fun and ebullient excitement that Scotty enjoyed as he managed the works during May and June were to be clouded as the threat of war with Germany grew. The latter part of July was spent moving his governor's furniture from London into the new house. At the factory, work continued on the German flying boat which was substantially completed by the end of July, but war rumours were growing stronger and Scotty became both excited and apprehensive. He was concerned that the factory should make a contribution to the forthcoming war effort, but there was no work on hand.

On Friday, July 31st, Billing, who had just purchased a new Rolls-Royce was away in London securing the views of Admiral Sueter, Director of Air Services in the Air Department of the Admiralty, on the likely requirements for aircraft in the event of war with Germany. The following day he arrived back at Steep Hill and discussed war plans for the factory with Scott-Paine. The two men decided that the emergency meant that they should take on work that was most likely to assist the national effort. They concluded that there would be a demand for light, land-based scout aircraft rather than for flying boats, and Scotty immediately set to work putting their ideas on paper. The project was dubbed PB 9 and Scotty worked all that night at Steep Hill, drawing out the machine. He was convinced that the aircraft would be 'of great note and moment in the world'. War was declared on Germany the next day and Southampton was suddenly full of soldiers of the British Expeditionary Force departing from the Docks for France. Scotty finished two elevations that day and passed them to the works draughtsman, Carol Vasilesco, to 'correct and make good'.[6] The outbreak of war naturally caused the cancellation of the order for the PB 7 and the machine was never completed.

The story of the creation of PB 9, has since become one of the popular tales from the pioneering days of British Aviation.[7] The machine was completed in a mere six days and ten hours, and acquired the sobriquet the 'Seven Day Bus'. Work started on August 4th. The drawings were completed, thirty new carpenters were started, the moulds were set out and the lines were chalked out on the mould loft floor. In a fanciful and romantic account of the creation of the 'Seven Day Bus', Billing was later to claim that the lines were chalked out on the factory walls and that he personally spent the week, day and night, without sleep, supervising the construction. In fact, he spent most of the week in London and it was Scott-Paine who worked day and night driving his craftsmen and teaching new hands their work. Sixty-eight men were employed on the project, and a boy was employed to play music on a gramophone as the work proceeded throughout each night. Scotty had to

Carol Vasilesco, Victor Mahl and Hubert Scott-Paine with PB 9 at Netley, near Southampton, August 11th, 1914.

undertake the installation of the Gnome rotary engine personally as all of his mechanics had been called away to French and British air stations.

Scotty was working twenty hours a day, and by the end of the third day, the fuselage was up and wired, the engine plates were mounted in the fuselage, the tail fin and rudder were completed and the oil and petrol tanks were installed. On the Saturday, August 8th, the wings were erected, covered and wired ready for tru-ing, all fittings of the chassis were finished and the main controls were completed. The project was speeded by Scotty's decision to use the wings assembly from the firm's Radley aircraft, which was so arranged that the assembled wing cellule could simply be slipped over the fuselage and bolted in position. Work continued throughout the Saturday night and again Scotty had no sleep, and by Sunday the wings were ready for mounting onto the fuselage.

Billing returned from London at 12.30 PM on the Sunday. An exhausted Scott-Paine was not pleased to see his governor whom, he knew, would claim all the credit for his remarkable achievement. Scotty went off home to his digs and slept. He was back at the works at 4.30 AM on the Monday morning and by midday PB 9 was finished. 'It was', Scotty wrote, 'a world's record

never before has there been a machine designed and built in a week before'.

Arrangements were made to carry out the test flight of PB 9 at Netley Common, near Southampton. At 4.00 AM the next morning, Tuesday 11th August, Pemberton Billing towed the wing cellule to Netley behind his Sheffield Simplex car. Scott-Paine followed in the work's lorry, towing the fuselage and all the gear needed for the test flight. The aircraft was quickly assembled and the wing cellule slipped into position before being fixed by U-bolts round the bottom longerons. Tommy Sopwith had lent his chief mechanic Victor Mahl and his test pilot Howard Pixton to assist Scott-Paine with the trials and Mahl was given the task of taking the machine into the air.

A mishap occurred when Mahl, carrying out a taxi-ing test, crashed a wing tip into a fence. Scotty sent for men from the factory to repair the damage and soon the machine was ready to fly. After a short take-off run of thirty-six yards, Mahl took PB 9 into a steeply banked climbing left-hand turn. A reporter from *Flight* was present and estimated the rate of climb to be in the region of five hundred feet per minute and the speed to be about 75 mph: Mahl reported that the machine was exceptionally good to fly. The aviation press was mixed in its praise of Scott-Paine's achievement. *Flight* described the event as 'another fine achievement for Mr Pemberton Billing', while *The Aeroplane* offered the more caustic comment that 'Mr Pemberton Billing has produced an aeroplane that flies . . .'.

Scotty spent the rest of the day trying, without much success, to erect a canvas hangar for PB 9 in the field before joining his triumphant team in a visit to a local cinema and a riotous party of celebration. At the cinema, the revellers took over the front two rows of seats and Ross commandeered the piano, playing music quite inappropriate to the film then being shown. The party was evicted by the manager and Scotty went off to bed to sleep for twenty-four hours.

The next few days for Scotty were spent sleeping, tidying his digs or with Brenda. On August 17th, he set off with PB 9 for Brooklands airfield in Surrey where military trials were to take place. He towed the wings behind the Sheffield Simplex car, while Billing followed in his Rolls-Royce, towing the fuselage. The next day Jack Alcock, later of Atlantic fame, took the machine up on a test flight. It behaved beautifully, but after a landing from a second flight Alcock managed to damage the tail. Brooklands was under the control of the Army, and as the team retired to bed for the night, the garrison gaily sang in the Blue Bird restaurant next door.

The next day Scott-Paine was up early to repair the damaged tail, and after great difficulty, he managed to get a carpenter to strip off the empennage and splice in new longerons, and to fit a replacement landing skid which he had found on a nearby scrap heap. Alcock had the machine out twice on the following day, but all was not well. Alcock began to criticise the aeroplane, complaining that it had some peculiar fault, and Scott-Paine noted in his diary that 'Alcock suffers from cold feet'. Alcock then got a Sopwith mechanic, H.C. Millar, to look over the machine; he came back with the comment that if the machine had been designed and built in a week, it certainly looked like it. Scotty was worried, and that night he had a nightmare for the first time in years, dreaming that the machine broke up in the air. On Friday, August 21st, Alcock had PB 9 out for one more circuit prior to taking it to Farnborough, landed safely and absolutely refused to take it up again.

Billing chose this moment to return to Brooklands from London and, on hearing Alcock's refusal, he stormed into the cockpit saying that he would take it up himself. When he had obtained his Royal Aero Club Certificate the previous year, the observer, Mr Rance, had commented that Billing had shown great aptitude but, 'If he thinks he knows anything about flying—God help him!'. He had not been in an aeroplane since that celebrated occasion, but climbed into the cockpit of PB 9 with confidence. Alcock swung the propeller, Billing turned PB 9 into the wind and as the motor roared the undercarriage buckled. Billing got out, puffing in his anger, jammed his monocle in his eye, summoned up as much dignity as he could, yelled to a furious Scott-Paine, 'Put the Damn thing away', and drove off in a swirl of dust.[8]

Scott-Paine, frustrated and angry, was left to take the wrecked machine back to Southampton. He piled the wings on top of the Sheffield Simplex and, towing the fuselage behind, he arrived back at the works after a three-hour trip. He returned to a factory that was completely without work to discover that his brother Philip had been badly injured in an air crash at Stockbridge in Hampshire. Bitterly he wrote: 'PB 9 wings and shop work looks fairly vacant and rotten, no special news at all. Mater income stopped through war. Phil broken up & so much worry for me. Oh Shut up. We're shut down at works, all salaries halved, mine included, My Aunt, What a Blag Billing is, 72 hands sacked and just 14 kept on.'

The factory was left to fend for itself, without staff and without work. However, Scotty was determined to make something of it and he carried on with some development work on PB 9. The wings were rearranged and the old Farman floats were fitted in an attempt to converted the 'Seven Day Bus' into a seaplane, an arrangement later designated the PB 13. The Canton Unné engines were tuned up for sale and were accepted by the Admiralty Inspector, Mr Markham, on September 15th. Billing, piqued by the lack of official interest in PB 9 lost all interest in the Aviation Works and all who depended upon it for their livelihood. He obtained a commission in the Royal Naval Air Service and, as he later claimed in his autobiography: 'I offered the factory to the authorities as a gift for the duration of the war. It was refused. We closed the gates.'[9]

But Scott-Paine was still in control of the factory and he was determined that he and the works should make a contribution to the war effort. His two brothers had joined up and Scotty wanted to use his mechanical skills in the armed forces. During September, he examined the possibility of a job in Russia, but nothing came of this. His relationship with Billing became more strained and, on October 2nd he was ready to give in his notice to 'Kaiser Billing', but then Pemberton Billing came up with the bright idea of turning the factory over to the production of light motor cars that were to sell at £500 each, the 'Rolls Royce of light busses'. The car

PB 9, the 'Seven Day Bus' altered for use as an election husting by Noel Pemberton Billing in 1916.

was to be known as the 'King Car'. Billing proposed that Scott-Paine should take charge of the scheme, but, after working for some time on the design, Scotty decided that the whole project was nothing but hot air on Billing's part. Billing continued to make extravagant promises to Scotty that he would be able to get his protégé an important post in the Army, but all he was able to come up with was a job as an air mechanic in the Royal Navy. A furious Scott-Paine wrote in his diary: 'I told him some things I can tell you, he must think I'm a fool, you know, to go out as a sort of a chauffeur to Billing. My Hat.'

There was still no work at the factory and Scott-Paine spent much of his time undertaking jobs for Sopwith who was still leasing part of the large shed at Woolston. One event of note was the crash of a Sopwith machine being flown by Victor Mahl in which Sopwith's chief designer, Reginald Alston was

killed. Scott-Paine co-ordinated the salvage of the wreck, which had sunk near Netley, and the recovery of the body. In the meantime, he kept on at Pemberton Billing who in November acquired some fame as the organiser of an adventurous aeroplane raid on the German Zeppelin sheds on Lake Constance. On October 29th, Scotty got a letter from the Admiralty ordering him to report to the Heavy Transport Section at the Wormwood Scrubs Airship Sheds, but on his arrival nobody knew anything about the summons and the day was wasted. Scotty also made enquiries amongst his old friends at Shoreham Aerodrome but nothing came of this.

Billing then proposed a scheme for the construction of armoured cars for use at the Front, but again the scheme came to nothing. Scotty still insisted that he could find work for the factory, whereupon Billing suggested that Scotty should take total charge of the works. The initial offer was not good enough for Scotty who had now set his sights on acquiring the works from Pemberton Billing. The arguments continued for some weeks but Scott-Paine drove a hard bargain, successfully. On December 5th, 1914, he recorded in his diary: 'Made arrangements with P-B to take over complete charge of the factory. I find it over £800 in debt, no credit anywhere and only 6 men in the place, a very big handful to get on with I'm sure.'[10]

CHAPTER 3
A Personal Fortune

Scott-Paine walked round the deserted factory: The company was in debt. The old Farman aircraft, the works lorry and a motor launch had been sold. There were still four aircraft in the silent sheds, but none of them could fly. There was the PB 7 built for the German Government, the ill-fated PB 9, the old Radley-England Waterplane and an incomplete machine listed as PB 13 (which may have been the mysterious Char-a-Banc, which Scotty had been working on before the outbreak of war). However, the balance sheet that was drawn up when he took over showed that the total assets of the company were valued at more than £11,000, and before long they were to be put to good use as Scotty secured orders for the construction of aeroplanes designed by other firms and for the repair of machines damaged at the Front.[1]

Although Billing retained some interest in the Supermarine Works at Southampton, Scott-Paine was now owner of the factory for all practical purposes. At the suggestion of the famous sportsman, Alfred Delves-Broughton, the factory had been registered as Pemberton Billing Ltd, a limited liability company, on 27th June, 1914. When Scott-Paine acquired control, it was agreed that the title of the company would be retained and that experimental new designs would continue to bear the PB designation.

Gradually the works at Woolston returned to life and the number of men employed grew. Scotty was much liked and admired by his employees and was capable of generating great affection from those who worked for him. Testimony of this came with the sudden death of the nineteen year old Carol Vasilesco who collapsed and died on his way to the Royal South Hants Hospital in Southampton on Christmas Eve of 1914. Scotty wrote to the young man's bereaved parents who lived near Regent's Park, London, a gesture that was much appreciated. Vasilesco's father wrote back to Scott-Paine on

January 7th, 1915, 'I wish to offer you a father's heartfelt thanks for all the kindess you have shown to my boy in life and death. My daughters have told me that you did all you could for his spiritual as well as for his temporal happiness and we feel that your efforts must have been crowned with success all the same. Thank you for your last beautiful token of friendship which my children saw from the grave.'[2]

A few days before the sad death of his draughtsman, Scotty had become formally engaged to Brenda Hockey. On Saturday, December 19th, he wrote her words in his diary: 'Hu and I go shopping in the evening when I come the proud possessor of a gold and diamond circle. Quite an eventful day.' It was to be a long engagement for Scotty and Brenda Hockey were married two years later on November 22nd, 1916.

Scotty managed to obtain contracts for the repair of Sopwith, Avro, Bristol and Royal Aircraft Factory aircraft, and the future of the Woolston Works was secured finally with the receipt of a major contract to build twelve Short S.38s on June 25th, 1915. In the meantime, Scotty continued development work on new designs, for he was convinced that government departments should base their requirements on new designs, designs that should remain frozen once they were agreed upon so that production could proceed without interruption. As a designer and entrepreneur, Scott-Paine would always be ready to commit expenditure on experimental, private venture designs.

Throughout 1915 he continued a close working relationship with the Air Department of the Admiralty led by Sir Murray Sueter, for the Air Department had been allowed to continue its own research and development of aircraft despite the official embargo on new designs by the Royal Aircraft Factory. As a result of this, the Admiralty made a great impact on the theory and practice of aircraft design, and Scott-Paine's next venture owed some of its design features to Harold Bolas, a designer in the Technical Department of the Air Department. The machine was designed as a single-seater scout with a single pusher propeller. It was designated PB 23E, but soon acquired the nickname, 'Push-Proj', an abbreviation for 'Pusher-Projectile', referring both to the engine arrangement and the cigar-shape of the small fuselage.

PB 23E made its maiden flight at Hendon in September 1915, but it proved unsatisfactory, and a modified version, the PB 25, was introduced, with swept-back wings designed to correct the centre of gravity. Despite continuing unsatisfactory reports about its flying qualities, PB 25 was the first of Scott-Paine's aircraft to be put into production. Twenty of the 'Pemberton Billing Scout' aircraft were ordered on November 15, 1915, with a delivery period of a mere twenty-four weeks. Although the production version was flown at both Eastchurch and the Isle of Grain, the flying characteristics continued to be unsatisfactory and none of these ever saw active service.[3]

The threat posed by German Zeppelins then led Scotty to consider a machine specially designed to counter the airships. He expended £6000 on a private venture scheme, a remarkable quadruplane which emerged in 1915 as the 'Nighthawk'. The quadruplane had a large wing area and high aspect ratio which allowed it to cruise at slow speeds at night in search of enemy airships, which could then be shot down with the aid of a gimbal-mounted searchlight and a 1½-pounder Davis non-recoil gun. Unfortunately, the machine crashed and was wrecked at Chingford in Essex on February 12th, 1916, but Scott-Paine immediately set about construction of a

The Supermarine 'Night Hawk' quadruplane designed in 1916 by Scott-Paine and Pemberton Billing to counter the German Zeppelin.

second, refined, quadruplane at his own expense. The aircraft was completed in record time and on March 6th, Admiral Sueter sent his technical assistant, Harris Booth, to Woolston to evaluate the likely performance. Scotty was hoping for an order for six aircraft but he was not too disappointed when, on March 28th, he received an order for two of the modified version, designated PB 31E.

The 'Nighthawk' episode was to prove to be the occasion for Scotty to acquire sole ownership of the Supermarine works. He had worked for almost a week without sleep to finish the prototype PB 31E, when, at the end of the week, Billing appeared in the factory complaining about delays in the delivery of certain instruments for the aircraft. He stormed up to Scott-Paine's office to telephone the Air Department, but was told over the telephone that his complaints would have to wait. His frustrations rose to bursting point and in a rage he flung the receiver on the floor and smashed it, saw his service cap lying on the table, threw it on the floor and jumped on it as a symbol of 'officialdom and its deadly Red Tape'. Scotty coolly told Billing that the telephone receiver was company property and that he would have to pay for the damage. Billing, blaming all the problems on official dislike for him, stormed out, saying that if he could not influence the government departments from his position in the Royal Naval Air Service, then he would resign his commission and would go into Parliament to fight for an effective procurement policy.[4]

Billing entered Parliament on March 22nd as Member for East Hertfordshire, having used PB 9 as an election husting. He claimed in Parliament that British airmen were being 'murdered rather than killed' by the poor design of aircraft and he supported his outrageous and poorly researched claims in his book, *Air War and How to Wage it*, in which he promoted the PB 25 and PB 31E as the types necessary for an effective aviation policy. However, Billing received so much criticism that he was out to profit from his campaign that he decided to sell his interest in the Woolston Works. He later recalled that he could only realise about one quarter of the £50,000 that he felt was his due, the price he had to pay, he remarked, for his patriotic attack on the aircraft policy of the government.[5]

Considerable speculation surrounded the transfer of the Supermarine works to Scott-Paine and *The Daily Chronicle* published a story that Billing had disposed of his aviation works for £25,000: this was then officially denied by Scott-Paine who had become sole owner of the company as well as manager of the works. On September 20th, 1916, Scotty registered his new company as the Super-

marine Aviation Company Limited. It was a name that was earn a major place in the annals of British Aviation.

Scott-Paine continued his close association with the Air Department of the Admiralty which had hired the famous yacht designer, Linton Hope, for its Technical Department during 1915. During 1916, Hope had worked up some ideas for an experimental flying boat hull with a monocoque structure based on oval hoops connected by stringers and covered with double diagonal mahogany planking.[6] Scotty's uncanny sense of design told him that the immensely strong and flexible hull would be a great improvement on anything then in service, and he knew that his company was well placed to put these ideas into practice. Scotty entered into detailed discussions with the Air Department and became closely involved in the development of the design of a new type of flying boat. His interest in design was empirical rather than technical and George Selman, who was later to join Scotty designing motor torpedo boats for the war against Hitler, recalled Scott-Paine visiting the National Physical Laboratory test tank at Teddington at this time. Selman was introduced to Scotty who then complained that he was impatient with the academic and detailed work with models; Scotty pulled out a pocket game of 'Put-and-take' and the two men spent the afternoon betting pennies on the outcome.[7]

Supermarine secured a contract to build two prototypes of the Admiralty Design Flying Boat on May 28th, 1916. The craftsmanship of Scott-Paine's workforce at Woolston did justice to the bold design of the AD Flying Boat. One of the prototypes spent seven hours at sea in a 38 mph wind, during which the boat was taken off and landed repeatedly. The wings were damaged but the hull withstood all the shocks. Other AD boats were stalled at heights between thirty and one hundred and twenty feet, and one machine withstood thirty-six heavy landings in one day and only shipped twenty pounds of water.

On May 12th, 1917, Scotty obtained an order to build twenty production AD flying boats. The factory expanded and women were taken on for the first time, working in many areas including the stores and on the doping of wing fabric. Supermarine soon became the second largest employer in Southampton and it was this experience of organising wartime work forces that was to put Scott-Paine at the forefront of employing women in his factories during World War Two. Amongst new recruits were his brother, Victor, who helped out at the factory when on leave from service with an artillery regiment in France, and a young draughtsman who was to achieve immortality as the designer of the Super-

26

marine Spitfire. The twenty-one year old draughts-man was Reginald Joseph Mitchell who had applied to Scott-Paine for a post in the Supermarine drawing office. Mitchell had just the mix of knowledge and practical inventive skill that made him a natural recruit of the ambitious Scott-Paine who was struggling to transform the Woolston Works from Pemberton Billing's plaything into a successful aircraft factory. Mitchell participated in the design of the Nighthawk Quadruplane and then worked as Scott-Paine's personal assistant before being appoin-ted Chief Designer.

Scott-Paine collaboration with the Air Depart-ment led to contracts for the construction of two further prototypes at Woolston. The first was for the construction of two Navy floatplanes, ordered on March 24th, 1916. As usual, Scotty was able to impress his customer, in this case by completing the first of the floatplanes within eight weeks of receiving the drawings. Admiral Murray Sueter was so impressed that he sent Scott-Paine a letter of congra-tulation. The second prototype was a single-seater fighter flying boat, designed at Woolston with the

assistance of R.J. Mitchell, in response to an Admiralty specification. Three Supermarine N.1B Baby flying boats were ordered on June 28th, 1917, but the order was cancelled at the end of the war by which time only one had been completed. The Baby was to be the most successful design to come out of Woolston during the Great War. While the AD flying boat was to bring Scott-Paine a fortune, it was the Baby that was to bring him fame.[8]

Scott-Paine's determination not to close the factory in 1914 had been vindicated. By the end of the war, he had built up a sophisticated design team and a skilled workforce at the Woolston Works. The man who had opened a post office account with £7 four years earlier was the owner of a successful aircraft factory and had become well known in aviation circles. He had become a rich man, and was later to recall that some of his detractors called him an 'armaments baron'. Suddenly, with the signing of the Armistice, the factory found itself without work. Henri Biard, who later joined Scott-Paine as a pilot, recalled that the Supermarine works was practically deserted and that the factory was reduced to making

Aerial view of the Supermarine Works, South-ampton, about 1919.

a few wheelbarrows. He even recalled that he test drove the wheelbarrows 'which I tested with Mitchell—the famous Spitfire designer—in them . . .'.[9]

Scotty's vision and enthusiasm remained undimmed. He had rescued the firm before from the brink of extinction and he could do so again. He decided that with the arrival of peace he could pursue his old interest in the use of flying boats for passenger carrying civil aviation. He knew that at least sixteen of the AD Flying Boats, that had taken up the last two years of his life, were somewhere in store, and, in a flash of entrepreneural genius he bought them back from the Admiralty.

Scotty was not alone in his belief that the future lay in civil aviation for the Air Ministry was to form a Department of Civil Aviation in February 1919. The wartime development of large aircraft and reliable engines had made long distance flight possible and this had been dramatically demonstrated when Jack Alcock, who had tested the ill-fated PB 9, and

Lieutenant Arthur Whitten Brown made a non-stop crossing of the Atlantic in a twin-engined Vickers Vimy bomber during 1919. Scott-Paine's close friend Alliott Verdon Roe, who had built an aircraft factory at Hamble near Southampton during the war, had seen the potential of commercial aviation and had formed an air transport branch of his company, and on August 5th, 1919, the first cross-channel scheduled air service was to start between an airfield at Hounslow and Le Bourget in France.[10]

In February 1919, Scott-Paine began to convert the AD Flying Boats into what were to be called the Supermarine Channel flying boats. Resurrecting his pre-war scheme, he planned to use the aircraft to fly regular services between Southampton and Ryde, Sandown, Shanklin and Ventnor on the Isle of Wight. He recruited a band of seven pilots including Henri Biard, Basil Hobbs and Commander James Bird, who was to become a fellow director of Supermarine, and, as soon as the first certificates of airworthiness were issued in July, Scotty started

One of the Supermarine Channel flying boats used on the first international flying boat service between Southampton and Le Havre in September 1919.

28

using his aircraft for pleasure rides. The first scheduled passenger service was started between Woolston and Bournemouth on July 23rd, by which time three machines were converted and ready for use.

The chartering of the flying boats for private use also kept Scott-Paine's pilots busy during August. One flying boat was used to fly members of various yacht clubs to watch the Cowes Regatta from the air and one aircraft was chartered by a Colonel Wingfield on August 7th so that he could fly over HMS *Renown* as she set sail for Canada with the Prince of Wales. On August 16th, the Mayor of Southampton inaugurated the Isle of Wight Service and was enthralled by the novel experience of flying low over Southampton Docks and looking down into the immense funnels of the liners in the port. One first for the pioneers was the replenishing of a shipping service with fuel delivered by air. On August 12th, the motor launch service run by Spencer Brothers from Ventnor ran out of petrol and one of the Channel flying boats was chartered to fly to the

Island with a supply of Shell motor spirit to keep the service going.[11]

Scotty was quick to take advantage of the railway strike of September 1919 which closed down the Southern Railway cross-channel steamers operating out of Southampton. The *Southern Daily Echo*, a Southampton-based newspaper, contracted Scotty to fly papers from Southampton to Bournemouth: the proprietors were impressed with the flight time of forty-three minutes. Scotty then advertised a scheduled cross-Channel air service, announcing that the advertised schedule would be maintained, whatever the weather conditions. This undertaking caused some hair-raising adventures for Scotty's band of seven pilots. The flamboyant Henri Biard was later to recall one adventure that nearly cost him his life. Two men, a Naval officer and a Belgian millionaire had arrived at Woolston and, despite the fact that a howling gale was in the offing, Scotty assured his visitors that a flying boat would take them to Le Havre. As the passengers climbed into the aircraft, Scotty presented the Belgian with a bottle of

A Supermarine Channel flying boat delivering petrol to Spencer's launches at Ventnor, Isle of Wight, September 1919. Henri Biard is seen in the centre.

rum to keep him warm in the exposed passenger compartment. He was not to know that the bottle would almost cause the loss of the aeroplane. The weather during the five-hour flight was appalling, and at one stage the Belgian took a drink from the bottle and turned to pass it to Biard who was behind and above him. The slipstream caught the liquor and blew it into the face of the pilot who almost lost control. He got his own back, however, for the Belgian then proceeded to open a gold-handled umbrella which, he hoped, would protect him from the hail and icicles. Biard realised that it would instantly blow into the propeller and cause them to crash, and hit the unsuspecting passenger over the head with the empty run bottle. Such were the trials of the pioneer flying boat services.[12]

Before the war Scotty had prepared Billing's motor boats for the Monaco Hydroplane races and

he had retained his long standing fascination with speed, both on the water and in the air. The post-war years had ushered in an era in which national prestige was often at stake, as it had been before the war, as brave and often foolhardy men and women sought to break speed records on land, in the air and on water. The war years had seen the development of improved and efficient engines and, with the acquisition of his considerable personal fortune, Scotty enthusiastically joined the ranks of the record breakers.

The Royal Aero Club announced in August 1919 that it would hold the next contest for the Jacques Schneider Trophy at Bournemouth on Wednesday, September 10th. The last contest had been won by Howard Pixton in a Sopwith flying boat at Monaco in 1914 at a speed of 86.7 mph. Scotty knew that his Supermarine Baby, which had achieved a top speed

The Supermarine N1.B Baby single seater, pusher scout/fighter flying boat completed in 1918.

of 116 mph, was a natural contender for the trophy. Scotty instructed Mitchell to redesign the N.1B to take a Napier Lion engine and the Baby was christened 'Supermarine Sea Lion'. The Lion engine had been developed as a private venture by Napiers during the war and was was to become a principal British aero engine of the 1920s. Under Scott-Paine's influence, a marine version was later to be developed and was to power Britain's first motor torpedo boats. The work on Sea Lion again saw Scotty's boundless energy as he worked day and night throughout August, getting the racer ready. The new engine was completed and installed, new wings and a new tail assembly were designed, built and fitted, the forward section of the hull was modified between the announcement of the contest and the actual date of the race five weeks later.[13]

Squadron leader Basil Hobbs was chosen by Scott-Paine to pilot the Sea Lion in the race. The machine was ready for the eliminating trials on September 8th but, because of the short notice, there was only one other serious contender, the Italians with a Savoia S.13 flying boat. The arrangements for the competing teams and their aircraft turned out to be totally inadequate and the contest threatened to turn into a fiasco as fog covered the whole of the course on the morning of September 10th, the day of the race. The sun began to break through about midday and at one o'clock, Sea Lion arrived with Hobbs at the controls, and tied up alongside Scotty's racing motor boat, *Tiddlywinks*. By late afternoon, the organisers decided that the weather had cleared sufficiently for the contest to begin and just before five o'clock the Sea Lion started up. The engine was started by another Supermarine pilot, Captain Hoare, who then jumped overboard to be picked up by Scotty in the waiting motor boat. Hobbs took off successfully. Unfortunately, there was still fog at Swanage. Thinking that visibility might be better near the water, Hobbs brought the machine down and alighted to work out his position. He then took off in an attempt to locate the Swanage marker boat and, as he left the water, the hull crashed into an unseen floating object. The flying boat continued without any problem despite the accident, so Hobbs decided to continue in the race. He went up above the fog and, seeing the Purbeck Hills, he satisfied himself that he had been round the Swanage marker boat and set off for Hengistbury Head. He came down to make his first landing near the marker boat to the east of Boscombe Pier as he was required to do by the rules. He made a perfect touchdown but the damage to the hull was greater than he had realised, and the machine immediately filled with water and turned over with its tail in the air, throwing Hobbs into the water. Scott-Paine and commander Bird raced up in *Tiddlywinks*. They managed to secure a line around the Sea Lion, and towed her into shallow water before she sank.[14]

The Sea Lion was out of the race, but Scott-Paine joined the public outcry when the Race Committee awarded the trophy to the Italian contender despite the fact that the Italian pilot Jannello had been disqualified for failing to go round the Swanage marker boat. Scotty was proud of his team's achievement and the performance of the Supermarine flying boat. Sea Lion was eventually repaired and Scott-Paine's contribution to the design and development of flying boats was recognised when the Science Museum in London accepted Sea Lion into the national collection of outstanding technological achievements.

Supermarine Sea Lion after its accident during the Schneider Trophy Contest held at Bournemouth in September 1919.

CHAPTER 4
In Pursuit of a Vision

As Hubert Scott-Paine celebrated his thirtieth birthday, he was able to look back with some satisfaction over the six years since he had taken PB 1 to Olympia as Billing's mechanic. He was now the owner of a successful company, he was well established as an industrialist and pioneer, and he had made his mark as a sportsman, supporting the British quest for supremacy in the air. He had a comfortable home in Chessel Avenue, near Bitterne, only a mile from Woolston, and his happiness had been made complete when his first child, Joyce Mary, was born in August 1917.

The first year of the new decade, 1920, saw Scott-Paine spreading his business interests across the world. Although the settlement of the railway strike the previous year had brought an end to his pioneering cross-Channel flying boat services, he had successfully established the role of the passenger carrying flying boat in civil aviation. Other countries soon became interested and in June 1919, Scotty obtained an order for Channel flying boats from the Norwegian government. The contract was obtained in spite of fierce opposition from Vickers, and it was to be the beginning of a long association between Scott-Paine and the aviation and naval authorities in Norway. Also, in 1920, Scotty launched a new venture in association with his friend A. V. Roe and the Beardmore Aero Engine Company with the formation of the Bermuda and West Atlantic Aviation Company. Three Supermarine Channels were soon pioneering an inter-island service and two further machines were then dispatched to Trinidad to carry out an aerial survey of the Orinoco Delta in Venezuela.

In April 1920, the Air Ministry announced that it would be holding competitions to encourage the development of civil aviation, and that one of the competitions would be for amphibious seaplanes that were to be 'safe, comfortable and economical for air

travel and capable of alighting on and rising from land as well as from water'. It was stipulated that the entries were to be capable of carrying at least two passengers in addition to the crew, and were to have a range of at least three hundred and fifty nautical miles. As soon as he received news of the proposed competition, Scott-Paine knew that his unique experience in building and operating flying boats put him well ahead of any competitors. He gathered a small team around him in his office at Woolston and told the assembled company that he intended to enter the competition.

The new aircraft, designated the Supermarine Commercial Amphibian, was to be designed mainly by Scott-Paine's protege, R.J. Mitchell. Scotty's driving energy ensured that, despite the short timescale, it was designed, built and tested in time to fly to Martlesham Heath, near Felixstowe on the east coast, for the contest during the following September. The machine was powered by a Rolls-Royce Eagle engine and, with its enclosed passenger cockpit, was a great improvement on the earlier Channel flying boat. Scott-Paine's entry was the only aircraft to complete all the competition trials satisfactorily, but it was under-powered with its Eagle engine, and in view of its limited speed, the prize was awarded to the Vickers Viking Amphibian. The Air Ministry observers were so impressed with Scotty's Supermarine Amphibian, however, that it doubled the second prize of £4000 to £8000, a well-earned tribute to the Woolston team.

Following the success of the Commercial Amphibian, the Air Ministry gave Scotty a contract to build a three-seat, deck-landing amphibian that emerged as the Supermarine Seal Mk II in May 1921. However, the amount of work from the Air Ministry appeared to be limited for the foreseeable future and Scott-Paine widened his international contacts, selling the Supermarine Channel boats. During

The Supermarine 'Commercial Amphibian'
entered for the Air Ministry Competition in
September 1920.

1921, Scotty sold Channel flying boats for service in New Zealand, Aukland and Onerahi. In July 1921, a Supermarine Channel became the first aircraft to visit Fiji, and Scotty was amused to see the photographs of a Southampton-built flying boat in a makeshift hangar of palm fronds on a romantic tropical beach.

Scotty never missed an opportunity to impress a potential customer and when a Japanese delegation visited Woolston on March 14th, 1921, he decided to demonstrate the seaworthiness of the Channel flying boat despite a full gale and a spring tide. A heavy sea was blowing even in the sheltered waters of the River Itchen and waves of some four to five feet were plunging against the Supermarine slipway. Not deterred, Scott-Paine placed his passengers in the flying boat and the skilled Biard managed to lift the boat off the water in a mere five seconds. The delegation was so impressed that it placed an immediate order for three Channels for use at the Kasumigaura Air Base. The year also saw sales of the Channel boats to Sweden and a flying boat was sold to Chile, who received a Channel Mk II in 1922.[1]

Following the success of the Commercial Amphibian, Scott-Paine got Mitchell to progress with the design of a passenger carrying flying boat for use on a scheduled airline route. Mitchell developed

his design on what was to emerge as the Supermarine Sea Eagle during 1922. The Sea Eagle was an amphibious flying boat that could carry six passengers in the comfort of an enclosed cabin. Scott-Paine then decided that, if he could build the necessary aircraft, he would establish Woolston as a marine airport and operate his own services between Southampton and the Channel Islands. The next step was to establish his own airline, and the British Marine Air Navigation Company was registered on March 23rd, 1922. The Asiatic Petroleum Company (Shellmex) was a major shareholder as was the London and South Western Railway that owned Southampton Docks. Scotty made Commander Bird a director of Supermarine and established him in a London office to concentrate on negotiations with the Air Ministry over the proposed route. Three months later, in June 1922, the Air Ministry approved Scotty's scheme for a service between Southampton, Cherbourg and Le Havre, as well as to the Channel Islands, and agreed to provide the British Air Navigation Company with an annual operating subsidy of £10,000 and to pay for the aircraft with a grant of £21,000.

As plans for his new airline gradually came to fruition, Scott-Paine cast around for further challenges. The quest for speed was still in his blood.

One day, during that summer of 1922 he took Henri Biard aside and said, 'How would you like to fly in the Schneider Trophy this year?' Biard could hardly believe that his energetic employer was serious, but then Scotty took him to a secret shop and showed him a diminutive flying boat that Mitchell and his colleagues had been making ready for the contest to be held at Naples during August. The flying boat, already christened Sea Lion II, was based on the successful N.1B Baby design, and had been built as the Sea King II the previous year, as a single-seater sportsman racing machine. The aircraft had never found a buyer, and as soon as he heard that the British government was not willing to finance an entry, Scott-Paine immediately decided to offer the Sea King as the British contender. The venture was likely to prove expensive so Scotty had arranged to see H. T. Vane, Managing Director of Napiers, who had agreed to lend a Napier Lion engine for the development of the Sea King into a formidable racer. A similar approach had been made to the directors of Shell and Wakefield who agreed to provide petrol and oil. Scotty also put a considerable amount of his own money into the project and even offered to sell his Rolls-Royce to finance it.

Biard was sworn to the greatest secrecy as work on the new racer was carried out in the factory's 'secret shop'. Suddenly, the Italian authorities announced that the date of the contest would be brought forward by fourteen days, but Scott-Paine who had produced the 'Seven Day Bus' in less time than this, worked his team by day and by night to finish the aircraft on time. Matters were made worse by the onset of summer gales which delayed the maiden flight. Day after day the team waited for a break in the weather, while Biard strode around the shed with fuming impatience. One day the weather moderated and, soon after sundown, the wind dropped sufficiently for Biard to order the machine out. It was wheeled out of the shed, started up and after a short run, Biard took off. Suddenly, when the machine was about two hundred feet above Southampton Docks the engine cut out. With great skill, Biard managed to land between the forest of masts and funnels and the fault was quickly rectified.[2]

During the hurried test flights, Sea Lion II

Sea Lion II, piloted by Henri Biard, during the Schneider Trophy Contest at Naples, 1922, when it regained the Trophy for Britain at a speed of 145.7 mph.

attained a speed of 150 mph and appeared to be a fitting contender for the trophy. A new problem them emerged as the continental railway companies told Scotty that they could not guarantee to deliver the flying boat to Naples on time. As Biard later wrote: 'It seemed that the stars in their course fought against us; but Mr Scott-Paine had his own way of overcoming the stars.' At that critical moment Scotty managed to persuade the General Steam Navigation Company to put the ss *Philomel*, then in Southampton Docks, at the disposal of the racing team. The shipping line agreed to carry the flying boat to Naples; Captain Field and his crew carefully packed Sea Lion on board with the help of Supermarine workers and Scotty, with his small band, sailed for the Mediterranean.

Henri Biard won the Schneider Trophy on August 12th at an average speed of 145.7 mph. The achievement was a tribute to Mitchell and his design team and a particular tribute to Biard whose skill in piloting an aircraft based on a five year old design outwitted the somewhat faster Italian flying boats. It was a triumph for Britain and for Scotty who afterwards was taken by Biard to see the crater of Mount Vesuvius. Scotty had a bad cold and as he looked into the crater, the sulphurous fumes made him choke, much to the alarm of Biard who later wrote: 'But the same spirit that won the Schneider Trophy for England made him risk everything because he intended to see the crater—and there you are!'[3]

Scott-Paine's determination to wrest the Schneider Trophy from the Italians was a gesture of sportsmanship that has largely gone unrecognised in the history of British aviation. He had of course realised that if the Italians had won a third time they would have retained the trophy outright, but Scotty's spirit of adventure made possible the later series of contests which led to the British win of 1931. It was these later contests that gave Supermarine the skill in high-speed aircraft design that was to lead to the development of the Supermarine Spitfire of World War Two.

The return to Southampton was jubilant. Scotty and Biard were received by the Mayor of Southampton and the party then returned to the Supermarine works, where the Woolston floating bridges were decked out with flags, and the population turned out, ringing hand bells, beating shovels, clashing tins and generally creating a joyous havoc.

As soon as the celebrations were over, Scott-Paine turned his energy to the completion of the three Sea Eagles that were needed to maintain the schedule agreed with the Air Ministry for his new commercial airline. The first Sea Eagle was ready for its maiden flight the following summer, and in June, 1923, Biard and Major Wright of the Air Ministry, took the machine up for the first time. Wright reported that it was the finest sea-going machine that he had ever flown, and the flying boat received its certificate of Airworthiness on July 17th. Scotty's plans for the airline were going well and he decided to enter the Sea Eagle in the Circuit of Britain King's Cup Race. Biard took the Sea Eagle to Hendon Airfield for the start of the race on July 13th. The race was a glorious failure for Biard who completed the circuit despite hair-raising adventures, but was disqualified after bursting a tyre at Newcastle and landing on the wheel rim at Glasgow.[4]

On Sunday, August 5th, 1923, Scott-Paine went to early Mass at Woolston, before meeting the Director of Civil Aviation, Sir Sefton Branker at the Supermarine sheds. Branker, a short, jaunty, relentless man, sporting a prominent moustache and a rimless monocle, had arrived for a special flight in the Sea Eagle. Branker was accompanied by Lord Apsley, Junior Member of Parliament for Southampton, and both men were highly impressed with the aircraft that was to establish the new flying boat passenger service to the Channel Islands. The flight took them over the yachts assembled for Cowes Week and they were given a demonstration of the machine's seaworthiness when taxiing through the lines of moored yachts in Cowes Harbour.[5] A week later, Scott-Paine welcomed Branker back to Woolston, this time for a proving flight that was to cover the whole route of the intended air service. The Sea Eagle was again piloted by Henri Biard, and the comfortable passenger cabin was occupied by Scotty, Sir Sefton Branker, Lieutenant Colonel Sir Francis Shelmerdine, Senior Assistant to the Controller of Aerodromes and Licensing, and C. H. Biddlecombe, a navigation expert in the Air Ministry.

Fog delayed the start of the journey but at 10.10 AM the flying boat took off from the glassy stillness of Southampton Water and landed fifty-one minutes later at Cherbourg. The VIPs were given lunch by the French authorities who then took the party to Deauville where it rejoined the Sea Eagle on the famous beach. Fifteen ·minutes after taking off, Scotty and his party arrived at St Peter Port, Guernsey, where another tumultuous reception awaited them. A banquet was held to celebrate the prospect of this important new means of communication with the mainland, which was both fast and safe, and extremely comfortable. In fact, the return trip to Southampton on the following day, was so leisurely that some of the passengers fell asleep, a tribute to the comfort of the modern flying boat.[6]

Scotty's vision was soon to become a reality. Customs and immigration facilities were established at Woolston, which became the first designated modern airport in the world, and final arrangements were made for the reception of passengers and cargoes. Eventually all was ready and regular scheduled flying boat air services began on September 25th, 1923. Scott-Paine had established the flying boat as part of British civil aviation policy, and this type of flying was to remain immensely popular until the cost of maintaining separate marine bases made the flying boat routes uneconomical in the early 1950s.[7]

While he was working up the new Sea Eagles and supervising the complex arrangements for the inauguration of passenger services, Scotty again found time to interest himself in the Schneider Trophy competition. The 1923 contest was to be held at Cowes and Scotty was content to leave the task of defending the trophy to others until it became clear that the proposed British entries were likely to be inferior to the Supermarine Sea Lion. He made a quick decision; if British honour were to be defended, then he was going to defend it with his tried and trusted flying boat. The financial commitment represented by the construction of the three Sea Eagles made it impossible for him to construct a new flying boat, so he called Mitchell to his office and discussed ways and means of increasing

the speed of the 1922 competitor. Sea Lion II was retrieved from the Air Ministry and Mitchell set about modifying the lines and wings, while Napier's came up with a new 525 hp Series III Lion engine. It was a challenge: Sea Lion was based on a wartime hull design and had been built to the limits of high-speed racing only twelve months previously. Severe competition was expected from the Americans with their Curtiss CR-3 floatplanes, and as Biard predicted, Sea Lion III, proved to be 'playful' and difficult to control, having a tendency to hydroplane free of the water before flying speed had been reached. The contest took place on September 28th, 1923 and Scotty thought that Sea Lion III, which had achieved 160 mph in trials, had a good chance of winning the trophy. However, the American floatplanes were much faster than anyone had anticipated and America won the trophy at an average speed of 177.38 mph, compared with Biard's 153.17 mph. Although Scotty was disappointed by the failure of Sea Lion to take the trophy for a second time, he was satisfied that his entry, backed only with the resources he could muster as an individual, had put up a good performance against the American team with its vast amount of government backing.[8]

Scotty was aware that the management of his fledgling airline was likely to take up much of his

A Sea Eagle flying boat at the Supermarine 'International Airport', Southampton, 1923.

effort so he appointed James Bird as Managing Director of Supermarine, with a specific responsibility for extracting further orders from the Air Ministry for the factory. The dearth of post-war orders then came to an end with an undertaking from Air Vice-Marshal Sir Geoffrey Salmond that the Air Ministry would order up to eighteen Supermarine Seagulls over a two-year period. This was followed by an order for a twelve-passenger transport amphibian, in response to which Scott-Paine instructed Mitchell to design the first twin-engined flying boat, the Supermarine Swan, which was to make its first flight on March 23rd, 1924.

However, Scott-Paine was more interested in the development of larger flying boats for civil aviation, and saw a role for the Swan on the Channel Island route. In the event, the machine showed so much promise during its trials with the Royal Air Force, that it was developed into the world famous Supermarine Southampton, although the prototype Swan was loaned to Imperial Airways and used on the Channel Island service in 1926 and 1927. In the meantime, Scott-Paine's path was diverging even further from that which his fellow director, James Bird, wished to follow. C.G. Grey, the editor of *The Aeroplane*, recorded in his unpublished autobiography, *Bats in my Belfry*, that Scotty and Bird had a great argument during which Bird said heatedly:

'What will you take to get out of this?'. Scotty responded by naming a sum that Grey recalled as £200,000, whereupon Bird slapped his hand on the table and said, 'Done with you!'[9]

The event was of sufficient importance for Scotty to revert to his old and largely abandoned habit of writing in his diary. On November 16th, 1923, he wrote in a volume devoid of other entries:[10]

This day after nearly 3 months of negotiating I sold all my patents and shareholdings in Supermarine for £192,000. I am very sorry indeed to part with all that I have built up singlehanded. I very much appreciate the men who have worked with me, only 3 staff hands ever left in the whole eleven years, and I only dismissed one. We had a wonderful works, a wonderful spirit, never any troubles, no stickers, the way we worked together and pushed together was outstanding. I do intend to continue my work on the flying boats i.e. marine aircraft to join the National Air Company. My ambition being to place British Aircraft all over the world. Just as our mercantile marine is today, there's my object and to use these splendid wonderful boats which I brought into being in putting our flag over the seas in the air the world over.

CHAPTER 5
A Second Career

Scott-Paine left Supermarine with a considerable personal fortune to take up the new challenge of promoting the role of the flying boat as a director of the newly formed national airline, Imperial Airways. Early in 1923 the government had reviewed its policy of providing subsidies to small independent airlines such as Scott-Paine's British Marine Air Navigation Company, and concluded that the national interest would be served best by the creation of one national airline. Imperial Airways was formed out of the merger of four existing airlines; the British Marine Air Navigation Company, Daimler Airways, Handley-Page Transport and Travel Limited and the Instone Airline. Amongst Scotty's fellow directors were two men who were to become closely involved with him during World War Two. Colonel Frank Searle and the General Manager of the airline, George Woods Humphery.

Flying boats were to play a vital role in the development of the Empire Routes following the introduction of the Empire Air Mail Scheme in 1934 when Imperial Airways ordered twenty-eight C-Class boats from Shorts of Rochester. The Empire flying boats were to become a familiar sight in Southampton in the years before World War Two. Woods Humphery was to present Scott-Paine with a silver, desk-top model of an Empire flying boat that carried an inscription recording his appreciation of the fact that these great airliners owed their existence to Hubert Scott-Paine's inspiration and foresight.[1]

During 1922 Scott-Paine had bought a large, rambling house in Weston Lane overlooking Southampton Water. Called 'The Cliff', the house had been built as a vicarage and was ideally suited to the larger Scott-Paine family. Their eldest daughter, Joyce Mary, called Jack Emma by her doting father, had been born in 1917, followed by Elizabeth a few years later; in 1925 by the only son John, and the next year by the youngest, a third daughter,

Rosanne. The house had a large estate, and a particular attraction for Scotty were the rambling stables and outhouses that were ideal for the storage of his personal collection of aero engines and as workshops where these could be made ready for installation in racing boats that were his pride and joy. Within a short time of moving to 'The Cliff', the household establishment, which already included a cook, a housemaid and a parlour maid and a nanny, was increased with the arrival of Len Parfitt as mechanic to look after the racing boats as well as Scotty's several motor cars. The motor cars included two Rolls-Royces, one with an aluminium body built by Supermarine, and one, a yellow car that had belonged to Pemberton Billing, that Scotty had claimed as his own when he took over control of the Supermarine works.[2]

The Scott-Paine family enjoyed all the trappings of a wealthy life style in the 1920s. An old yacht, the *Sula* was bought by Scotty and was moored at Bursledon on the nearby River Hamble. The yacht was an eighty-ton auxiliary ketch, built in 1879 by Stowe and Sons at Scotty's home town of Shoreham. The family enjoyed cruises around the Solent in the yacht, often going on longer cruises with, in many cases, VIP guests such as Sir Eric Geddes, Chairman of Imperial Airways. Life in the Scott-Paine household was lively and full of fun; the ebullient Scotty, known as 'Fuzz' to his wife, Brenda, was larger than life and often around the house singing at the top of his voice or playing practical jokes on the unsuspecting members of his family or staff. The jokes did not always go down well with Brenda and their relationship often became strained. 'Nanny' White, who worked with the family for about eighteen months as nanny to John and Rosanne, recalled one such incident. A dinner party was to take place and the guests, including Reginald Mitchell, had just arrived and were smoking and having a drink in the lounge.

Their host was upstairs, singing at the top of his voice in the bathroom, and Scotty then emerged to greet his guests, much to the embarrassment of Brenda who saw that he was dressed only in his bathrobe.[3]

Dinners at 'The Cliff' were important affairs for Brenda Scott-Paine who attached great importance to developing social contacts. Frequent guests included the country's most prominent men in aviation such as Sir Sefton Branker, Sir Samuel Instone, Sir Eric Geddes, Woods Humphery, A.V. Roe, whose children were close friends of the Scott-Paine children, the Master of Semphill and, occasionally, Noel Pemberton Billing. Sporting personalities such as Betty Carstairs, Amelia Earhart and Sir Alan Cobham were frequent visitors, often closeted away with Scotty in his study, where servants were not allowed to enter and where schemes for the development of high speed motor boats were discussed in secret detail.

As a sportsman of international repute Scott-Paine played a prominent part in the affairs of the Royal Motor Yacht Club which did much to promote the development of fast motor boats. The Club had its headquarters at Hythe on Southampton Water and had hosted the British International Motor Boat Trophy contest for the Harmsworth Trophy in July 1920. A challenge had been received from Commodore Garfield (Gar) Wood, an American industrialist and keen hydroplane racer, who brought over two boats: *Miss Detroit V*, a 38-foot hydroplane, and *Miss America*, a diminutive 26-foot single-stepper. Both were powered by two Liberty Packard aero engines. Three British boats defended the trophy which had been won in 1913. There was *Maple Leaf V*, powered by four Sunbeam engines, and *Maple Leaf VI*, a single-stepper powered by two Rolls-Royce engines and piloted by Harry Hawker, the well-known wartime pilot and associate of Tommy Sopwith. The third defender had been a boat called *Sunbeam-Despujols*. Gar Wood won the trophy in *Miss America* at a speed of 51.8 knots and so began an unbroken series of wins which it became Scott-Paine's driving ambition to break.

It fell to amateur sportsmen such as Scott-Paine to carry on the development of high speed craft after the Admiralty disbanded the Coastal Motor Boat organisation in 1926. Scotty's principal racing boat at this time was *Tiddlywinks*, a 21-foot speed boat built by Supermarine in 1919. It was reputedly an old flying boat hull, suggested by some to be the hull of the unfinished PB 7, built for the German government in 1914.[4] The boat was kept at the Imperial Airways sheds at Woolston, where it was looked after by Len Parfitt. Parfitt had been recruited by Scotty while he was completing his apprenticeship at Dixon

Brothers in Woolston, where he had been given the job of installing a Beardmore aero engine into the speed boat. On hearing that Parfitt had six months of his time left to serve, Scotty went up to the office at Dixon's and told the manager that if he did not release his protégé into his employment, he would take his business elsewhere. Thus Len Parfitt came to join Scott-Paine's little band just as his new master had joined Pemberton Billing's 'litte bodyguard of fellows' twelve years earlier.

Scott-Paine certainly made an impact on the local scene with the trials of *Tiddlywinks* in the River Itchen. The boat was fitted with a three-foot surface propeller with direct drive and no clutch, so that when the engine was started, the boat roared off at speed. On the first occasion with its new Beardmore fitted, the engine was over filled with oil and, when it was started up, the whole of the Itchen was blotted out in a great cloud of blue smoke. *Tiddlywinks* roared off across the river, leaning over on her side as she shot past the Supermarine works with the result that Parfitt and Scotty were thrown over. Parfitt saved himself by grabbing a sparking plug on the engine, but Scotty got his foot caught on the throttle cable so there was no way of slowing the boat. Eventually when she came back on her bottom, Scotty managed to stop the boat and a launch came out to tow it back. Scotty was nothing if not a practical experimentalist and he ordered Parfitt to remove one of the two rudders to see if this would improve the steering. The effect was that the boat just went round in huge, concentric circles despite what was done with the helm. Roaring up the River Itchen, out of control, the boat eventually came to rest about a mile upstream, underneath Northam Bridge, where the two men just sat and laughed at their madcap escapade.[5]

Scotty and Len Parfitt spent many hours trying to improve the performance of what was potentially a very powerful racing boat. Scotty's mechanical skills, together with his knowledge of high performance aero engines soon put him in the forefront of high speed boat development. Some of his experiments appeared foolhardy to those who knew him, as recalled by Len Parfitt who took *Tiddlywinks* from Southampton to Cowes on the Isle of Wight:

. . . we ran down in the ordinary way to Hythe and she went porpoising, hit the water and jumped. Like that all the way and we went on to Cowes, down to Saunders one day. We ran into Cowes Harbour and tied on to a bouy, went ashore. Sam Saunders came out to see us, and of course he was thunderstruck and said, 'You never came from Southampton in that thing!' Scotty replied, 'Yes we did, and we are off now—let go everything, let go the ropes, let go the moorings and don't try and grab us when we go.' We started to crank her over, whoosh, she was gone and we left them. It was funny! We came porpoising out of Cowes and all the way home like a kangaroo. And we got home and gave Saunders a ring to say that we had arrived safely—Sam said he was very very surprised'.

Two strands in Hubert Scott-Paine's life were about to come together. As a sportsman and an official of the Royal Motor Yacht Club he was keen to promote a wider interest in the sport of racing motor boats. As an entrepreneur of considerable experience he realised that any growth in popular motor boating would be to the benefit of American boat builders as nothing was being done to encourage the British motor boat building industry to take advantage of the popular interest in the sport. Whilst motor boating had tended to be the exclusive preserve of rich enthusiasts who were willing to devote huge amounts of money to compete for prestigious international trophies, there was a tremendous growth of popular motorboat racing in America. A major step forward

in Britain had been the presentation of the Duke of York's International Trophy for 1½ litre hydroplanes in 1924 and the development of a single class 17-foot boat, designed by Sammy Saunders, and powered by a 50 hp Sunbeam engine. The type had achieved fame at the hands of the Standard Oil millionaire, Marion Barbara (Betty) Carstairs, who did more to popularise fast motor boat racing in Britain than any other racer for many years past.

Scott-Paine watched the decline of the British motor boat industry as American boats, particularly the Chris-Craft, made inroads into the expanding British market, much as the American motor car manufacturers had done at the end of the Great War. Scotty saw it as a patriotic duty to help to turn the tide of American imports and he saw the revival of interest in popular motor boat racing as crucial to the renaissance of motor boat building. During 1926, he persuaded the Royal Motor Yacht Club to join forces with the British Motor Boat Club in finding a solution. The outcome was the joint promotion of a new 'one-class' design of racing boat, the 'Puma' class, designed to Scotty's specifications by Saunders' chief designer, the young and innovative Fred Cooper.

The new 'Puma' class was intended to bring high

The prototype Puma class racing boat, P1, with Len Parfitt and Scott-Paine. His wife and daughters, Joyce and Elizabeth, are on the *Sula*.

speed racing within the means of the moderately wealthy citizen and so encourage British boatyards in the face of the flood of mass produced boats from the United States. It was a 30-foot multi-step hydroplane, designed to be capable of continuous service with the minimum of attention to either hull or machinery; it could be used as a comfortable cruiser in sheltered waters such as the Solent or as a powerful racer, capable of over 40 knots. The prospective purchaser would also be assured by the agreement between the racing clubs which meant that there was no danger of it being outclassed and rendered obsolete for racing purposes by newer boats of a different design. The 'Puma One-Class' hydroplane cost £1,200 and could be ordered from Saunders or any other boat builder approved by the racing committees of the clubs. The British engine manufacturers were not producing any light-weight, high-powered marine engines at this time, so Scotty's choice, with all his Supermarine experience, was the 240 hp Siddeley 'Puma' aero engine, which was available in large numbers from the Aircraft Disposal Company. This was installed to drive a single propeller up to 1400 rpm through a Joe's reverse gear mounted amidships.[6]

Scott-Paine, architect of the scheme, ordered the first 'Puma' boat, to be called *Panther*. The ceremonial unveiling of *Panther* took place in Sammy Saunders yard in East Cowes on the Isle of Wight, on March 9th, 1927. A number of eminent motorboating enthusiasts were there with Scotty on that Wednesday morning. There was A. H. R. Phillips and T. D. Wynn Weston, respectively Treasurer and Secretary of the Royal Motor Yacht Club, Lieutenant Commander Tristram Fox RN of the British Motor Boat Club, Flight Lieutenant F. L. Luxmoor, a well-known racing enthusiasts, and Colonel Darly, joint Managing Director of the Aircraft Disposal Company.

Scotty, smartly dressed in a double-breasted suit, with yachting cap set at an angle over his well-brushed red hair, welcomed his guests. The boat was uncovered and subjected to much scrutiny and admiration. After a short ceremony, the party was taken to the Gloster Hotel as guests of Sammy Saunders, who, after a splendid lunch spoke highly of Scott-Paine's achievement in bringing the two major clubs together in promoting this new racing class. 'No other man', he concluded, 'could have accomplished that.' Scott-Paine responded with a short speech in which he told the assembled company that the Americans had great designs on the British market for motor boats and that he knew personally of two or three American companies that were seriously considering a campaign to flood the market

with cheap imports, much as the American motor car manufacturers had successfully done. 'They must be stopped', he said, 'British firms must capture the market!'[7]

The entrepreneurial instinct that had made his fortune at Supermarine told Scotty that, if there was a market for mass produced motor boats in Britain, then he certainly had the experience and background to manufacture and sell boats himself. There was no-one else with comparable technical and practical experience of the design of fast motor boats and their machinery, together with experience in the mass production of wooden hulls. Six months later he had bought his own yard and had set out to capture the market.

The significance of the event led to its being recorded in Scotty's rarely used pocket diary. On Friday, September 30th, 1927, he noted, 'Bought Hythe Shipyard'. The brevity of the entry hardly indicated that the decision was to change his life and was to lead to the creation of a legend in his own lifetime. Bill Sheaff, who had joined Scotty as his chauffeur on June 7th that very year, later recalled how the news was broken to him. 'I was up at the garage doing a job . . . I don't know if I was de-coking the old Morris or not, and he came back to me and he looked at me—he said, "Bill, I have bought a boatyard." I said, "Whatever for?" Knowing that he had retired and was enjoying life. "Oh!" he said, "I don't know, just for something to do, a bit of a hobby." "Expensive isn't it?" "Oh", he said, "I don't know, I bet you sixpence I make five percent on it in five years!" Bill Sheaff never did get his tanner but he was to witness the development of the most sophisticated boat building yard in the world.[8]

Len Parfitt's recollection was similar to Bill Sheaff's. On the morning of the sale he was at White's Yard at Itchen with the *Sula* when the office boy came round to tell Parfitt that he was wanted on the telephone. It was Scott-Paine who shouted down the line, 'That you Len . . . go and launch *P1* [*Panther*] and bring her over here to Hythe!' Scotty went on tell Parfitt: 'I have bought so much bloody stuff at the sale at Kemp's Yard I have had to buy the whole bloody yard to keep it in!' Scotty was excited and kept on laughing. He again joked that he had not gone there to buy the yard, he had gone there to buy gear, but had to buy the whole yard to keep it all in. *P1* was kept at the Imperial Airways sheds at Woolston so Parfitt ran down the road to Woolston where the tide was out; he just managed to get the speed boat afloat and sped off across Southampton Water to Hythe. He had no idea of how much water there would be at Hythe, but just managed to get into the yard basin and stay afloat. Parfitt could not get ashore but, by the time Scotty made an appearance, the tide had turned and the boat was well afloat again. Parfitt secured *P1* to the jetty and clambered out to find the yard a hive of activity with people carrying benches and workshop equipment here, there and everywhere. He later recalled: 'Everybody was on the move carrying something, nobody knew whether they had bought it or not, take out what you like, nobody cared!'

Eventually Len Parfitt cornered a member of the auctioneer's staff and enquired what it was that Scott-Paine had bought that he had to then purchase the whole yard to keep it in. Parfitt recalled: 'The auctioneer got out some keys and showed me this room [the size of a small sitting room] and in the middle was about ten or twelve bags of ¼ inch BSF bolts and nuts and one of those big round lamp shades, like what they used to have in offices . . . ''What else?'' ''That's all as far as I know.'' ''No, there is some more somewhere'', Parfitt insisted, ''he didn't buy the whole blooming yard to keep that in!'' ,

Finally, Parfitt bumped into Scotty who was walking around the yard with Noel Van Raalte, a friend and motor boat enthusiast who, it was rumoured at the time, provided some of the finance for the purchase of the yard. Scotty admitted that he had been joking as he got Parfitt to take him back to Woolston in the speedboat. 'I want you to go over in the morning, first thing, and take charge', were his instructions as he climbed out of the boat at the Imperial Airways Sheds. 'What have I got to do?', asked Parfitt. 'Just keep you eye on the place', was the reply.[9]

CHAPTER 6
The Hire'em and Fire'em Yard

Although Scott-Paine joked with his staff that he had bought the shipyard for the frivolous pursuit of a hobby, he had very real plans to make it into one of the most up-to-date, mass production boatyards in the country. Much of the yard was in a derelict condition, although a mere five years earlier the *Yachting World* had described the Hythe Ship Yard as one of the most up to date in the country. At that time it had been acquired by Mr R. Kemp who had started a marine engineering concern on the River Itchen in 1913, the year in which Scott-Paine and Pemberton Billing had founded the Supermarine yard. Kemp had carried out 'high class yacht work' at Hythe, the site being recommended to owners as 'conveniently close to railway links with London, while being far enough removed from Southampton to render it free from the smokey pollution that often affected the delicate outside painting required on yachts'. At the time the yard had boasted extensive hauling out facilities, boat building sheds, fitting out

The Hythe Shipyard *circa* 1936.

berths, mould lofts and, for the convenience of owners, an entertainment hall complete with raised stage, electric light foot-lights and a self-contained kitchen'.[1]

Scotty could stand at his home in Weston and look across Southampton Water to his new yard at Hythe. He could reach the yard in a matter of minutes by boat, but the journey by road was considerably longer as he had to drive through Southampton, and down the narrow lanes of the New Forest shore. He gave Len Parfitt instructions to find some labour in the village, which he did by recruiting a local bosun, Dan Ewan, who soon rounded up about five workers to assist in the demolition of the older buildings. One recruit was Reg Holley, who had been retained by the previous owners to look after the site prior to the sale. Holley had been born and brought up in the Hythe Ship Yard before the Great War, and had spent much of his working life in the yard. Reg Holley was to stay with Scott-Paine until the closure of the yard in 1947.

Scotty and his men carried out a rapid survey of the buildings. They decided that one large shed, with balconies on three sides, had to come down, once Reg Holley had reported that it was dangerous to walk on the upper levels. Similarly the old yacht store, constructed on stilts with storage for masts beneath was soon declared unsafe for future use. The small workforce set about demolition, driven by Scotty's ceaseless energy: the stilts below the shed were all sawn through and, when the time came to saw the last one, Scotty was called over to give the shed a final shove to push it over.[2]

As Scott-Paine joined in the massive physical effort of clearing the old buildings, his mind was working on his plans for the future. First of all he needed a name for the yard, and several brain-storming sessions were held with those around him. Len Parfitt later recalled that it was during one such session, held with himself and Noel Van Raalte, in one of the old lofts, that the name the British Power Boat Company was decided upon.

Recalling the exciting days when he had created Supermarine with his old 'governor' Pemberton Billing, Scotty set about building up his team. Having found his own mechanic at Dixon's yard at Woolston, he then pirated Dixon's yard manager, Stuart Barker, as his own yard manager. Scotty also wanted the very best designer in the business and was able to recruit Fred Cooper, who had already made a name for himself as a motor boat designer with Saunders of Cowes. Gradually, he built up a close-knit team that was to remain close to him, maintaining a special relationship as his 'bodyguard of faithful fellows', even when the yard employed over fifteen

hundred men and women at the height of World War Two. Scotty had the capacity to draw out the most intense loyalty and love from his close employees.

During 1928, Scotty's plans for the yard gradually took shape. About thirty employees were taken on, many on a seasonal basis, and Scotty set about training shipwrights and longshoremen in production techniques that had more in common with the production lines of an aircraft factory than the traditional work of a boatyard. During these early months the payroll cost Scott-Paine £120-£130 per month, and there was considerable additional expense on the reconstruction, all of which had to be met from his own resources. The local people watched the work with interest and expressed cautious interest in the techniques of mass production which appeared to be so different to their traditional boat building ways. One local timber supplier came up to Scotty who was working in the yard, and offered him a good stock of grown oak—the naturally shaped timber which formed the keel of boats. To the man's amazement, Scotty told him that he was not interested, that he was going to build Scott-Paine craft, and was not going to use grown oak for his keels. The man went away wondering what Scott-Paine's strange ideas were, and what these strange boats were going to look like.[3]

The first type of boat designed by Fred Cooper and put into production as part of Scotty's plan to popularise motor boating, was a small hydroplane, approved as a 'one-class' design by the Royal Motor Yacht Club. The first of the so-called 'Puppy Dog' Class was built in 1928 and christened *Bow Wow*. It was a single-step hydroplane, 16 feet long and powered by a 9 hp sports model Riley car engine, driving through a reverse gear and developing 40 hp at 4,000 rpm. Although the stepped hydroplane was more expensive to build than the stepless hard-chine hull of the popular American Chris Craft, higher speeds could be attained with a small engine and, with a top speed of 35 mph, the 'Puppy Dog' Class soon proved popular. With the racing enthusiast in mind, Scotty then produced a powerful stock racing boat, a 21 foot 6 inch hydroplane powered by the American 135 hp Scripps engine that was to become the standard engine for the International 5½ litre racing class that Scotty was to bring to the world's attention two years later with his specially designed *Miss Britain I*.[4]

In choosing Fred Cooper, Scotty had obtained a designer of outstanding talent, whose technical skills could augment his own practical sense of design. During 1928 the two men developed a unique system of hull construction in which a conventional clinker hull was built in such a way that the overlapping

The prototype 'Puppy Dog' class hydroplane,
Bow Wow, 1929.

planks were laid diagonally so that the exposed edges of the planks faced aft, and away from the keel. The result was, in effect, a thirty-step hull, built with all the advantages of economy that were possible using much shorter and straighter planks. This new type of boat was offered as a 13-foot utility craft fitted with an outboard Evinrude motor and capable of speeds of up to 35 mph. Len Parfitt had the task of testing the first model, taking it over to Howard's timber yard on the Itchen with instructions to try to turn it over. His conclusion was that not only was it a safe boat, but that any youngster could get in and drive one around. At the yard they were later to be known as 'Butchers' Boats' after their popularity with Southampton tradesmen delivering supplies to yachts in the area.[5]

Scott-Paine and Fred Cooper were particularly interested in the development of the hard-chine hull for motor boats. Despite its popularity in America, the type found little support amongst motor boat enthusiasts in Britain at the time. With its tendency to pound in a seaway, the type was considered to have none of the advantages of seaworthiness of round bilge boats, and was without the advantage of speed that the stepped hydroplane enjoyed. Scotty had come to the view that, although there appeared to be little to recommend the hard-chine stepless planning hull, it might actually have tremendous

potential. He knew that this type of hull could be built using modern mass production techniques as it avoided the use of complicated shapes of timber in the hull, and he told Fred Cooper that it must be possible to develop the lines in such a way as to reduce the tendency for such boats to pound, whilst the speed could be maintained with the right choice of engine. There was no doubt in his mind that the hard-chine type of hull was capable of development into a fast, seaworthy and economic type of motor boat, and that it could bring fast and comfortable motor boating within the reach of many who otherwise would never take to popular boating.[6]

As work progressed at Hythe during 1928, Fred Cooper designed the hull which was to fulfil Scotty's expectations and was to put the British Power Boat Company ahead of all its competitors. It was a 23-foot hard-chine planing hull that was soon available in two versions, a basic cruiser powered by a 100 hp Chrysler engine and a more expensive 'Junior Express Cabin Cruiser' powered by a 135 hp Scripps engine. The Cabin Cruiser was designed for comfort; it could carry nine passengers on a day cruise; it had sleeping accommodation for two; and it had the necessary luxury of a WC.

By the winter of 1928, Scotty had increased his workforce, and was building a range of five different boats for the 1929 season. Many of these hands were then laid off at the beginning of the new 'selling' programme. For those employed on piece work, where a job was incomplete, the balance of the sums earned would only be sent on when the boat was eventually completed. Men were selected and then carefully supervised during their first week of work, at the end of which they were either kept on or laid off if Scotty decided that they were not one hundred per cent suitable. The yard soon acquired the sobriquet the 'Hire-em-and Fire-em-Yard'.[7]

Scotty also realised that the promotion of motor-boating as a sport relied upon the owner having the facilities to berth and look after his boat. The Hythe yard was ideally suited to provide a facility for the motor boat enthusiast, especially the racing enthusiast, as Southampton Water was the venue for many of the established motor boat racing events at the time, and Hythe itself was the home of the Royal Motor Yacht Club. Scotty made sure that the British Power Boat Company was widely advertised as a 'marine garage' for the use of boat owners, and, by the end of 1928, over one hundred boats were laid up at the garage for the winter season. The wide range of facilities for owners included twelve slips, petrol pumps, storage facilities for boats, car parking for up to fifty cars, expert mechanics to assist at any time, a rest room for owners' mechanics, a club house and, as Scotty proclaimed to visiting journalists, 'every-thing you could wish for'. The facilities were soon admired by the popular press and one reporter, visiting the yard in March 1929, enthused that it was 'delightfully clean and up to date, even to the minutest detail. This establishment has already become a popular centre for those interested in this fascinating hobby. The reason is not difficult to discover for, with twelve slipways, all interchange-able, special hauling up gear, quick service and exceptionally modern plant. The devotee of motor boating can be assured of the attention which he deserves.'[8]

Scott-Paine had a flair for publicity and he knew that the success of his boats in the international racing scene would be sure to focus the attention of the motor boating world upon his emergent British Power Boat Company. His stock boats were soon winning awards in all the major events including the Lido Championship of Europe, the Potsdam Cham-pionship of Germany, the Atlantis Gold Trophy, the Lucinha Challenge Cup, and many others. During the autumn of 1928, he then heard that Henry Segrave, who at Daytona Beach the previous year had become the first man to travel at over 200 mph on land, wanted to compete against Gar Wood's new *Miss America VII* the following March. Scotty had a meeting with Henry Segrave and his patron, Lord

Wakefield of Hythe, and told them that he could design and build the boat that would beat Gar Wood. Scotty's ideas were revolutionary and he proposed a small single-engined racing boat to compete against the American's multi-engined *Miss America*. Gar Wood had retained the Harmworth Trophy in Detroit in August 1928 in *Miss America VI*, powered by two Packard engines with a joint power of 2,200 hp, but Scotty proposed a boat powered with a single 930 hp Napier Lion engine of the sort that had already been used to break the world speed records on land and in the air. The Napier Lion engine had powered the Supermarine S5 which had won the 1927 Schneider Contest at Calshot, as well as Segrave's record breaking car, *Golden Arrow*.

Scott-Paine carefully explained his theory to Henry Segrave who had to drive the boat. He was convinced that success lay in the design of smaller, single-engined boats and that trophies such as the Harmsworth Trophy would be brought back through the skilful driving of such boats rather than through the brute force of several marinised aero engines. He went on to demonstrate that breaking water speed records was unlike similar attempts either in the air or in motor cars. The movement of water due to current and tide, the effects of the wind, disturbances due to boats or even relatively distant ships, semi-submerged objects such as water-logged wood, all provided hazards even on a seemingly ideal day. Time after time, Scotty told his audience, he had seen boats tearing along at 40 to 60 mph hit some disturbance and jump high in the air. He went on to remind them that the newspapers were still covering the story of how the plucky Betty Carstairs and her mechanic had been thrown clear out of their boat when it had hit a slight swell during the Harmsworth Trophy earlier that month. They had been lucky not be killed. Even a flat calm could conceal a rise and fall due to a disturbance that perhaps originated many miles away.[9]

Scotty knew better than anyone the terrible feeling of climbing into the air, out of the water, and the boat clearing the surface, twisting around the torque caused by the propeller. The slightest mis-use of the throttle at that vital moment could cause the instant death of the pilot and his mechanic. Closing the throttle, he told Seagrave, could draw the boat down as it re-enters the water, with catastrophic conse-quences. On the other hand, if the engine is racing as the boat comes back down on the water it causes too much torque and the pilot can find the boat capsized. Scotty argued strongly, from his experience of both flying boats and racing boats, that Segrave's best chance of success lay in mastering the manoeuvr-ability of a small boat, and the skill in handling one

Scott-Paine on *Miss England* at Hythe, with
Henry Segrave at the wheel.

propeller, designed for extremely high revs.

Segrave and Lord Wakefield were convinced, and
agreed that Scott-Paine should build *Miss England* for
the World Championship. Scotty hurried to Hythe
to discuss the project with Fred Cooper and his newly
recruited design assistant, Tommy Quelch. Cooper
came up with a design for a 26-foot single step hydroplane with the engine mounted as far as possible
against the transom which thereby acted as a second,
riding step when the boat was at speed. The broad
forward step acted as a balancer and carried
relatively little weight so that there would be little
tendency to submerge forward while the boat was at
speed. The hull construction incorporated all of
Scotty's experience of motor boat racing, and he
personally supervised the marine conversion of the
Napier engine that was to drive a single propeller at a
revolutionary 6,800 revolutions per minute. The

drive from the engine extended forward to a reverse
gear which made it possible to keep the axis of the
propeller shaft parallel with the water whilst
mounting the engine in the stern of the boat. The
unorthodox propeller was designed and made at the
Hythe yard after Scott-Paine had conducted numerous experiments. Many entirely novel features were
designed, including a water-lubricated bearing for
the tail shaft and a special water cooling arrangement
for the engine.[10]

Scotty drove his small band to work all hours while
the boat was designed and built in the greatest
secrecy at Hythe. The marathon efforts of the 'Seven
Day Bus' or the race to prepare Sea Lion I in time for
the 1919 Schneider Trophy were as if rehearsals for
the efforts to get *Miss England* built on time. Even Leñ
Parfitt found that his employer's insistence on
absolute dedication to the job in hand, and on his

team working long hours without extra pay, was too much. Scotty turned his back on anyone who argued and for Len Parfitt the straw that broke the camel's back was finding himself at Southampton West railway station at two o'clock in the morning with instructions to locate and pick up the propeller shaft for *Miss England*, and to transport it to a boat moored at Town Quay. He had no-one to help him but Scotty's response the following day was, 'If you don't like the bloody job—clear out! I will soon fill your vacancy!' Len went at the end of the week.[11]

The plans for the boat were completed on Tommy Quelch's drawing board in a remarkable three weeks and four days.[12] The construction of the hull took only seven weeks and two days. It was a formidable achievement, but delays in the delivery of the engine meant that there was no time for trials before the boat had to be shipped to America. There was time, however, for a bit of publicity and Scotty took the diminutive racer to London for a special showing at Boots Ltd, Piccadilly. *Miss England*, was then returned to Southampton and loaded on board the RMS *Majestic*, which was preparing to sail for New York on January 31st, 1929.[13]

Miss England was an immediate success. Early in March a jubilant Scott-Paine received a cable from Daytona Beach, Miami, Florida.[14]

Mile timed today at 78 on 3/4 throttle. Boat ran dead horizontal, handles beautifully, no wash. Hull simply wonderful. Motor wonderful. Congratulations—Segrave.

Scotty's triumph was then made complete with the news that Gar Wood had been beaten for the first time in nine years. Fresh from his record breaking dash along the sands of Daytona Beach in *Golden Arrow*, Segrave had raced Gar Wood in his *America*

VII in two races over a twelve-mile course. In the first heat Gar Wood was leading by half a lap when *Miss America* broke her steering quadrant and was eliminated, leaving Segrave to complete the course at an average 60 mph. Although *Miss England* was beaten on the second heat, during which it reached the speed of 87.2 mph, it was decided that the overall winner of the World Championship was Henry Segrave and *Miss England*.

The following day Segrave tried for a world speed record. The single-engined boat averaged 91.91 mph over six runs, not quite enough to break Gar Wood's existing record of 92.8 mph. But the championship had been won and Scott-Paine's design had been proved successful.

Segrave returned home to a hero's welcome in Southampton and again in London. A grateful King conferred a knighthood upon the sportsman who held the nation's honour in his hands. Sensing the national mood of rejoicing, Lord Wakefield donated *Miss England* to the Science Museum in London where it joined Scotty's Schneider Trophy Sea Lion. Segrave then recorded his appreciation of Scott-Paine's contribution in a letter to *The Times*:[15]

My sole purpose of going to the States with the *Golden Arrow* and *Miss England* was to regain for Britain the land speed record and the world's motor boat championship. But I could never have achieved this purpose without the aid of the great genius Captain Irving, who accomplished the remarkable task of designing a motor car that has made practicable the speed of 231 miles an hour; and Mr Scott-Paine who built the first British motor boat to capture the world's championship from *Miss America*—which was, incidentally, a boat of considerably more that twice the power of *Miss England*.

CHAPTER 7
The Crest of a Wave

Scotty was quick to make the most out of *Miss England's* success, proclaiming that the boat had been 'designed and built by Hubert Scott-Paine'. Fred Cooper was furious that his contribution had not been acknowledged by Scotty and he too left the British Power Boat Company after an acrimonious argument. Lord Wakefield took Cooper's side, and refused to give Scott-Paine the chance to construct his next boat, *Miss England II*, which was to be designed by Fred Cooper and was to break the world record at 110.28 mph in 1931.[1]

Notwithstanding the departure of Fred Cooper, the 1929 season was an outstanding success for Scotty, both in the sale of boats and in the achieve-

The hull shop at Hythe in the early 1930s.

ment of numerous racing honours for British Power Boat Company craft. During the year, Scott-Paine developed new techniques for the mass production of hard chine hulls, using jigs and templates for the production of frames and other components. A distinctive feature of the production techniques was that the hulls were built and planked upside down, and then turned over for the construction of the decks and deck houses and the fitting out of the machinery and accommodation. The hulls were constructed of double diagonal planking below the chine, while the sides were single planking screwed to seam battens. The technique allowed for the use of short, straight lengths of planking that were produced in the sawmill prior to finishing and fitting in the hull shops.

By the end of 1929 the firm was employing three hundred men, although many were employed during the winter months and laid off during the subsequent 'boat selling' season. Over twenty different trades were employed and the payroll at the end of 1929 was £1,500–1,600 per week. By this time, the works, with its stock and equipment, were valued at over £100,000, in addition to which Scotty had spent nearly £50,000 on building up his personal fleet of racing craft. The winter of 1929/1930 saw a building programme of boats valued at £40,000. Most of the work was speculative but Scotty worked on the principle that if boats were completed and ready for sale, customers would buy them rather than foreign boats, which were normally available within three to four weeks of ordering.[2]

A new building shop was under construction at the end of 1929, and by January 1930 a new saw mill had been completed. Scotty inspected every part of the works every week, ensuring that the highest standards of tidiness and workmanship were adhered to. He issued all the workforce with white overalls which he insisted were laundered regularly so that a pride in the workplace became second nature to all employees. Scotty was insistent that good work came from contented employees and he introduced many schemes for employee welfare, including incentive schemes to assist apprentices in building up their own tool kits, and mobile canteens to bring refreshments to workmen in the sheds and building shops.

Scott-Paine was making one of his regular inspections during January 1930, when he took a reporter from the magazine *The Motor Boat* around the factory. The two men looked over the new saw mill that had just been completed. A new building shed was going up and Scotty pointed out over three dozen completed outboard safety dingies, nearly a dozen speedboats, two Junior Express Cruisers and at least seven other hulls in course of completion. Most were versions of the 23-foot hull which had been re-

designed for the 1930 season to provide a drier ride, and four 35-foot cruisers were under construction. The first of these, *Miss Pamela II*, had been tested during January and had proved to be an exceptionally comfortable and dry boat, even in bad weather conditions and heavy seas. It had been designed with sleeping accommodation for four and was powered by two 125 hp Chrysler engines. Marketed as the 'Sea Ace', the 35-foot cruiser was advertised at a price of £2,200. The reporter had no doubts about the success of Scott-Paine's enterprise and wrote that 'the running of such a large boat-building yard solely devoted to high-speed pleasure craft is an idea entirely new to this country, and if it meets with the success that it is due, it should benefit the public and have marked influence on the policy of the British Boatbuilding industry. Given good salesmanship, we think it can be done.'[3]

Salesmanship was something at which Scott-Paine excelled. The new range of motor boats sold during the 1930 season had names taken from the pack of cards. At the top of the range, the 35-foot Express Cruiser was called the 'Sea Ace'. The 23-foot boat was obtainable as the 'Sea King', 'Sea Queen' or the 'Sea Jack'. The 'Sea King', or 'Junior Express Cruiser' was a 35 mph runabout with seating for six, selling at £685, and with a top speed of 35 mph was capable of racing as well as comfortable cruising. The 'Sea Queen', which had less luxurious fittings, sold at £415, while the 'Sea Jack' was advertised as a 'Sea Lorry', a utility boat, capable of carrying a load equivalent to twelve people, and costing £398.

In January 1930, Scotty travelled to America to visit the New York Motor Boat Show and to study boat production in the United States. He carefully examined the displays at the Grand Central Hall, New York and came to the conclusion that although the boat building industry was considerable, there had been no advance on design over the previous five years. Word was spreading about Scott-Paine's outstanding designs and at least five eminent boat builders approached Scotty, asking if they could build his boats under licence in America. Scotty travelled across the States, looking at boat yards from the east coast to the west coast and concluded that none could approach Hythe for efficiency in design or operation. He also talked to the naval authorities about their requirements for coast guard vessels, but it was to be some years before Scott-Paine boats were to be purchased by the United States Navy. Scott-Paine returned to England on the *Aquitania*, carrying details of American marine accessories such as petrol cookers, many of which were novel to the British market, and convinced that his yard led the world in motor boat design and construction.[4]

While he was in America, Scott-Paine made a special visit to the Yachtsmen's Association of America in his capacity as Chairman of the Joint Racing Committee of the Royal Motor Yacht Club and the British Motor Boat Club. The RMYC and the donors of the Harmsworth Trophy had asked him to negotiate a change to the rules arising from the deed of gift of the Harmsworth Trophy. Scotty told his hosts that they wished to eliminate those parts of the rules which insist that should a boat not finish the course within three hours of the winning boat it shall be entirely disqualified. The rules, he explained, were framed in the years when it was desirable to encourage reliability from the engines of the competing boats, but now engines were extremely reliable and the rule was unfair to boats that might meet with an unexpected accident such as striking some floating object or the fouling of the propeller on floating debris. Scotty's American hosts were courteous but unobliging. It had proved impossible to get all the committee together as many of the American members were at Miami. Although Scotty could have insisted upon the change according to the rules governing voting, he was anxious not to press his American friends before all their members could be consulted.

While he was with the Committee, Scotty also proposed alterations to the rules governing weight restrictions in the new 5½ litre racing class. The 5½ litre Class had been proposed a year earlier, to bring motor boat racing within the means of the moderately wealthy citizen. A chance meeting of racing enthusiasts in Florida early in 1929, at the time that Henry Segrave had raced *Miss England*, discussed the future of international motorboat competitions. It was generally recognised that the competitions were restricted due to the immense sums of money involved in designing, building and entering craft for the Harmsworth Trophy. The gathering concluded that the establishment of a class in which hulls and motors were restricted so that an average man could afford to enter a boat, would be a great stimulus to competition, and would generate public support through events that were full of interest from a spectator point of view.[5]

Hubert Scott-Paine proposed a modification of the rules of the 5½ litre class so that boats could be designed as cruisers as well as racers for this event. He was sure that this would widen the market for such boats and so help the rejuvenation of the boat building industry. As he sailed on the *Aquitania*, he was under the impression that his suggestions had been adopted and, as soon as he arrived back in Southampton on February 14th, he announced his intention of building a boat for the contest. To his amazement, he then heard from the Yachtsmen's Association of America that the American motor boat racing establishment had disagreed with the removal of the weight limit. He gave immediate instructions to abandon the hull under construction in his 'secret shop' at Hythe and sat down with Tommy Quelch to design a revolutionary boat that was to emerge as *Miss Britain I*.

The building and testing of *Miss Britain I* was undertaken in the greatest secrecy at the Hythe yard. As the work progressed, so the revolutionary nature of the design became apparent. Scotty had created a hull in which the exceptional strength came from a deep and rigid centre girder, the structure of which owed much to his experience in aircraft design. The engine itself was used to assist in the dispersing of stresses through the engine bearers and, higher up, through the top of the 'fuselage' fore and aft members. When at rest the boat had no freeboard, resting on the water like a dinner plate. This improved the aerodynamic quality of the boat which proved itself to be exceptionally seaworthy in heavy weather. The waterline length of the boat was 20 feet ½ inch, with a maximum beam of 5 feet 8 inches. The main fore and after structure was built of spruce fastened by ply gussets, the inter girder frames being mahogany. The stock Scripps Model 124 engine, developing 135 hp at 3,000 rpm, was mounted aft, driving a single propeller through a reverse gear specially designed at Hythe. The rudder arrangement drew particular attention from the racing enthusiasts, as the conventional interconnection between the stern and bow rudders was dispensed with in favour of an arrangement in which the fore rudder was controlled by the foot, as in an aircraft, while the stern rudder was controlled through a system patented by Scott-Paine. As the rules of the 5½ litre trophy meant that all bouys were to be left on the port side, Scotty placed the stern rudder offset on the starboard side, thus avoiding the slipstream of the propeller. To further reduce drag Scotty had designed the rudder strut as a hollow casting through which the cooling water for the engine was collected.[6]

Scotty was immensely excited by the boat. The significance of the challenge led him to take out his rarely used pocket diary and on Saturday 16th August, 1930 he wrote: 'Brenda and I sailed for America in *Berengaria* with my own designed and built *Miss Britain I* with which I have challenged the Americans in the new 5½ litre boats.'[7]

Miss Britain I astounded the crowds gathered at Detroit for the 5½ litre Detroit News Trophy event. Not only did Scotty's boat look remarkable, but those watching the race were impressed by her manoeuvrability. During the first heat she demonstrated her seaworthiness in heavy seas when Scotty stopped to assist the crew of a capsized contender. Scotty's attention to detail in the design meant that the boat achieved 48 mph, a remarkable speed for a stock engine of only 135 hp. The challenge was successful and, on Wednesday, September 24th, Scotty again took out his diary and wrote, 'Arrived back from America with Brenda, *Miss Britain I* and Detroit International News Trophy, the first American trophy ever to be won from America.'

Two months later, on Wednesday, November 26th, 1930, Scotty again made an entry in his diary: 'Beauforte-Greenwood and Norrington etc. down to see mock-up of their new launch I've invented for them.' It was the first breakthrough in a campaign that Scotty had been quietly undertaking to persuade the government service departments to try out his new hard-chine boats. Flight Lieutenant W. E. G. Beauforte-Greenwood MINE AMINA was the Head of the Marine Equipment Branch of the Air Ministry and was responsible for the provisioning of RAF marine craft for use with the flying boat squadrons. At the time, the Air Ministry relied upon an Admiralty designed, round bilge boat for use as tenders to service the flying boats, but Scotty was convinced that his hard-chine launches were safer, faster, more manoeuvrable and cheaper to build and operate. With his experience of flying boats both at Supermarine and with Imperial Airways, which had adopted the Short Calcutta flying boat for its Empire Routes in 1928, Scotty knew that his boats were absolutely ideal for flying boat co-ordination work.

Early in the year Scotty had approached Beauforte-Greenwood and had suggested that the Air Ministry borrow one of the 35-foot cruisers he was building and try it out as a Seaplane Tender in place of the ageing 35-foot tenders, powered with a Brook engine, then in service. Beauforte-Greenwood had visited Hythe during the summer with his assistant Flight Lieutenant Norrington and Flight Lieutenant Jinman, Officer in Command of the Marine Craft Section of No 209 Squadron, based at RAF Cattewater, Plymouth. They had been impressed with the demonstration that Scotty had laid on and with their host, had worked out a specification for an experimental 37-foot 6-inch boat that would suit the Air Ministry requirements. Despite the fact that the Air Staff were reluctant to commit funds for the purchase of boats rather than aircraft, Beauforte-Greenwood had managed to obtain authority to purchase one experimental Scott-Paine launch for service trials.[8]

The new launch, powered by two 100 hp Brook engines, underwent yard trials at the end of 1930. Beauforte-Greenwood was highly impressed and the Air Ministry agreed to purchase the prototype which was designated *RAF 200*. The boat was then delivered for service trials at RAF Mount Batten, Cattewater, Plymouth on March 17th, 1931. The trials were conducted by Thomas Edward Shaw, Air-craftman 1st Class, in the trade of Aircrafthand (General Duties). Shaw, better known as Lawrence of Arabia, had been posted to Station Headquarters at RAF Cattewater in February 1929 and had been detailed to the Workshop and Marine Section which was responsible for the fleet of motor boats employed in ferrying crews, mooring and re-fuelling of flying boats.

The trials of *RAF 200* by T. E. Shaw, who put the prototype through its paces, were to be the beginning of a partnership between Shaw and Scott-Paine that was to be of profound significance. Shaw became a powerful advocate of Scott-Paine boats and it was to be largely as a result of his enthusiasm that the first motor torpedo boats emerged in 1936. Scott-Paine listened to Shaw's criticisms of *RAF 200* with interest once the requisite fifty hours of running had been completed on April 2nd, 1931. *RAF 200* had behaved well in all weathers and, on one occasion, had run up the channel from Falmouth to Plymouth against a strong wind and in heavy seas and had shipped solid water only once. The boat handled well in narrow water, could turn in her own length and, in Shaw's opinion, was better and safer than any other service marine craft.

Scotty had good reason to be pleased with the design and the workmanship of his Hythe craftsmen. There was one problem, however: the Brook engine was heavy, and out of date by American motorboat engine standards. Apart from the use of marinised aero engines for racing boats, the standard power units of Scott-Paine's larger boats were all American, either the 100 hp Chrysler engine or the well-known 135 hp Scripps engine. Scott-Paine was well aware that the supply of engines to power the large number of hulls being produced in his yard remained the outstanding obstacle to the development of a self-sufficient industry. Scotty was convinced that if he could find a suitable engine in the United Kingdom, the output of his British Power Boat Company would alone be sufficient for a manufacturer to produce a marine version.

During 1930, Scotty had travelled the length and breadth of England interviewing engine manufacturers. The breakthrough came when he met Wilson Hamil of Meadows at Wolverhampton who showed Scotty the Meadows engine used both in the Vickers tank and in the 'Invicta' motor car. Scotty's experience with marine engines was second to none, and he was sure that a marine version of the

RAF 261, one of the 'RAF 200' Class 37 foot 6 inch seaplane tenders. This boat, fitted with radio aerials, was built in 1937.

Meadows engine could be easily designed. Hamil introduced Scotty to his engineers who were given the task of re-designing features such as the oil feed system so that the engine could be installed in boats at an angle of seventeen degrees to the horizontal.

The Meadows engine, which had six cylinders and which could produce 100 hp at 3,000 revolutions per minute, had a power-weight ratio ideal for high speed planing boats. Scotty concluded an exclusive deal for the manufacturing rights of the 'Power-Meadows' engine, and six experimental engines were put into production. One was continuously run on a test bed and two were installed in an experimental hull at Hythe during March 1931, while the other three were left unassembled for the modification of parts. Scotty was delighted with the outcome of these trials and, after making some modification to the design, he placed an order for one hundred engines. The order was entirely speculative, but it was a stroke of entrepreneurial genius. The exclusive use of the most efficient British marine engine put the British Power Boat Company in a unique position in

T. E. Shaw and Scott-Paine.

the production of high speed craft and in a position of considerable advantage over rivals such as Vospers of Gosport. The 100 hp Power-Meadows engine was a great success and was soon followed by the exclusive production by Meadows of the 'Power 12/48' engine, designed as a 'super sports model', and a four-cylinder 'Power 8/28' utility engine.[9]

In April 1931, Shaw was seconded from RAF Cattewater, by then re-named RAF Mount Batten, to test the installation of the new Power-Meadows engines in *RAF 200*. During this visit, and his many subsequent stays at Hythe, Shaw lodged in a room at Myrtle Cottage, in John Street, overlooking Southampton Water. His landlady was Mrs Biddle-combe, whose husband, George was Scott-Paine's steward on board the yacht, *Sula*. Shaw tested the engines in the yard's experimental hull, driving the boat up and down Southampton Water, before installing two Meadows engines in *RAF 200* under Scott-Paine's personal supervision.

Even before the new engines had been installed in *RAF 200* during the early part of May, the Air Ministry had placed an order for seven more of the 37-foot 6-inch cruisers. Shaw wrote to his friend Dick Knowles: 'the RAF is at last trying to get some marine craft of modern design, a need I have been urging on them (per C.O.'s signature) for 18 months . . . that was my notion of what motor-boats should be fit for.' The installation of the Power engines was accompanied by numerous teething problems as Shaw wrote to Clare Sydney Smith. 'The boat has been suffering from one engine trouble after another for the past fortnight, and everybody (there are the maker's people here, besides Mr Scott-Paine's fitters) at their wits' ends to keep her going or make her right . . . nothing radically wrong with the engines, you understand, but minor defects that have to be put right as they occur'.[10]

Gradually Scott-Paine was able to sort out the problems and Shaw was able to report the considerable advantage of the Meadows engine over the old Brook engine. For instance, the starter motor on the Meadows could be removed in five minutes, compared with the six hours it took to perform the same operation on the Brook engine. The trials continued throughout May and June and, on the 16th day of the trials, Scotty was able to welcome the Air Ministry top brass, including the Air Officer Commanding Coastal, Air Officer Commanding No 10 Group and various staff officers for a spectacular demonstration of their new boat.

The work was arduous for Shaw who wrote to the Smiths at Mount Batten, 'I confess the truth I have had almost all the speed boating the most confirmed water rat could want.' Shaw was then given orders to transport *RAF 200* to Mount Batten, so Scotty invited Beauforte-Greenwood, Jinman and Norrington to lunch on board the *Sula* and suggested that *RAF 200* should make the trip by sea under her own power. It would be a formidable trial for the craft, but Beauforte-Greenwood agreed to Scotty's proposal and on June 6th, 1931, the boat left Hythe. The trip was a great success and it was a tribute to Scotty's design that the voyage to Plymouth was completed in a remarkable seven hours and thirty minutes. At the end of June, *RAF 200* was allocated to the Marine Craft Training Section at RAF, Calshot. The return trip to Southampton Water was the best advertisement for his hard-chine launch that Scott-Paine could have wished for. Except for taking on one sea, the boat only took on spray, and the report submitted to the Chief Instructor of the Marine Training Section at Calshot concluded: 'I am sure there are not many boats of this size which would be able to stand up to the seas we encountered.'[11]

During the summer of 1931 the Air Ministry increased its order for the new seaplane tender by a further eight craft. The adoption of a high speed, hard-chine motor boat by the armed services was the breakthrough that Scotty had been working for and he was determined to impress the Air Ministry with his ability to deliver the boats in record time.

Earlier in the year it had been decided that the return match for the Detroit News Trophy, in which Scotty had to defend his title to the coveted trophy, would be the star event of the Southampton Motor Boat Week during that July. Scotty had secretly built *Miss Britain II* to defend the trophy, and at the same time had built an almost identical boat, *Whyteleaf III*, which had been commissioned by the well-known Lloyd's broker, Fred White, for the contest. The other principle British entry was to be Betty Carstairs, piloting her *Newg II*.[12]

The American challengers failed to enter for the contest at the last minute, so the contest was between the British motor boats. The three contenders undertook their speed trials under a grey sky, with a fierce northerly wind and a choppy Southampton Water. But the sun shone as the regatta, presided over by Lord Louis Mountbatten, opened on Tuesday, July 21st. A crowd of vessels, including several large and notable steam yachts, were gathered off Hythe to watch the racing.

The first event, the Rear Commodore's Cup was won by a Flight Lieutenant Luxmore, racing one of Scotty's own fleet, *Panther II*, while Scotty came third in *Twinkletoes*. At 2.45 in the afternoon the loudspeaker on board the yacht, *Florinda*, announced that the Detroit News Trophy event would start in fifteen minutes. The atmosphere was electric when the spectators gave a gasp of surprise. Scotty's *Miss Britain I* flashed into view. Where was *Miss Britain II* which everyone had heard of and which had been built specially for this race? The rumour went round that something must be wrong with the new boat and that Scott-Paine would soon be out of the race. In fact Scotty, in a sporting gesture, had decided to use his older boat to give his friends a chance as the Americans were not entering the race. It was a grand gesture, particularly appreciated by Fred White, who realised that Scotty, having built his boat, was giving him a sporting chance to win the trophy.

However, it was to be Scott-Paine and *Miss Britain I* who were to be the stars of the day. Even before the smoke from the starter's gun had cleared in the stiff breeze, Scotty was away in front, with Betty Carstairs hard at his heels. *Newg II* was the faster boat, but Scotty's skilful handling of the turns kept him in the lead. The *Newg II* broke down, and although Betty Carstairs did get going again, Scotty went on to win the heat. *Whyteleaf III* was never really in the race and was handled indifferently by the less experienced Fred White in the choppy sea. Scotty's winning speed was 36.43 knots. The second heat was equally exciting. Betty Carstairs' boat overturned, throwing the pilot and mechanic into the water, but Scotty and Fred White quickly stopped to go to their assistance. *Newg II* was saved from sinking by some quick action by a nearby RAF pinnace crew. *Whyteleaf III* went on to win the race although Scotty had the best lap time at a speed of 40.22 knots. Betty Carstairs withdrew from the contest and the final heat was between the two Scott-Paine boats. *Miss Britain I* went on to win at an average speed of 38.66 knots, compared with the speed of 36.20 knots of the newer *Whyteleaf III*. Again Scotty, proud of his achievement, and honoured by the motor boat world for his sportsmanlike behaviour, was presented with the Detroit News Trophy. The presentation was made by Lady Brecknock at the regatta dinner held at the South Western Hotel in Southampton; it was to remain with him for life.[13]

Scotty went on to win other trophies at the Southampton Motor Boat Week, including the Rear Commodore's cup which he won in *Twinkletoes*. He did well in the Lucinha Cup and his own Scott-Paine Cup and, on the last day of the contests entered *Glitterwake*, designed and built by him at Hythe, for the Sea Mile Contest for the 'Motor Boat' Trophy. The trophy was won by Betty Carstairs in *Estelle IV*, at a speed of over 72 knots, but it was an exciting climax to the week.

Scotty took his racing fleet back to his Hythe Yard where *Miss Britain* was being made ready for the international events to be held at Stockholm on August 8th, at Geneva on August 15th and at Venice on September 13th. He was riding the crest of a wave. His racing boats were famous the world over; his Marine Garage at Hythe was housing hundreds of motor boats for private owners; his workshop assembly lines were producing a popular range of motorboats from little outboard runabouts to luxury cruisers. The first batch of Air Ministry Seaplane Tenders were under construction and he had developed the most successful marine engine produced in Britain, enjoying exclusive rights over its use.

Scotty could look out over Southampton Water from the Cliff at Weston and see his yard in the distance. He would look first for the massive World War One flying boat sheds owned by Vickers Supermarine at Hythe, and then for the nearby, smaller sheds that were his own. He loved his yard with a passion, and had good cause to be satisfied with the progress that he had made over the last four years, building it up from nothing into the most sophisticated boat yard in the world.

The local policeman was cycling along the Shore Road at Weston at 6.30 AM on the morning of the Bank Holiday Monday, August 3rd, 1931, when he looked across Southampton Water and saw smoke rising from the opposite shore. He pedalled furiously up Weston Lane to The Cliff, summoned a startled Scotty from his bed, and delivered the dreadful news that his factory was on fire.

CHAPTER 8
The Phoenix Rises

A distraught Scott-Paine gathered his family on the patio, and with tears streaming down his face said, 'Look at my factory burning!' He lifted the six year old John onto his shoulder so that he could see over the garden hedge, and took heart from his son's comforting reply, 'Never mind Dad. You can build it again'. Scotty ran to his Rolls-Royce and watched the flames that he could see amongst the clouds of smoke as he drove through Southampton and down the coast road to Hythe. By the time he arrived, the fire, which had started in the roof of one of the building shops, was well established and fire engines were already fighting the flames.

It was dead low water and the fire engines were unable to find enough water to stop the fire from spreading, and soon most of the British Power Boat Company Yard was ablaze. Bill Sheaff had been on board *Sula* but because the harbour had dried out, was unable to get a launch ashore, and he watched helplessly as the fire spread. Soon gangs of men were helping Scotty salvage what they could as the flames spread through the sheds. Stuart Barker arrived and risked his life on several occasions rescuing equipment as gas bottles exploded around him in the heat. However, little could be saved, and even boats that were dragged from the sheds were consumed in the fire as they could not be launched into the safety of the harbour.

The destruction was almost complete. That evening Scotty went home, tired, blackened with smoke and with his hopes in ruins. The way in which the fire had started, the fact that the yard was deserted for the Bank Holiday, and the coincidence with the lowest tide for weeks, convinced Scotty that the blaze was the work of an arsonist bent on destroying his business.[1]

Not even the destruction, the loss of four years' work, could dampen Scott-Paine's enthusiasm, and he threw himself into the massive task of reconstruc-

tion. Perhaps the greatest loss was the destruction of the almost complete seaplane tenders being built for the RAF, together with all the drawings and manufacturing templates. Scotty's racing fleet, including the untried *Miss Britain II*, was almost totally destroyed, the only survivors being *Glitterwake*, and *Black Panther* which escaped with minor damage in the fire, and *Panther III*, which happened to be on the River Thames for the Sussex Motor Yacht Club International Race. Fifty racing craft were lost, including a new 12 litre boat which had been built in great secrecy for the Venice meeting to be held between September 13th and 30th.[2]

Despite the loss of his racing fleet, Scotty was determined to attend the Venice meeting and to show the world that he was not beaten. He left for Italy with Brenda at the beginning of September and both of them won honours during the event. Scotty drove *Panther III* to victory in the 6 litre Coppa San Marco and in the 120-mile race between Vienna and Trieste in honour of the King of Italy. *Glitterwake* won the 12 litre Coppa Federazione, while Brenda raced *Panther III* to victory in the Coppa Achille event for ladies. When he got home, Scotty used the accumulated prize money to have a trophy made, in the form of a Viking longboat with a motor boat below. The inscription recorded the fact that the boats were made ready for the Venice event in a mere seventeen days after the great fire at Hythe.

Every employee helped with the massive task of clearing the debris of the fire. Additional men were drafted in from the village, including Harry Banks, who was to remain with Scott-Paine, as one of his 'bodyguard of faithful fellows', until the yard closed in 1947. Scott-Paine had insufficient money to pay wages on a regular basis and often there was no wage packet forthcoming at the end of the week. For many months, the standard response to creditors was that all the paperwork had been lost in the fire and that the

The Hythe yard following the fire of August 3rd, 1931.

company was unable to make payments.[3] Eventually the insurance companies paid out £264,000 towards the loss, but Scott-Paine still had to meet a personal loss of £24,000.

It was important for the motor boat world to know that Scott-Paine was still in business and announcements were placed in the yachting journals with details of the arrangements that could be made for clients' boats at Hythe, together with details for proposed new buildings for the proper storage of boats. Scott-Paine was going to use the last four years' experience to re-build the yard as the most efficient motor boat factory in the world.

On October 10th, Scotty made a detailed inspection of the remarkable progress that had already been made in the reconstruction. One of two new building shops was well under way to completion; it was 300 feet long by 70 feet wide and 35 feet high. The 8 inch concrete floor could take the loading of the biggest boats, while the single-span structure of steel and asbestos was ideal for the mass production of boats.

The interior was to be painted white for maximum light while runs of pipe and electrical conduit were to be picked out in bright colours for ease of maintenance. Overhead tracks were to be provided for the movement of boats and for the movement of engines from the adjacent engine shop to the place where they were to be lowered into the completed hulls.

A new two-storey building was already nearing completion, on the first floor of which there was a new machine shop. Scotty had paid close attention to detail and even the new lathes were enamelled in white, picked out in black. There was a new coppersmiths shop and sheet metal shop, a new chromium plating plant, raw material store and a new buffing shop. Plans were in hand for a new sawmill to be built on the south side of the new boat building shop, so that the incoming timber could go straight from the timber stores into the sawmill and then directly into the production shops. The best of modern power tools such as the Black and Decker 'hicycle' equipment was installed throughout the works. Modern facilities were being laid down for the handling of clients' boats, while new waiting rooms and other accommodation for owners visiting the marine garage were planned.[4]

As the production of boats for the 1932 season got underway, Scotty increased his workforce, introducing what were then seen as revolutionary methods of management. A new costing and works control system, providing information to department heads, was designed and introduced. There were new systems for stores control and Scotty introduced new ideas such as industrial psychology and time and motion studies into the yard. The welfare arrangements such as the tea ladies to bring refreshments to the craftsmen, in their white boiler suits, on the shop floor, were continued from the pre-fire days.

Early in 1932, Scotty showed a reporter from the magazine, *Yachting World* around the factory. He told his visitor that he looked upon the Phoenix-like recovery of the British Power Boat Company as the birth of a new national industry, and that the yard would be the most efficient in the world. 'The re-building', wrote the reporter, 'is unparalleled in the annals of British motor boating and a triumph of determination and endeavour.' Perhaps the most remarkable achievement was that the sixteen RAF Seaplane Tenders were completed and delivered within the original contract time and, on March 30th, eight of the boats were out on Southampton Water, demonstrating their manoeuvrability in a tight 'V' formation at 30 mph.[5]

Production at Hythe was now exclusively devoted to the range of hard-chine boats based on the original 23-foot hull design of Fred Cooper, all of which were powered by Meadows engines. The 35-foot 'Sea Ace', with a single 100 hp Power Meadows engine was selling at £950. The 24-foot 6-inch 'Sea King', also powered by a single 100 hp engine, cost £700, while the 23-foot 6-inch 'Sea Prince' was being advertised for £525. A new introduction to the range was the 'Sea Joker', a 16 foot dingy, powered by a 30 hp engine.

Scotty was beginning to develop an idea for a larger, sea-going, hard-chine boat, that might be used by the RAF for aircraft co-ordination work or even by the Royal Navy as a small, torpedo carrying warship. However, he knew that the satisfactory development of a larger boat depended upon the availability of a more powerful marine engine. In February 1932, Scotty purchased twelve second-hand Napier Lion engines from the Air Ministry and set about extensive experiments, converting the engines for marine use, installing them in experimental hulls, including *Whizz Bang*, a 30 foot hydroplane of the 'Puma' class, built by Saunders in 1928. Scotty was encouraged by the results and

approached his old friend George Wilkinson, Chief Engineer of Napier to discuss the possibility of manufacturing a production version of the marinised Lion. George Wilkinson was not enthusiastic, saying that it could not be done, but Scotty, persuaded him to let him have the use of the Napier Lion test bench so that he could experiment with carburettors. It was necessary to do away with the complicated down-draft induction pipes of the Claudel-Hobson aero carburettor which, if they had been left in their original position, would have been in the bilge of a boat in a marine installation. Scotty was assisted by L.A. Hall, Chief Engineer of Imperial Airways, and the two men cracked the problem using a standard Amal lorry carburetor with a heated extension to the induction pipe manifold. Mr Binks of Amal was called in. As Scotty was to later recall:

> . . . our own engineers from Hythe fitted the ahead, neutral and astern gears which we built at Hythe, and which I patented because we turned it into a unit that contained all the auxiliary gear necessary for the modification or convertion of an ordinary aero engine, or any other engine, into a marine engine. We had our salt water pumps and their drives, electric starting gear, electric generator drive and other auxiliary drives for operating gun gear, etc, if necessary, and main thrust and astern races. There were innumerable other major changes we had to make after vast experiments and tests.

Once the engine had been converted it ran five hundred hours before Scott-Paine invited George Wilkinson down to Hythe to see it. The Napier engineer was surprised and delighted with the work. Scotty then hammered out an agreement for exclusive rights over the new engine, and the Board of Napiers agreed that the new engine should bear the identity of the British Power Boat Company and should be re-named the Power-Napier Sea Lion. The development of a practical and reliable 500 hp marine engine, of only 2⅔ lb per brake horse power was to make possible the development of a new generation of sea-going hard-chine craft which was to lead to the first motor torpedo boats. By 1938, over two hundred Power-Napier engines had been fitted to boats as Hythe.[6]

Despite the success of the *'RAF 200'* Class of boat, the Admiralty was not convinced of the wisdom of hard-chine craft. Scotty, on the other hand, could see endless opportunities for the use of such boats in the Navy, as pinnaces, supply boats, tenders for warships and even Admirals' barges. In October 1931, the Admiralty had appointed a Coastal Motor Boat Committee to investigate possible roles for high-speed offensive motor boats, and Scotty had

T. E. Shaw piloting a 16 foot RAF dingy of the
clinker-built 'Sea Joker' type.

started working on ideas for a torpedo carrying hard-
chine motor boat. In March 1932, T. E. Shaw wrote
to his old friend Geoffry Dawson, Editor of *The
Times*, suggesting that he send his 'marine man'
down to Hythe to see the RAF boats, promising that
the reporter would be given a good show.

Today it struck me, that as editor you might be
interested in the new type of motorboat that we
have been producing lately for the RAF. I'm
partly the guilty cause of them—after a big crash
at Plymouth Sound, which showed me convin-
cingly that we had nothing in the Service fit to help
marine aircraft in difficulties. Nor could the Navy
supply even an idea of the type of craft we needed.
The Navy is rather Nelsonic in its motor boats. I
suppose it knows something about steam . . . so
the RAF (partly, as I confessed above, at my
prompting) went into the science of it, and have
had produced for them, by the Power Boat works
at Hythe here, an entirely new type of seaplane
tender. They are 37 feet boats, twin-engined,
doing 30 mph in all weathers, handy, safe, and

very cheap. Many of their features are unique.
They cost less than any boats we have every
bought before. All this has been done through the
Admiralty, in the teeth of its protests and
traditions. Now the boats are finished and sailors
are beginning to take notice, and wonder if there
isn't something in it.[7]

Dawson dispatched reporters to Hythe and Scott-
Paine's boats received widespread publicity through
several feature articles in *The Times*. At the end of
March, the aeronautical correspondent of *The Times*
accompanied Shaw on an epic voyage from Calshot
to Donibristle in the Firth of Forth. At his request
Shaw was not mentioned in the subsequent article
about the voyage of *RAF 210*, describing how the
remarkable journey, during which the dimunitive
boat met exceptionally heavy weather, demonstrated
the seaworthiness and endurance of the new RAF
boats. As it entered the Firth of Forth the weather
was so bad that it had been pronounced unfit for the
existing motor boats stationed at Donibristle. *RAF
210* covered the 742 miles from Calshot in thirty-five

hours and ten minutes running time, an average speed of 21 mph (18.3 knots). The day after its arrival it was put to work at the RAF Station without anything having to be done by way of servicing or repairs. The epic voyage was the best advertisement that Scotty could have wished for in promoting the British Power Boat Company, and it confirmed Scotty's belief that a larger sea-going launch could be designed and built using his hard-chine planing hull.[8]

The success of the 'RAF 200' Class led to the development of other specialist boats for the Air Ministry. In November 1931, Shaw had been back at Hythe testing small boats based on either a 16 foot or an 18 foot hull. The boats, powered by the new Power-Meadows 28 hp engine, were to be used for ferrying crews and stores and as a special bomb dingy and fuel carrying dingy.[9] Shaw remained at Hythe until the Donibristle run in April 1932, testing the '200' Class boats and the dingies. The work was arduous and was carried out in all weathers. In February, he wrote to the Sydney Smiths: 'I wish life at Hythe was easier. I work all day on the boats at the yard; and at night with reports or logs or handbook. No music: no books: no rides. Too much motor boating.' He worked on a lengthy technical description of the '200' Class boats which he finished in March. 'My *Notes of the 200 Class*, are finished', he wrote to Clare Sydney Smith, from his lodgings at Hythe, 'a small book of about 40 pages, I expect: and they may appear as an Air Ministry Publication. That will make me laugh, if it does. I am revising them now, for submission to the Publications Department, and preparing an index. Ever so dull, these notes, and entirely impersonal. Nobody could guess that anybody had written them. They seem just to have collected themselves.'[10]

Early in 1932, the Air Ministry Member for Research and Development suggested that there was a need for a marine craft that could withstand a hit by an 8½ lb practice bomb dropped from an aeroplane.[11] There was a need for a fast, unsinkable target so that air crews could practice bombing on shipping. Beauforte-Greenwood approached Scott-Paine who immediately put his inventive mind to work, asking Tommy Quelch to prepare sketches for a boat, based on the 37 foot 6 inch hull, but with an armoured deck, and designed to be unsinkable by being built of water-tight compartments filled with cellular rubber. Scotty then travelled to Sheffield where he discussed the production of armour plating with Captain Nicholson of Hadfields, a world famous steel manufacturer. He wanted a light-weight armour that could withstand the impact of an 8½ lb practice bomb dropped from 10,000 feet, with

a striking velocity of 890 feet per second. As the plans progressed it became clear that the weight of the boat, with its armour and specially strengthened hull, meant that it would have to be propelled by at least 300 hp. As the production version of the Napier was not then ready, Scotty decided to experiment with the installation of three 100 hp engines. He ordered his men to construct a full-size engine room mock-up for the installation of three 100 hp Power-Meadows engines, with the two outer engines driving through 'V'-drives, and the centre engine with direct drive. It was a revolutionary arrangement in which all three propellers would rotate in the same direction.

In March 1932, Shaw wrote to Clare Sydney Smith, 'in April, there are two target boats to test. This is a new proposition and should be curious and perhaps exciting.' In early June, Shaw delivered two experimental 37-foot 6-inch target boats to Bridlington where they were to be fitted with armoured decks. Even with the weight of the armour, the boats managed operating speeds of 25 knots on the bombing ranges at Bridlington, where, with their decks painted bright yellow, they were easily visible, although their speed and manoeuvrability made them difficult targets for the bombers.

Shaw's time with Scott-Paine at Hythe was to come to a temporary end in September 1932 when articles appeared in the *News Chronicle* and the *Sunday Chronicle* about his work with high speed boats, particularly the dare-devil piloting of the armoured boats. The publicity embarrassed the Air Ministry and arrangements were made for Shaw's immediate return to Mount Batten. An Air Ministry minute of September 5th, 1932, stated that the current programme for the construction of new marine craft had been completed and that only repair work and repeat orders were being carried out at Hythe, so the retention of Shaw at the Power Boat Yard could no longer be justified.[12]

During the summer of 1932, Scott-Paine undertook a special commission that was further to enhance his reputation in motor boating circles. The Baron Empain wanted a high speed tender to go with his steam yacht, *Heliopolis*, and he approached Scotty. The Baron insisted that the boat should be able to travel at 60 mph and that it should not be longer than 27 feet 6 inches as it had to fit between the davits aboard the yacht. Scotty's mind immediately leapt to consider the Napier Lion engine that he had just finished developing. He decided upon a wager. In the event of the top speed not reaching the specification, the purchase price would be lowered by £100 for every mph below 55 mph; conversely, Scotty was to benefit from a top speed in excess of the

T.E. Shaw with British Power Boat and Air
Ministry personnel inspecting a 37 foot 6 inch
Armoured Target Boat at Hythe, 1932.

specification. The two men shook hands and Scotty went straight to his office to draw out a sketch of what he had in mind.[13]

The 27 feet 6 inches tender was an outstanding success. Leather seats, electric cigar lighters and glove compartments contrived to give the six passengers luxury usually associated with a limousine motor car. The driver sat in the boat as in a car, with a steering wheel, a reverse gear at his left hand and a throttle lever on the wheel. The powerful 500 hp Power Napier Sea Lion could be started at the turn of a switch and at 2 mph, the boat was as easy to handle as any motor launch. A slight twist of the throttle and the multi-step hydroplane would lift up its bows and, before the passengers would be aware of any change, the boat would be speeding at 60 mph. In fact, the tender was to reach a speed of 63.01 mph during a demonstration over Scotty's measured mile at Netley in April 1933. Its manoeuvrability was outstanding: shutting the throttles quickly just brought the boat to a gentle halt, with the engine quietly ticking over. As one would expect from a limousine, the engine, with its three large vertical exhaust pipes, and the reverse gear were quiet, and the boat took no spray, even in moderate seas.[14]

CHAPTER 9
The Red Fox of Hythe

During 1932 Scotty had considered building a challenger for the 1933 Harmsworth Trophy race to be held at Detroit. He wanted to build a single-engined boat to challenge the giant *Miss America X*, with her four Packard engines. He had approached Rolls-Royce with a request to use one of the Rolls-Royce 'R' engines which had powered the Schneider Trophy winning Supermarine S6B in 1931, but Scotty had been told that there was no engine available, and had quietly dropped the idea of building a challenger. Then came his success with the Power-Napier engine in 1932, brilliantly demonstrated in Baron Empain's runabout, and Scotty again considered the idea of building a contender. There was not much time because, under the rules governing the British International Trophy, the Royal Motor Yacht Club had to lodge a challenge with the Yachtsmen's Association of America before March 1st of any year. At the end of February 1933, however, Lieutenant Colonel Bersey, the Commodore of the RMYC sent a cable communicating Scotty's challenge to America, announcing that the name of the challenger would be *Miss Britain III*.

No details of the boat were announced but Scotty did reveal that, through the generosity of Napiers, it would be powered by a supercharged Napier Lion engine developing some 1,350 hp. As *Miss America X* was powered by a total of 7,800 hp, many observers thought that Scotty's information was a deliberate deception and that he was actually building a much larger boat. Scotty told the racing committee that the boat, which he was going to pilot himself, would be built in the greatest secrecy at his Hythe yard at a cost of between £15,000 and £20,000. He was aware that the Napier Lion engine was low powered by 1933 aero engine standards, and he made it clear that if the boat failed to come up to his expectations during trials, he would not take it to the race on Lake St Clair. He went on to tell the committee that he would

only go to America if he really had a chance of beating Gar Wood, the wily 'Old Fox of Algonac'. Nobody doubted that if *Miss Britain III* was taken to America, the national honour would be safe in the patriotic hands of Hubert Scott-Paine.[1]

Work on building *Miss Britain III* was carried out in Scotty's secret shop at Hythe. Only a select few of his trusted 'bodyguard of faithful fellows' were allowed in the shop that was guarded at the door by Charlie Chiverton, who had been given a list of those who were to be allowed in. The work was carried out at a tremendous pace; *Miss Britain III* was designed and built in nine weeks and four days. It was a remarkable achievement, more impressive even than the record breaking design and construction of *Miss England* four years earlier.

Scotty invited a select group of journalists from the motor boating press to Hythe during June 1933, and showed them the almost complete *Miss Britain III* in the secret shop. The revolutionary nature of the boat took them all by surprise. Everyone had expected a boat of conventional wooden construction, but the new record breaker, which they likened to a 'silver fish upon a platter', was made of metal. Scott-Paine and Tommy Quelch had come up with a masterpiece. While the side and bottom stringers were of wood section reinforced with metal, the frame structure was covered with a skin of 'Alclad', a clad aluminium alloy comprising an aluminium based copper alloy, clad on each side with pure aluminium. The outer covering of pure aluminium was a mere eight per cent of the total thickness. The metal skin was fastened to the frames with thousands of duralumin screws with countersunk heads.

The 24 foot 6 inch hull was built as a stepped hydroplane, with one main step and several subsidiary steps forward. As with *Miss Britain I*, a central girder construction of mahogany sandwiched between 'Alclad' plates, made the structure enor-

The unveiling of *Miss Britain III* at Hythe, June 1933.

mously strong. The overall weight of the boat was 3,360 lb, representing a mere 2.5 lb per bhp. The engine was installed at the rear of the boat, driving a single propeller through a reverse gear at 9,000 revolutions per minute. Every bit of Scotty's ingenuity and experience had gone into the construction of his masterpiece.[2] Tommy Quelch and Scotty's mechanic, Gordon Thomas, and all the boatbuilders had brought all their experience and craftsmanship to the project. Scotty rewarded his team well: Gordon Thomas, for instance, had his wage packet increased by 30s per week for his work in designing the cooling water scoop that had been built into the rudder bracket.[2]

Once the boat had been completed, trials were undertaken in the greatest secrecy. *Miss Britain III* was taken out on Southampton Water early in the morning so that the speed runs could not be seen by prying eyes. In the dark, the flames from the exhaust were often the only clue to the boat's whereabouts on the water. Scotty used an unsupercharged Lion

engine developing 900 hp during the trials, but even with this limitation, the challenge to Gar Wood looked serious.

Designing a propeller for *Miss Britain III* posed particular problems, and this almost cost Scotty his life. During one of the speed trials a blade broke off the American 'Games' propeller that Scotty was using, and shot straight through the boat, just behind the pilot's seat. Scotty concluded that his faith in his two medallions of St Christopher placed on the dashboard was well founded. He called George Selman, whom he had first met in 1917 at the National Physical Laboratory, and who had become one of the country's leading propeller experts. He had already consulted Selman about the propeller for the boat, so the designer hurried to Hythe where he was taken by Scotty to the secret shop. He looked at the damaged *Miss Britain III* and Scotty pointed out the hole in the boat. Selman said, 'What happened?' 'Oh', came the answer, 'It was mice! Actually, you were dead right . . . you told me that propeller wasn't strong enough, the blade came off. I'm lucky to be here!' Selman then designed a new propeller for *Miss Britain III*, a propeller that was to make racing history.[3]

Scotty sailed for America on the *Empress of Britain* on August 12th. His team of six included Steve Biggs, the foreman of the secret shop team and chief boatbuilder on the project; the mechanic, Gordon Thomas; Norman Jeans, Jim Rousell and Reg Holley, all of whom had worked in the secret shop gang; and the mechanic who had been seconded to the project by Napier's. The race committee had decided that the race was to take place at Algonac, on the St Clair River, about 45 miles north-east of Detroit. This made Scotty furious as he had specially designed *Miss Britain III* for the wider turns of Lake St Clair which originally had been chosen as the venue. However, he was confident of victory as he settled his team in a houseboat on the river and went out to meet a host of journalists and photographers. The team found bottles of liquor stashed beneath their bunks; Scotty concluded that the American opposition was not beyond a bit of sabotage and reckoned that this was an attempt to reduce the effectiveness of his team.[4]

The American press referred to the forthcoming contest as between the 'Red Fox of Hythe' and the 'Grey Fox of Algonac'. The British press, confident that right, if not might, belonged to Scotty, described it as a contest between David and Goliath. On September 4th, over thirty-five thousand spectators gathered on both the American and Canadian sides of the river to witness what was widely seen as the most exciting motor boat race of recent years.

The excitement was intense, but a fairly strong wind, together with the disturbance caused by the thousands of spectator craft, made the eight mile course too rough. The race was scheduled to start at 3.00 PM but it was not until 6.00 PM that the contestants crossed the starting line. *Miss America X* took the lead in the first heat of five laps, and although Scotty managed to clock 88.226 mph in the fifth lap, he was nearly three miles behind the American defender at the end of the race. Although the American boat was much more powerful, its average speed was just over 82 mph, compared with an average of 78.5 mph by Scott-Paine.

Scotty installed his second 1,375 hp Napier Lion for the second heat held on Monday, September 6th. At 5 PM, the two boats crossed the starting line neck and neck. Gar Wood slowly took the lead, leaving Scotty in rough water behind. Scotty went full out, and the skill of his driving took the breath away from the spectators, who could see daylight under *Miss Britain III* as the boat flew out of the water in pursuit

of Gar Wood. Going slightly faster and cutting the corners brought Scotty up to his rival, but Gar Wood, with his four 1,600 hp engines pulled away again to make a lap speed of 89.3 mph. In the fifth lap, Scotty appeared to be closing up and the excitement, transmitted live from the Commentators' barge to the BBC in London, was electric. Gar Wood crossed the line twenty-two seconds ahead of the diminutive challenger from Hythe. For the last four laps Scotty's speed had been in excess of Gar Wood's; the American's average was 86.937 mph against Scotty's 85.789 mph. Although Scotty had not won the trophy, he was a hero; not only was he the only challenger to have completed two races since 1920, the public on both sides of the Atlantic were satisfied that David had very nearly beaten Goliath. All Gar Wood could say was, 'What a loser!' In fact, Scotty might very well have beaten him if the race had gone on for another lap, for when Gar Wood took *Miss America X* out for a demonstration lap after the race, he broke a propeller shaft and came to a halt half way around the circuit.[5]

Scotty came home to a hero's welcome, ready to face further challengers. He was determined to show the British public that his creation was capable of even higher speeds than those he had attained in the Harmsworth event. On September 24th, three days after his return from Detroit, he took *Miss Britain III* to a racing event at Poole where he clocked up a speed of 95.08 mph. On this occasion disaster almost overtook the record breaker, when a broken petrol feed caused a fire to break out in the engine. It was quickly extinguished but Scotty had a fright and his language matched the occasion. His wife Brenda and some other ladies were nearly in the committee boat, which came up to the burning *Miss Britain III*. The ladies called out to see if Scotty was alright, but retired quickly in the face of the brusque answer, 'I've just fucked up a bloody good boat!'[6]

The damage was quickly repaired and on November 16th, 1933, on a cold and still Southampton Water, Hubert Scott-Paine, together with Gordon Thomas, became the first men to travel at over 100 mph in a single-engined boat. *Miss Britain III* had been fitted with the supercharged engine used during the first heat of the Harmsworth Trophy and shortly after 12.00 noon, as the sun broke through the mist, Scotty set off on his first run. A sharp cross-sea caused the spectators concern as they watched the sheets of spray sent up by the racing boat, but the average of the first two runs was 97.77 mph. Scotty tried again. He reached just over 98 mph, took a wide turn and then roared up Southampton Water, against the tide, at an average speed of 102.105 mph. The average for the runs was 100.132 mph (86.95

Miss Britain III at speed with Scott-Paine and
Gordon Thomas on board.

knots), a record that was to remain unbroken for over
fifty years.[7]

The following month, Scott-Paine was again in the
news. During December, the author and biographer
of Lawrence of Arabia, Captain Liddel Hart, wrote
an article in *The Daily Telegraph* describing the
dramatic role of Scott-Paine's armoured target boats
and T. E. Shaw's role in testing them. The development of the boats had continued; shrouded by
secrecy, since the prototypes had been delivered in
July 1932. The boats had proved remarkably
effective in improving the efficiency of aerial
bombing at sea, and had proved much cheaper than
the earlier practice of using old battleships. Liddel
Hart praised the courage of the crews, who took the
boats to sea for twelve hours at a time and who had to
wear ear defenders, crash helmets and gas masks to
protect them against the concussive effect of the
practice bombs filled with smoke compound. The
revolutionary design of the boats which could not
sink, even when pierced in an unprotected part, was
quite remarkable. *The Daily Telegraph* editorial joined
Liddel Hart in praising the human resourcefulness

and courage, and the readiness of men to face risks in
pursuing a line of scientific investigation: 'We are
told that the experiments have contributed not only
to military progress, but to marine engineering
knowledge and his countrymen, who so recently
followed with bated breath Mr Hubert Scott-Paine's
gallant attempt to wrest from America the laurels of
motor-boat racing, will be interested to learn of his
contribution to water-craft design in a different
sphere.'[8]

During 1933, Scott-Paine had pursued his idea of
a torpedo carrying motor boat and with Tommy
Quelch, had sketched out an idea for a 60-foot boat,
carrying two 18 inch torpedoes and powered by three
Power Napier Sea Lion engines. On his return from
the Harmsworth Trophy challenge, he heard from
contacts in the Admiralty that the Coastal Motor
Boat Committee, which had been established in
October 1931, was about to report with a recommendation that tenders should be sought for experimental torpedo craft from a number of companies,
including the British Power Boat Company. Scotty
went on the offensive at once. He telephoned a

reporter from *The Daily Mail* and invited him down for dinner at 'The Cliff'. The two men sat talking in Scotty's study for hours and the reporter was given a glimpse of Scott-Paine's vision of a navy armed with mile-a-minute battleships which would turn with the dexterity of a speed boat and out-manoeuvre any aircraft. 'The thing is not a dream', Scotty told his guest, 'It can be done and must be done if there is to be any future to the Navy. The battle today is not with the strong—it is with the swift. This is true in war and in commerce. The fact is that with the accepted design of ships the limit of speed has been reached. You can get a few more miles an hour out of them by piling engines into them until they are quite impractical, but everyone recognises that that is getting nowhere.' Scotty warmed to his subject, 'A ship today, to be a real pace maker, should be a mile-a-minute ship, and I am not differentiating at the moment between war craft and mercantile craft . . . already I think I have solved the problem of speed. This has been tested practically in the 37 ft boats which we supplied to the Royal Air Force. They are 30 mile an hour boats. The will travel anywhere in any sort of weather, and they are already seven years old. This was the first step. Now this winter I hope to build a 60 ft boat, built on the hull designs of those RAF boats to travel at that speed.' Scotty went on to predict that large fleets of these, which could be built for the price of one destroyer, would be invincible in the restricted waters of the Channel and the Mediterranean. 'Here then', he told his guest, 'to my mind is the secret of future ships of war. I maintain that a fleet of these mosquito craft would more than justify themselves at this moment and their building affords no difficulty.'[9]

Scott-Paine got the coverage he wanted in the newspapers and in October the Coastal Motor Boat Committee recommended that a new Coastal Motor Boat should be designed so that the Navy could keep abreast of developments. The report concluded that this would stimulate high speed engine design and that tenders should be sought from a number of companies, including the British Power Boat Company, for an experimental 55 foot boat, capable of carrying two 18 inch torpedoes and two to three Lewis guns.

Conservative opinion in the Admiralty argued that there was no identified operational requirements for such boats, and that ordering one experimental boat would not provide a sufficient experimental basis for assessing new designs. Despite the widespread coverage of Scott-Paine's vision of a 'mile-a-minute' navy, and despite the success of the 37 foot 6 inch boats with the RAF, the Admiralty rejected the conclusions of the Coastal Motor Boat Committee.[10]

Scott-Paine's words did reach the sympathic ears of a small group of naval officers who were growing increasingly interested in hard-chine motor boats. The Admiralty was persuaded to borrow one of the Power Boat 16 foot dingies for a trial and, despite official reluctance to recognise their usefulness, several destroyer captains purchased these boats for their personal use. Subsequently, the Admiralty ordered considerable numbers of the 16 foot dingies, and issued specifications for competitive tendering for their construction by rival boatyards. Peter Du Cane of Vosper's won a tender to construct a number of these boats, much to Scott-Paine's chagrin who argued that this was tantamount to piracy of his designs. A considerable rivalry developed between Scott-Paine and Du Cane who later recalled that his difficulty was the purchase of suitable engines as Scotty had cornered the market with his exclusive rights over the Power-Meadows engine. The first batch of Vosper 16 foot planing dingies were delivered to a new destroyer flotilla in time of the Jubilee Review of King George V. Scott-Paine dingies had been supplied to a previous flotilla and Du Cane later recalled that there was intense competition between the flotillas to keep their boats running reliably. Du Cane received an urgent call from the flagship of the flotillas carrying his boats, demanding a replacement dingy to replace a faulty craft. Examination showed that this dingy, together with all the others in the flotilla had been sabotaged with bird feathers in the fuel tanks, 'so it was concluded that there had been dirty work at the crossroads from some source.'[11]

Scotty continued to press his ideas for a 60 foot torpedo boat upon the naval staff and the forceful presentation of his views caused much resentment in the Admiralty. T. E. Shaw shared Scott-Paine's vision and pressed home the arguments when he had a chance. In March 1934, he wrote to an old friend, Lionel Curtis, criticising the defence policies of Lord Rothermere and Lord Beaverbrook. 'The defence of surface craft against aircraft', he wrote, 'will be found in manoeuvre:—in being able to turn quicker on the water than the plane can in the air—not difficult, with small ships, as the water gives you a firmer rudder. So I expect to see the surface ships of navies in future limited to small, high-speed manoeuvrable mosquito craft, none larger than the destroyers of today.'[12]

The arguments gradually had their effect and Scotty was supported by Admiral C. E. Kennedy-Purvis, Assistant Chief on Naval Staff and Captain de Meric, Director of Naval Equipment, together with his successor, Captain C. L. Woodhouse. Scotty's most powerful ally was Admiral Sir R. G.

16 foot clinker built Royal Navy Jolly Boat on
Southampton Water.

(Reggie) Henderson GCB, Third Sea Lord and
Controller of the Navy between 1934 and his
untimely death in 1939. There was much 'sub-rosa'
criticism of Admiral Henderson at that time and his
critics complained that he had been 'mesmerised by
Scott-Paine', and that he 'rather fancied himself
dashing around in a speed boat'. The Materiel
Departments of the Admiralty did not like the novel
constructional techniques of Scott-Paine's boats and
the Naval Staff could not identify any operational
requirements for them. However, Scotty received a
considerable boost when the Commander-in-Chief
Mediterranean recommended the introduction of
Fast Motor Boats into his fleet. Again, the conservative detractors in the Admiralty complained that
he had been influenced by the sight of liberty boats of
the US Navy swirling around his slower Admiral's
Barge, and there was a wide feeling that Lordships
acceded to the growing clamour and approved the
purchase of Fast Motor Boats against their better
judgement, and against the advice of the Naval
Constructors Department which claimed that they
were expensive, flimsy and difficult to maintain.[13]
   Gradually Scott-Paine's hard-chine boats were

introduced into the Royal Navy. A 24 foot 6 inch
Admiral's barge was ordered for HMS *Enchantress*, a
new sloop fitted out as the Admiralty yacht.
Following this, a number of 24 foot 6 inch boats were
ordered as destroyers' motor boats and these were
followed by a 25-foot Fast Motor Boat that was to
become standard throughout the Navy. A 35 foot
twin-engined seaplane tender was produced for use
with aircraft carriers and eventually Scotty
persuaded the Admiralty to replace its old steam
picket boats with a new hard-chine planing 45-foot
picket boat. Although Scotty received the lion's share
of orders for these new boats, much to the chagrin of
other boat builders, the Admiralty used his designs
as the basis for specifications issued for competitive tendering and other companies, particularly
Vospers, were invited to build identical boats. Scotty
saw this as an outrageous attack on his commercial
rights, arguing that as the inventor of these new types
of boats, he should be protected from the Admiralty's
competitive tendering policies. The arguments did
little to enhance Scott-Paine's reputation amongst
what he called the 'bowler-hatted brigade' in the
Admiralty.[14]

25 foot Fast Motor Boat produced for the Royal
Navy as a destroyer's tender.

CHAPTER 10
A Visit to Devonport

Although Scotty was sure that the future prosperity of his yard would ultimately depend on the design and production of boats for government departments, he was determined that it should still lead the world market in the production of sporting and pleasure motor boats. Unlike other boatyards, which tended to show their new designs at the Olympia Boat Show in the autumn of each year to generate orders for the winter months' construction period, Scotty believed in keeping his range of boats under wraps until it was too late for any competitor to copy the new season's designs. In March 1933, he had instituted a special exhibition at Hythe which had attracted widespread publicity, and he decided to repeat the experiment the following year.[1] The 1934 Hythe Motor Boat Week was held between April 16th and 28th and was widely billed as the biggest high-speed craft exhibition in Europe. Scotty arranged for a large laying-up shed to be given over to the display, at the centre of which was the world famous *Miss Britain III*. Twenty-three types of hard-chine boat were on display, ranging in price from £156 to £4,500. The luxury end of the cruiser market was represented by two new 40 foot models, the 'Sea Emperor', powered by a 500 hp Napier Sea Lion engine, and the 'Sea Lord', powered by two 100 hp Power Meadows engines. There was a 37 foot 6 inch 'Sea Monarch' and a new 35 foot 'Sea Flash' which could carry twelve passengers and which was described as a marine equivalent to a Rolls-Royce or Bentley car. The pack of cards, 'Sea King', 'Sea Queen', 'Sea Jack' and 'Sea Joker' were still available in various forms and, the smallest boat was the 'Sea Swallow', a 13 foot runabout, with a deck made of aeroplane fabric and powered by a 28 hp Meadows engine.[2]

Several types of boat were specially designed for use abroad. The 'Sea Hunter' was a 24 foot 6 inch boat designed for tropical use, having open sides with a fixed awning roof of two layers of canvas on a wooden frame. The 23 foot 'Sea Jack' was used by Imperial Airways both in Iraq and on the Cape-Cairo route, and in 1934 a 'Sea Jack', fitted with canvas awnings and with wicker chairs for the pilot and his passengers, was sold for the transport of dates from Basra to Shatt-el-Arab on the River Euphrates.

The 35 foot, triple screw *Sea Flash*, described as the 'Rolls-Royce' of motor boats.

The bottom of the hull was copper sheathed as a protection against worm, while the upper deck of teak was not varnished in view of the intense sun. In December 1934, a number of 20 foot boats were sold to Burma for use on the River Irrawaddy and in August 1934, a 37 foot 6 inch seaplane tender was supplied to a private German flying boat station at Nordeney.[3]

Scott-Paine offered his customers boats specially designed for their particular requirements. There was a 37 foot 6 inch whaling boat with a harpoon gun mounted on the fore deck and a 37 foot 6 inch fire float with two pumps linked to the two 100 hp engines, and twin foam installations providing a continuous stream from three monitors situated on the fore deck, amidships and on the after deck. Another adaption of the standard 37 foot 6 inch boat was a floating ambulance complete with an operating theatre. During 1933, the yard had produced a special version of the 37 foot 6 inch cruiser, the 'Sea Coach' which was designed as a 'marine omnibus'. The 'Sea Coach' was used by the Southampton based ferry company, Red Funnel, to provide an express service between Southampton and Cowes on the Isle of Wight. The Power 'Sea Coach', *Island Enterprise*, which started a regular service at Whitsun 1935, could carry twelve passengers in a comfortable saloon to the Isle of Wight in twenty-six minutes, half the time taken by the ferry paddle steamers. As the regular Red Funnel engineers were more used to steam engines than high performance marine petrol engines, Scott-Paine undertook to provide Red Funnel with trained engineers and crews for the express service. Many apprentices who served their time at the British Power Boat Company worked in the crew of *Island Enterprise*.[4]

In 1934, Imperial Airways announced plans for its Empire Air Mail Scheme using a fleet of 'C' Class Empire flying boats which it then ordered from Short's of Rochester. Scott-Paine was already supplying Imperial Airways with marine craft associated with its flying boat operations and was able to use his position as a Director to ensure that the British Power Boat Company supplied the air-

Flotilla of 37 foot 6 inch tenders built for Imperial Airways.

line with all the marine craft, passenger tenders, re-fuelling dingies and maintenance boats required to operate the Empire Route flying boat services which started from Southampton in 1937. Scott-Paine's ability to provide boats fitted and marketed for specialised requirements, was made possible by his use of a relatively small number of standard hard-chine hulls which could be mass produced at the Hythe factory, and fitted out to the customer's specifications. A cartoon of the time depicted Scotty with a giant saw about to cut the stern off a hull while asking a customer, 'How long would you like it?'[5]

Scotty's fame as an international sportsman was again enhanced at the numerous British and European motor boat events during the 1934 racing season. He took *Miss Britain III* to Venice in September where the diminutive racing boat was the centre of attention. Scotty entered for two prestigious races, the Volpi Cup and the Prince of Piedmont Cup. During the first trial for the Prince of Piedmont Cup, *Miss Britain* failed to achieve her maximum speed and averaged just over 86 mph, but her performance during the second trial, held three days later, was outstanding. The competition was held over a measured mile and Scotty managed to extract a maximum speed of 111.111 mph out of *Miss Britain III*. He won the trophy at an average speed of 110.1 mph, the fastest speed of any single-engined boat and the highest ever achieved in salt water. *Miss Britain III* was also the star in the Count Volpi Cup race which Scotty won for Britain for the first time since 1929, when Henry Segrave had won it in *Miss England*. The Venice event almost cost Scotty his life when a seaplane landed across his bows during the record breaking run for the Prince of Piedmont Cup, causing *Miss Britain III* to break clear of the water and fly for a considerable distance. Scotty managed to keep the boat under control, but the impact caused severe damage to his back, although it was not until 1941 that his spine was X-rayed and found to have been broken in the incident.[6]

Two months later Scotty attended the annual three-day meeting of the International Motor Yachting Union at Antwerp, where he was accorded the highest honour by the assembled company, the International Gold Medal. The honour was presented for his achievements in 1934, and so great was the feeling that he deserved this above anyone else, when he was nominated by the British delegates, two other countries withdrew their nominations in his favour. The President of the International Union looked back over Scotty's career of twenty-five years in motor boat racing during which time he had won practically every race that he had entered. He had won one hundred and two first prizes in both national and international events, and unlike other sportsmen, he had never lost a race through mechanical failure. It was a fitting conclusion to a long and illustrious racing career.[7]

Scotty had decided to retire from racing so that he could concentrate all his efforts on developing a motor torpedo boat. Although the Admiralty did not express any formal interest in Scott-Paine's ideas for a motor torpedo boat during 1934, naval experts from Germany, Russia, Estonia, Denmark, Poland and Portugal, as well as from several South American countries, visited Hythe to examine his proposals. Scotty was aware of the dangers of war in Europe and refused to divulge details to representatives from Italy and France or to experts from German shipyards, although the latter were keen to negotiate agreements to manufacture the boat under licence. Extensive discussions were carried out with the Estonians, who were allowed to remove plans for the 60 foot boat from the yard. The Estonian government then infuriated Scott-Paine by publishing details as part of a specification for tenders from competitors' boatyards.[8]

Scotty's gradual move to the production of even larger hard-chine boats took a step forward during the summer of 1934 when he produced a 45 foot hull, powered by three 100 hp Power-Meadows engines, which was to be an outstanding success. The first of the larger boats to be built was a 45 foot armoured customs launch designed for the Chinese Maritime Customs to combat smuggling and piracy in Chinese waters. The 30 mph *Kuan Wei*, delivered in March 1935, had an operating range of 420 miles and was fitted with two tons of armour plating. It was capable of taking a further eight tons of load, which could be in the form of personnel, cargo or additional armour. Scott-Paine listened carefully to the requirements outlined by the Customs authorities and incorporated many special features, ensuring, for instance, that the door leading from the crew's compartment to the steering control compartment, was made of armoured steel. The door could be secured from the control side in the event of the native crew deciding to mutiny against their British officers. The boat was intended as the first of a fleet of such vessels and was designed to be equipped with four Lewis guns, teargas bombs and hand grenades.[9]

The persistent lobbying of the Admiralty continued until, in September 1934, aided and abetted by T.E. Shaw, Scott-Paine persuaded the Commander in Chief Devonport to try out an admiral's barge, based on the 45 foot design. Shaw wrote to Clare Sydney Smith:

. . . another contract was with Admiral (yes, he

had been promoted since) and Lady Fullerton. The Admiralty went on being mulish about Scott-Paine's motor-boats, and I lost patience and thought it might be rather a rag to force one down their throats. Also it would buck the Navy up to have a modern boat set against their primitive junks. So I pulled string after string, and all the bells rang, till finally Scott-Paine and I were asked down to Plymouth to explain these new boats. The Admiral put us up at Mount Wise for two nights, and behaved like the whitest sort of man. He really is a super-Admiral. Scott-Paine got a long way with him, and the Eyres-Monsell blew in, in a yacht. We roped him into the talk (he is a sort of S. of S. for the Navy, and a war-time partner of mine) and that about clinched it. So Scott-Paine got the order for a new Admiral's Barge for the C. in C.[10]

Scott-Paine was determined to impress his new customer and convert even the most ardent doubter in the Admiralty. With his flair for pulling rabbits out of hats by working all hours of the day and night, he delivered the barge in only twenty-six days. The achievement was all the more remarkable as the 45 foot hull had been built with the typical British Power Boat raked stem but naval etiquette required the Admiral's Barge to have a straight stem. Notwithstanding, the boat was altered and completed with its luxurious fittings and was delivered by sea for a demonstration in front of the Commander in chief, Admiral Fullerton, the First Lord, Viscount Monsell and the Board of the Admiralty on October 11th, 1934. Shaw wrote:

. . . we finished it in about three weeks, and down it went by sea, a great 45 ft thing, full of cabins and

The Board of the Admiralty inspecting the C-in-C Devonport Admiral's Barge, October 1934.

lavatories and chromium plate. The day after it got there happened to be an inspection day by the whole Board of the Admiralty. Seven Sea Lords and some Land Lords got into it at once and Scott-Paine nearly talked their heads off. The Admiral went on being as white as white and Lady Fullerton remembered how Jacky Fisher fought for new ideas and backed up.

Admiral Fullerton put Shaw, Scott-Paine and Bill Sheaff up at Mount Wise, outside the town, and invited Scott-Paine to make a presentation to the assembled Board of the Admiralty about his ideas for fast motor boats and, in particular, his proposals for a 60 foot motor torpedo boat. The Board had been impressed by the economic arguments for the introduction of a fast motor boat to replace the traditional Admiral's Barges. The steam barges were costing in the order of £700 a year in maintenance, and required a crew of six, while Scott-Paine's boat, which cost only £4,500 complete with three 100 hp Meadows engines, was estimated to have running costs of £200 a year and required a crew of only three or four.

Scotty's presentation was to the point and hard hitting. He painted a word picture of his career with Supermarine and the founding of the British Power Boat Company. He showed how the Navy could adopt a small boat policy, purchasing boats which ranged from 16 feet to 60 feet, standardising on six different sizes, constructed with two sizes of boat planks, and powered by the same engine. With such a policy, it would be possible to standardise on mechanical and electrical equipment, and engines could be changed in only two hours. He pointed out that since the purchase of the Admiral's Barge, the Engineer Admiral's Department of the Admiralty had incorporated Scotty's own design features in their instructions concerning the installation of petrol engines. Scotty then went on to describe his proposal for a 60 foot boat, powered by three Napier Sea Lion engines, which would carry two 18 inch torpedoes, depth charges, machine guns and an anti-aircraft gun. The boat would have a range of 800 miles and, unlike the Coastal Motor Boats of the Great War, it would be able to stay at sea in bad weather conditions. The motor torpedo boat, capable of operation independent of a shore base was a practicable proposition. Scotty urged the Board to purchase seven such boats as a matter of urgency so that an operational flotilla could be established, and he offered to turn over the entire output of the yard at Hythe to the experimental needs of the Admiralty.[11]

Discussions continued that evening over dinner. Lady Fullerton expressed interest in the proposed torpedo boat and asked Scott-Paine to show her the drawings. With a lady's eye for detail she immediately remarked, 'Good God, a boat without any heads.' Scotty wished his hosts good night and went to the billiard room, put the drawings on the billiard table and re-sketched the boat. 'Good God!' said the Admiral the next morning, 'How the hell did you get this?' 'Well, I worked all night on it', replied Scotty as he handed over the revised drawings.[12]

Scott-Paine's relationship with the Admiralty thawed and the following July, *The Times* reported that over thirty fast motor boats of various sorts had been delivered to the Navy since the Admiral's Barge had been demonstrated at Devonport. The occasion of the report was the delivery of a 45 foot Admiral's Barge for the Commander-in-Chief, Mediterranean Fleet, and the reporter had been given a dramatic demonstration of the boat's speed and manoeuvrability even when crossing the wake of a passenger liner in Southampton Water. After the demonstration, Scotty took his guests on a run to Portsmouth, pointing out the possibilities that such boats might have carrying guns and torpedoes. The passengers were impressed with the speed and the seaworthiness of the barge: 'There would be nothing', reported *The Times*, 'to prevent its further development with the object of producing a similar craft big enough to carry an armament suitable for use against orthodox naval vessels in the narrow seas.'[13]

Scott-Paine took every opportunity to publicise the advantages of the speed and seaworthiness of his larger hard-chine craft such as the 45 foot boat. A 45 foot Power Sportsman's Cruiser was advertised in a lavish catalogue as the acme of luxury motor boat cruising. During the summer of 1935, the seagoing qualities of the 45 foot boat led to its adoption by the Australian government for patrol and rescue work in the Timor Sea. Quantas Empire Airways had been operating flying boats over the 500 miles of sea between Darwin and the Island of Timor for the last year and it was felt that a rescue craft should be available in the event of a flying boat getting into difficulties. Scotty suggested a purpose-built version of the boat which he had built six months earlier for the Chinese Maritime Customs. It was to have a hull sheathed in bronze alloy to provide protection against marine borers and was to be fitted with a Marconi Direction Finding Radio with a radius of 500 miles. In the event of a flying boat coming down, the rescue launch, which would have a range of 950 miles, would be able to make contact with the aircraft and rendevous at high speed. The launch was designed to carry up to forty passengers in case of emergency, although the Empire Flying boats

British Power Boat Company 45 foot Naval
Picket boat.

operating between Southampton and Australia
carried a much smaller number.[14]

Beauforte-Greenwood had enthusiastically supported Scott-Paine's vision of large sea-going hard-
chine launches being used for aircraft co-ordination
and had played an active part in Scotty obtaining the
contract for the Timor Sea rescue boat. It was largely
as a result of their collaboration that the Air Ministry
issued a specification for a boat of between 60 and 70
feet in length, with an operating range of 500 miles
and a speed of not less than 35 knots. Tenders were
sought from twelve firms in June 1935 for the boats,
which were to be used with General Reconnaissance
Squadrons, to act as safety boats and navigation
markers for the over-water training of aircraft
crews.[15] The British Power Boat Company was the
only company in a position to fulfil these exacting
specifications, but Scotty still had to persuade the
Admiralty that he could deliver the boat wanted by
the Air Ministry. As he later recalled:

. . . all the well-known builders of Great Britain
replied that such a vessel was impossible to build.

The Air Ministry refused to accept my tender by
saying that they could not place a contract because
of the fact that the builders of Great Britain of
repute had categorically stated it was a quite
impossible task, and they were not going to be
faced with being overhauled in Commons by
placing a job on which they were going to spend
money, which everyone said was not going to
work. It took me many months to overcome this
decision, and it was only by my offering to cancel
the contract and return all progress payments if
the vessel proved unsatisfactory, that we obtained
permission to go ahead.[16]

The War Office also became an enthusiastic
supporter of Scott-Paine's boats and, in the summer
of 1935, ordered a version of the 45 foot boat as a
general service launch for patrol work, the transport
of stores and personnel and for target towing in the
training of coastal artillery. Scotty had first managed
to interest the War Office during the summer of 1934
when the Royal Engineers School of Electric Light at
Gosport arranged some night exercises for coastal

Advertisement for the British Power Boat Company featuring the 57 foot Army target towing launch.

Daily Mail

MONDAY, SEPTEMBER 9th, 1935

SPEEDBOAT DASH TO LINER

Mr. SCOTT-PAINE'S 30 M.P.H. RACE

Thrilling Account of Journey with " Daily Mail " Pictures

LIFE JACKETS READY

By HUBERT SCOTT-PAINE

The motor boat designer and racing pilot, who tells the thrilling story of his adventurous dash in a speedboat to mid-channel to pick up pictures dropped for the " Daily Mail " from a liner.

ON Friday, shortly after noon, The Daily Mail rang me up to see whether it would be possible to find the Orient liner "Orion" somewhere southwards of the Isle of Wight. The purpose was to take from her an important package of pictures showing the rescue of cruise passengers from the Cunard-White Star liner Doric which was in collision off the coast of Portugal on Thursday.

I told The Daily Mail that it would be a difficult, if not almost impossible, task, but they insisted upon its importance, and I told them I would let them know after luncheon.

Three Courses

In the meantime I sent out instructions to obtain weather reports, turned out large and small-scale charts of the vicinity of the Isle of Wight and the Channel between the Isle of Wight and the French coast, and sought local information about the Orion—happily a distinctive ship.

I found that her trial speed was 22 knots and that she would probably be making time for liner time.

With this information I laid off three courses that she would possibly follow. I marked them on three probable positions against the three lots of speeds that I thought she might be using. I then laid out my own boat's speed and charted it. After calculating, I agreed on a diagonal course that, providing the information was reasonably accurate, would bring me ahead of her between 7 and 8 p.m.

In the event of this not being so I proposed to run a 28-mile circle which would cover practically the whole of that part of the Channel.

One Boat

There was only one boat capable of carrying out the task—a luxury cruiser which I designed and built for myself, named Glitterwake II. She is between 45 ft. and 50 ft. long, has three

100 h.p. engines, and was built by my company, the British Power Boat Co.

Owing to the nature of the work, I proposed taking four picked men who have been accompanying me on various expeditions such as this over the last ten years.

At 5.40 we got our authority from the Customs. A few minutes afterwards we received wireless information from the Orion that she expected to be seaward of the Isle of Wight between 6.15 and 6.45.

By a stroke of good luck I had fitted a high-powered searchlight to the boat a few days previously.

I instructed the crew to clear the boat of anything that was unnecessary, for I meant to risk everything by running the machinery at the very limit of its capabilities.

We cleared Calshot at 6.21 p.m. Portsmouth at 6.40 p.m., left the Warner Lightship at 6.50 p.m., and were at sea alongside the Nab Light Tower at 7.5 p.m.

Our chase then had really started.

I think we all felt the excitement of it. By this time we were climbing up and down the big heaves of the sea which was working up the Channel, although the wind was light.

The impending darkness and the searching of the horizon for signs of smoke keyed all of us up a little more, although we are old hands in the racing game and had long since got over that kind of excitement.

Temptation

We sighted a small tramp steamer, and a little later the smoke of another steamer, evidently a big one. There was a great temptation to alter course and bear away for her. But we refrained from this and very soon brought her into view as being a single-funnelled liner, outward bound.

The sea by this time was deep enough for us to lose our horizon, and the light was rapidly failing. We were beginning to become very apprehensive of successful results.

Once again we saw smoke on the up-Channel side, that is the Dover side of our position.

The question was whether to alter course or carry on. I decided on the latter. This decision was no easy matter, and we were greatly relieved a few minutes afterwards to see that it was a P. and O. ship coming down Channel, outward bound.

Raised Hopes

It was now 7.45 p.m. and five minutes off the time that I had given to hold course. At 7.47 p.m. my chauffeur-mechanic friend, Bill Sheaff, thought that he saw smoke on our down-Channel side. It was the first trace of any life that we saw on the side that we expected to see it.

This raised all our hopes, and with eager peering and glancing, and gymnastic balancing on the part of Jack Banks, whom we call

bo'sun of our outfit, we tried to get a better sight of the vessel. Our own movements, however, were so short and sharp that it was impossible to focus the glasses, which were eventually lost overboard.

As we sped onwards, having now been running at the limit of our engine capacity for about two hours, we all felt that if this was not our ship the chase would be unsuccessful.

Success at Last

There was a feeling that she might turn out to be one of Fyffe's boats. I concluded, however, that she was too fast for that. Taking a good look at the large ship, as she now proved to be, I made up my mind that she was our quarry.

In a few minutes this proved to be undoubtedly the case, and I went through all the emotional delights that navigators invariably get on having made a good guess.

Immediately I got to work with my searchlight to make our recognition signals. Our time estimation had been right, our course had been right, the problematical course of the Orion had been judged correctly, and none of us would have changed places with the King!

You can imagine how delighted we were when, instead of getting any return signal from the Orion, we noticed that she was immediately altering course and steaming towards us.

Pictures in Barrel

At four minutes past 8 o'clock we were encountering the terrific swell of the wash of the steamer. At the same time we saw that she had thrown overboard the package of photographs that we were to pick up.

This package was most beautifully arranged. It was a small barrel to which was made fast a weight and floated staff with a white flag attached. Again attached to this was a calcium flare that immediately lit on contact with the water. We steamed slowly towards this, and the boys grabbed it with a boat hook.

I ordered the life jackets to be brought into the saloon, and, having corrected all our check-ups we had some hot tea and food and started back for

home at a slightly diminished speed as compared with our outward journey.

Obscure Moon

At 8.40 p.m. we lost the last of the light from the setting sun. With an obscured moon and heavy overhead clouds, we were alone in the middle of the English Channel with no light of any sort. Neither did we open up a light until about 9.10 p.m., when we collected the Nab Light Tower.

Our pictures handed over, in a few minutes we were under way again from Southampton Docks, back to the factory. We had forgotten that for two hours previously we had been driving in total and complete darkness at close on 30 m.p.h., entering into The Daily Mail's spirit in trying at all costs to get pictures for the British people in time for the morning paper.

Newspaper report on Scott-Paine's exploits in *Glitterwake*

---

defence searchlights at Stokes Bay, near Portsmouth. The searchlights were to be tested against 'enemy' landing forces and a small sum of money had been made available for the hire of civilian boats and boatmen to act as the landing force. When Scotty heard of this he immediately lent two fast motor boats without charge and made sure that they were crewed with his best men. The army observers were impressed with the speed and manoeuvrability of the boats which could not be held in a searchlight beam, and, as a result, the School of Artillery at Whale Island decided to order similar boats for towing practice targets for use in training coastal gunners.[17]

During September, Scotty's well-orchestrated publicity campaign took a step forward when *The Daily Mail* carried the banner headline 'Speedboat Dash to Liner—Mr Scott-Paine's 30 mph Race'. The Orient liner *Orion* was expected off the Isle of Wight carrying dramatic photographs showing the rescue of cruise passengers from the Cunard-White Star Line, *Doric*, which had been in collision off the coast of Portugal. *The Daily Mail* had contacted Scott-Paine and had asked if he could intercept the incoming liner, collect the pictures and rush them to Southampton so that they could be used in the early editions. Scotty had recently completed a luxury

35 mph express cruiser for his own personal use. *Glitterwake II* was based on the successful 45 foot boats, powered by three 100 hp Meadows engines, and was fitted out with extensive saloons and a luxurious ladies' stateroom, decorated in grey, silver and blue, with mirrors on every wall.[18]

Scotty quickly raised a hand-picked crew from his 'band of faithful fellows', including Bill Sheaff and Jack Banks. Speed was of the essence as it was 6 o'clock in the evening when the call came and the liner had to be contacted before darkness fell. The launch roared off down Southampton Water. Calshot was cleared at 6.21 PM at 7.05 PM, the boat was alongside the Nab Tower. Deep waves meant that the horizon was constantly lost to view and darkness soon fell. Scotty had worked out where the liner might be, but one or two false starts led to time being lost chasing the smoke of other ships. At 7.47 PM, after two hours of running at full speed, Bill Sheaff spotted the smoke of a distant ship. Scotty did a rapid calculation and decided that it must be *Orion* and the boat sped off towards its quarry. Scotty's hunch was right, and in response to signals from the searchlight mounted on top of *Glitterwake II*'s coach roof, the liner altered course towards the speeding launch. At 8 o'clock, *Glitterwake II* was pitching

Bill Sheaff with Scott-Paine's launch, *Glitterwake*,
and one of his Rolls-Royce cars.

around in the liner's wash to pick up a barrel
containing the photographs, which had been thrown
overboard.[19]

Hubert Scott-Paine's two-year battle to convert
the doubters in the Admiralty to his vision of a 'mile-
a-minute' navy was about to come to an end,
although his ostentatious marketing continued to
cause resentment in certain corners of the Admiralty.
Admiral Henderson telephoned Scott-Paine two
weeks after the national publicity over the *Doric*
pictures, and told him that he had at last persuaded
the Admiralty to order two experimental 60 foot
torpedo carrying motor boats of the sort that Scott-
Paine had been pressing upon him and his colleagues. Scotty was jubilant and was later to recall that,
'When we got that order, we did not get drunk, but
we were the craziest lot of fellows inside a factory.'

Scotty did not forget the contribution that T. E.
Shaw had made in promoting his boats in high
places. Shaw's death in May 1935 had been a

considerable shock for the nation and Scotty had
attended the funeral service at the village church at
Moreton in Dorset to mourn the loss of a national
hero and the end of a partnership. Although he did
not live to see the acceptance of Scott-Paine's vision
of the motor torpedo boat, Shaw did write to his
friend Robert Graves shortly before his death about
his contribution to his partner's battle with the
Admiralty:

That for eight years, and now for the last four I
have been so curiously fortunate as to share in a
little revolution we have made in boat design . . .
Now I do not claim to have made these boats.
They have grown out of the joint experience, skill
and imagination of many men. But I can
(secretly) feel that they owe to me their
opportunity and their acceptance. The pundits
met them with a fierce hostility: all the RAF
sailors, and all the Navy, said they would break,

sink, wear out, be unmanageable. To-day we are advising the War Office in refitting the coast defences entirely with boats of our model, and the Admiralty has specified them for the modernised battleships: while the German, Chinese, Spanish and Portugese governments have adopted them! In inventing them we have had to make new engines, new auxiliaries, use new timbers, new metals, new materials. Nothing now hinders the application of our designs to big ships—except the conservatism of man, of course. Patience. It cannot be stopped now.[20]

CHAPTER 11
The Motor Torpedo Boat

Scotty had been so confident of obtaining a contract for the experimental craft that he had secretly started work on one of the 60 foot hulls well before Admiral Henderson had telephoned with the news that an order was to be placed. The order for what were to emerge as Motor Torpedo Boats Nos 1 and 2 was officially placed with the British Power Boat Company on September 27th, 1935, although Scotty was later to claim that he did not get written confirmation of the order for another one and a half years. The hulls of the two boats were recorded as being 'laid down' on October 12th and October 22nd respectively, although the Scott-Paine method of building did not involve hulls being 'laid' in the traditional sense. His hand-picked team of mechanics, designers and craftsmen had been put to work on the project in his secret shop, knowing that Scott-Paine intended to beat all his previous construction records such as the 'Seven Day Bus' or, more recently, the delivery of the Admiral's Barge for the Commander-in-Chief Devonport. The first boat was to be launched only seventy-nine days later on December 14th. It was another remarkable Scott-Paine achievement, and succeeded in impressing officials at the Admiralty.[1]

As with all of Scott-Paine's hard-chine motor boats, the 60 foot hull was based on Fred Cooper's original hull design of 1927. The construction was of sawn frames with double diagonal planking below the chine and with a single layer of planking screwed to diagonal seam battens above the chine. Using his experience with *Miss Britain III*, Scotty proposed the use of 'Birmabright' aluminium alloy for the deck and wheelhouse. The material had been developed for boat building by the British Aluminium Company which had set up a boat building subsidiary, the Birmal Boat Building Company, on the River Itchen in Southampton.

The initial order for two experimental motor

torpedo boats was then increased by an order for a further four boats on October 19th, 1935. The fortuitous emergence of an urgent operational requirement for torpedo boats, so soon after the decision to order experimental craft, arose with the invasion of Abyssinia by Mussolini in early October 1935. The Commander-in-Chief, Mediterranean, insisted that a flotilla of offensive motor boats such as those proposed by Scott-Paine, were needed at Malta to counter the threat of Italian torpedo boats. Following his urgent representations to the Admiralty, a decision was taken to order a flotilla of the new torpedo boats as part of the 1935 Emergency Naval Building Programme. It was to the credit of the Admiralty that having taken the decision to develop this new branch of the service, it took steps to make it effective.

The work at Hythe took on a new pace as Scotty set about turning his vision of a 'mile-a-minute' navy into an operational reality. To speed the work up, Scotty purchased a number of second-hand Napier Lion aero engines from the Air Ministry to use in the construction of a full-scale mock up of the engine room layout, in which wooden pipes, flanges, junctions and other components were fabricated and later used as models for the production of operational components. This was later to give rise to malicious allegations that he had actually installed second-hand aero engines in the boats of the First Flotilla delivered to the Royal Navy. In fact, Scott-Paine's design philosophy was to make production drawings from built mock ups and full-scale replicas rather than undertaking the construction from theoretical designs produced on a drawing board.

The draughtsman who produced the production drawings for the Birmabright wheelhouse of the first 60 foot boat was Graham Cooksey who had joined Tommy Quelch's team some time earlier. They were based on a mock-up built in the secret shop at Hythe

The prototype 60 foot motor torpedo boat with a
single torpedo launching gantry.

and were passed to the Birmal Boat Building
Company who undertook the fabrication at their
Itchen yard. Cooksey was delighted when the
finished product fitted the hull of the first motor
torpedo boat perfectly. He was horrified, however,
when he noticed that Birmal had made one mistake
and that the windows were lower than those shown in
his drawings. Cooksey knew that this was the sort of
detail that Scotty would immediately notice and so he
went straight to Scotty's office. His boss was capable
of exploding when things were not done just as he had
intended, and Cooksey knocked on the door with
some trepidation. Scotty was in a Board meeting, but
he summoned Cooksey, who explained the problem.
Scott-Paine's response was short and to the point:
'Ah well', he said, 'We will have to find a short arsed
skipper!'

Scotty had spotted Cooksey as a talented draughtsman and it was typical that he encouraged and
supported employees who showed loyalty and
promise. At this time Cooksey was attending evening
classes on naval architecture and Scotty met him
leaving the yard. 'Where are you going, Cooksey?'

Cooksey replied, 'Evening class in Naval Architecture in Southampton.' 'Must you go so bloody
early?' 'Yes Sir', came the reply, 'I have to cycle.'
Scotty then retorted, 'Can't you buy a bloody motor
bike.' No Sir—I can't afford it.' 'Clear Off!' Scotty
concluded the interview. The next day Scott-Paine
came up to Cooksey and told him that he was to have
a £1 a week rise. This was later confirmed by a letter
to which Scotty had scrawled a post-script, 'This does
not include the wheelhouse.' The incident was
typical of the way in which Scott-Paine repaid loyalty
and dedication in his employees. [2]

Yard trials with the first torpedo boat were started
in December 1935 using three second-hand Lion
engines with no reverse gear or clutches. Scotty was
delighted that the wealth of practical experience
accumulated at the yard over the previous four years
meant that the engine fittings, propellers, rudders
and hull all performed perfectly in the prototype
boat. The trials continued and new marinised Napier
Lion engines were installed prior to the boats being
handed over.

During January 1936, Scott-Paine was informed

that the Naval Construction Programme Committee, which had until then referred to Scott-Paine's
boats as Coastal Motor Boats, had decided that the
new boats were to be designated officially Motor
Torpedo Boats. On February 28th, 1936, Scott-
Paine received from the Admiralty his 'License to
Dispatch or Deliver Vessels of War for his Majesty's
Service', as he handed over *MTB 01* and *MTB 02* to
Lieutenant Commander G. B. Sayer, who had been
appointed to command the 1st MTB Flotilla.[3] His
flotilla crew included two engineer officers, a gunner
and a handful of technical ratings.[4] Training in the
operation of the new vessels was undertaken in co-
operation with the builders, and Scott-Paine personally trained the coxwains how to handle fast
motor boats. Scotty would take the crews out on
Southampton Water, teaching them how to 'feel' the
water by seeking out the wash of the liners using the
port of Southampton. The MTBs would chase the
liners like terriers worrying their prey. Scotty showed
them how to detect the wash of a distant ship, to hunt
it and to feel their way near the ship whilst keeping
out of sight. He even blindfolded the helmsmen to
increase their feel for the behaviour of their new, high
performance boats. As Scotty later recalled: 'I blindfolded the men during the last month, and they all
developed a fairly good sort of catch hands and feet.
They could all move about the boat. They did
everything. They could pull reverse gears, discharge
torpedoes, and steer the ship, and all of them could
make a darned good cup of tea.' Scotty's training
techniques were developed further when the 1st
Flotilla was stationed in the Mediterranean and the
crews could pick up a training ship's wash at night,
go around at right angles, pick up the inboard wash,
and so find their way inside the fleet.[5]

Development work on the design of the torpedo
discharge arrangement was carried out by Scott-
Paine in association with the Naval School of
Torpedoes and Mining at HMS *Vernon*, Portsmouth.
Scotty had initially worked on a scheme for the discharge of torpedoes from cradles carried in recesses
in the sides of the boat's hull, forward of amidships.
He had proposed that the cradles should be projected
outwards by means of elastic cords and the torpedoes
then dropped into the sea. He set out his ideas in a
letter to Admiral Henderson on October 21st, 1935,
requesting that the scheme should be the subject of a
secret patent that would protect his commercial
interests. The idea was examined by Captain John
Carslake, the Deputy Director of Torpedoes and
Mining, who responded that Scott-Paine's scheme
was simply an amalgam of existing ideas and that as
the Admiralty was funding experimental work with
the British Power Boat Company through HMS

Vernon, there should be no question of any system
being the subject of commercial patents.[6]

Scotty then dropped the idea of forward-firing
side-discharge and concentrated his inventive genius
on developing an effective stern discharge. He came
up with a scheme that was supported by HMS *Vernon*,
in which two 18 inch torpedoes were carried on
overhead rails in the engine room compartment of
the boats. A lattice-work girder, normally stowed on
the after deck, was arranged so that it could be hinged
over the transom to form a continuation of the engine
room rails. Once the motors of the torpedoes had
been started, the boat accelerated towards the target
so that the torpedoes, which had guide wheels welded
to their casings to allow them to run on the overhead
rails, would run out of ports in the stern of the boat
onto the discharge rails. Once the torpedoes had
dropped into the sea, the MTB would turn off its
course, allowing the torpedoes a clear run to their
target.

Once the basis of the idea had been accepted by
HMS *Vernon*, Scotty set to work putting it into practice
on the first MTBs. Graham Cooksey was brought
into the project and was sent to a Midlands cycle
manufacturer to obtain bicycle frame tubing to build
a prototype discharge rig. Subsequently, the production versions were manufactured from aluminium
bronze by a Midlands firm, and the system was generally considered to be reasonably satisfactory. The
principal disadvantages of the stern discharge
arrangements were that the wheels welded to the
casing reduced the speed of the torpedoes in the water
considerably. Naval officers also realised that the
system might be operationally hazardous as it
required the MTB to run towards the target at
speed.[7]

Gradually, the 1st Flotilla was formed. The hulls
of *MTBs 03* and *04* were laid down on January 3rd,
1936, and the hulls of *MTBs 05* and *06* were laid
down on October 29th and 12th, respectively. The
press delighted in speculating about the new boats
which were dubbed by one magazine as 'Vest Pocket
Leviathans'. Scott-Paine's natural wish to publicise
his boats was constrained by Admiralty security
requirements.

But there were no such constraints imposed by his
old friend, Beauforte-Greenwood. Scotty's men put
the finishing touches to his prototype 64 foot Royal
Air Force boat in May 1936, and were preparing to
unveil it with a spectacular dash along the east coast
of England. The event was to attract as much publicity as the Donibristle run with T. E. Shaw had
done four years earlier.

Early in the morning of May 23rd, a small group
gathered on the jetty at the Hythe yard, where the

The prototype 64 foot High Speed Launch built
for the RAF, leaving Hythe for Grimsby, May,
1936.

boat was fuelled and prepared for its record breaking
run. It promised to be a fine day once the sun had dis-
pelled the chilling mists over Southampton Water.
Beauforte-Greenwood was accompanied by Flight
Lieutenant Norrington, together with his second
assistant, Mr McCue, Captain Butters of the Marine
Section of the Directorate of Equipment, and a
Corporal engineer. Scotty had decided that he was
going to bring along his General Manager, Stuart
Barker, and his personal servant cum chauffeur, Bill
Sheaff who was to provide the food during the record
breaking run. Mr R. Boyle, a Power Boat engineer,
was to tend the three Napier Lion engines. Charlie
Chiverton, foreman of the Secret Shop, was to tend
the boat and to act as seaman along with Bill Pusey.

Scotty took the boat, later designated *RAF 100*, on
to Southampton Water and opened the throttles. The
boat roared off towards the Isle of Wight. The
distance of 373 miles to Grimsby was covered in a
mere fourteen hours, and Scotty remained at the
helm during the whole voyage except for one relief of
twenty-five minutes. Heavy weather was encountered as the boat sped across the Wash. 'The weather
was just the kind of weather we were looking for',
Scotty told a Correspondent from *The Aeroplane*, 'and
for a considerable part of the passage I drove the boat
without any consideration for her. It was a very

confused sea such as I have seldom seen. In fact I
don't ever remember such confused sea conditions.'

The return trip to Hythe was delayed until May
26th due to fog, and when the launch left Grimsby at
nine o'clock, the weather was overcast with poor visibility. Cromer was sighted at 11.45 AM, by which
time the seas were running with waves up to six feet
in height. As the boat rounded the South Foreland at
3.45 in the afternoon, heavy seas were encountered.
Scotty's skill at the helm enabled the speed to be
maintained, even when the wash of a cross-channel
ferry off Dover threw the sea over the boat. The
heavy weather continued all along the south coast,
but Scotty persevered and the engines behaved faultlessly. It was an impressive performance of the speed,
reliability and seaworthiness of the 64 foot craft. A
tired but exhilarated crew cheered as the boat tied up
at the Hythe jetty at 7.59 PM, ten and three quarter
hours after leaving Grimsby. The record breaking
run had been made at an average speed of 36.2 mph.[8]

The 64 foot boat was an outstanding success and a
further twenty-one were built for the RAF between
1937 and 1940. The last one was delivered on July 7th,
1940, just in time to take part in rescuing airman during
the Battle of Britain.

As soon as he got back to Hythe Scotty threw himself
into preparing the first two motor torpedo boats, *MTB*

01 and *02*, for the visit of the new King, Edward VIII to Portsmouth. He had been told of the Royal visit some weeks before and had been delighted that the first naval ship to receive the new King was to be *MTB 01*. It was essential that everything was ready for an event that not only gave due recognition to this new arm of the Navy, but which was an important boost in his campaign to convince the remaining doubters in the Admiralty.

King Edward VIII arrived at HMS *Vernon*, where *MTBs 01* and *02* were to be formally commissioned, at 11.30 AM on June 30th, 1936. At the gangway of *MTB 01*, the King stood at the salute as he was piped aboard. He entered the wheelhouse whereupon the torpedo boat, under the command of Lieutenant Commander Sayer, started his engines and set off for Stokes Bay with Scott-Paine following, in command of *MTB 02*. The King was given a demonstration of

the new torpedo firing gear as a torpedo was fired at HMS *Amazon*. The round trip was made at speed, despite the rough weather, and within twenty minutes a wind-blown King Edward was back on shore with his party. Scott-Paine was then presented to the King at a luncheon held at HMS *Excellent*.[9]

The publicity that surrounded the Royal visit fuelled speculation in the press about the new 'mosquitoes' of the Royal Navy. Scott-Paine's reputation rode high, and was again enhanced by national publicity when *RAF 100* was handed over to the Royal Air Force in a ceremony held at Hythe on July 20th, 1936. Four days later a demonstration of the first High Speed Launch of the RAF was given on Southampton Water for the benefit of the world's press. A ferry steamer which normally plied between Southampton and Hythe was chartered to carry the

Scott-Paine at HMS *Vernon* after the Royal visit June 1936; greeting, left to right, Lt Commander Sayer, Captain Willis of HMS *Vernon* and Engineer Commander Meggs.

press party out to SS *Kenilworth Castle*, a Union-Castle ship that was laid up at moorings off Netley, in Southampton Water. It was an ideal platform from which to watch and photograph *RAF 100* as it roared past at speed. Later that day, over twenty reporters and photographers went on board *RAF 100* and, with Scotty at the helm, streaked down Southampton Water to Calshot. The boat, tuned perfectly and handled perfectly, reached a speed of 45 mph, despite its full load. In true Scott-Paine style, it was a demonstration that impressed all who had been invited.[10]

The trials of the first motor torpedo boats and the spectacular success of *RAF 100*, impressed the Admiralty, which, having reluctantly accepted the Motor Torpedo Boat in principle, took active steps to establish a coherent policy for these new boats. The week before the Royal visit to Portsmouth, the Director of Tactical Division, Naval Staff, had written a memorandum setting out the role of the new Motor Torpedo Boats in attacking shipping in enemy harbours and in protected waters. He was also aware of lengthy discussions that had been taking place between Scott-Paine and the Captain of the Anti-Submarine School at Portland over the previous months and concurred with Scotty's arguments that the new motor boats would be ideal for anti-submarine and mine-sweeping duties.[11] In August 1936, the Admiralty then decided that the approval for a further six boats which had been given by the Admiralty Construction Programme Committee in the previous January, should be amended to allow eight boats to be constructed.

Scotty had always believed in the importance of developing new, experimental types, and when he heard informally that these were to be ordered from him as part of the 1936 Construction Programmes, he was delighted that the Admiralty was at last beginning to listen to his philosophy of fast boat development. Of the six motor torpedo boats to be ordered, one was to be fitted for anti-submarine work and another for minesweeping. Two of the eight boats were to be experimental target boats; one, powered by a single Napier Lion engine, was to be fitted as a radio controlled target, and the other to be a hull, without engines, and fitted for being towed. The Admiralty was also aware of the limitations of the Scott-Paine 60 foot boat and Scotty was asked to come up with a design for an experimental 66 foot boat that could carry two of the larger and more powerful 21 inch torpedoes.[12]

As soon as *MTBs 01* and *02* had been commissioned at the Royal ceremony in June, the two boats had been sent back to Hythe for further trials until the remainder of the boats of the 1st Flotilla were completed. Scott-Paine's revolutionary technology took some getting used to in a Navy that had little experience of high performance marine engines. The Admiralty Engineers had, for instance, demanded a full astern trial at full power and revolutions of the engines in accordance with procedures set down when steam engines had first been introduced. Scotty pointed out that the angle of the propeller shafts would result in the boat being pulled under, even if it did not actually disintegrate, and the Admiralty dropped the requirements, accepting one-fifth power at the appropriate revolutions. There were further problems with the coupling of the propeller shafts of the wing engines through the reverse gears, which led to a spate of broken drive shafts. The problem was caused by a torsional condition but Scotty's engineers came up with a solution in the form of a pendulastic coupling that was to remain standard in coastal forces boats throughout World War Two. However, the naturally conservative nature of the Admiralty Engineer-in Chief's Department led to the imposition of a ban on a certain speed range which frustrated Scott-Paine and which was largely ignored in practice.[13]

In November 1936, Scotty helped conduct the rough weather trials of *MTB 01*, which were carried out off the Isle of Wight. *MTB 01* was under the command of Scott-Paine who had with him a Power Boat crew; Lieutenant Commander Sayer, Lieutenant H. Kidson, Officer Commanding *MTB 04*, and Lieutenant (E) Brockley were also on board. The boat was accompanied by the destroyer HMS *Amazon*, which had on board a number of officers who were to witness the trial. To the south of the Isle of Wight, the two vessels were exposed to gale force winds and waves up to twelve feet in height. The observers were amazed as the frail looking *MTB 01* maintained a speed of 30 knots, much of the time remaining invisible from the deck of the destroyer due to the height of the seas. As the destroyer passed St Catherine's it was rolling heavily, but *MTB 01*, under the skilful control of Scott-Paine, who guided it up and over the rolling waves to reduce the inevitable pounding, maintained a level keel and was able to keep up its speed with little discomfort to those on board.[14]

The rough weather trials of *MTB 01* impressed the naval observers and brought to a close a year that had been of considerable significance for Hubert Scott-Paine and the British Power Boat Company. By the end of 1936, both the Royal Navy and the Royal Air Force had accepted high-speed planing motor boats for sea going duties. After months of prodigious effort, Scotty had laid the foundations of what was to emerge as the Coastal Forces and the Air Sea Rescue service of World War Two.

CHAPTER 12
Competition with Vosper

Although the Director of Tactical Division had suggested in August 1936 that Hubert Scott-Paine should be asked to prepare a design for a larger boat capable of carrying 21 inch torpedoes, Peter Du Cane of Vospers had also approached the Admiralty with a request to build a torpedo boat, and was about to steal a march on his competitor. Financial provision had been made available in the 1936 Construction Programme for the development of a boat capable of taking 21 inch torpedoes, but Du Cane was told at first that no order would be placed with Vospers. Du Cane had friends at the Admiralty, though, and he held lengthy discussions, during which officials outlined the likely future requirements for MTBs in the light of the operational experience of Scott-Paine's 60 foot boats. Du Cane was told that future boats would be capable of carrying 21 inch torpedoes would be capable of operating the restricted seas such as the North Sea and would be capable of crossing to either the French or Dutch Coast under cover of darkness, and engage the enemy before returning to base. He was convinced that he could design a boat with superior performance to the Scott-Paine boats and he persuaded the directors of Vospers to design and build a boat as a private venture.[1]

Having regard to Scotty's near monopoly of suitable marine engines in Britain, Du Cane chose the 1,150 hp Isotta Fraschini marine engine, which had been developed in Italy for use in the Italian navy's MAS boats. The Directors agreed and by the end of August 1936, the lines of Du Cane's 68 foot torpedo boat had been completed in the drawing office.

Scotty had been aware of the Vosper threat to his company's superiority in the production of hard-chine hulls, as Vosper had been producing the 16 foot Jolly boat and a 35 foot hard-chine launch for the Navy for some time. He got to hear of Du Cane's

proposals for a larger MTB and soon realised that his competitor's boat was likely to be superior to his own 60 foot boats. The first MTBs had been designed using Fred Cooper's hull type of double diagonal planking below the chine, and single planking above, but the experience of the 1st Flotilla had shown that a stronger hull would be required to meet the 'ghost' Admiralty requirement for a larger and more seaworthy MTB. The pressure of work in completing the 1st and 2nd Flotillas meant that new design work had to take second place, but Scotty did get Tommy Quelch to sketch out a 66 foot boat, carrying two 21 inch torpedoes on engine room rails, as with the 60 foot boats. At the same time Tommy Quelch drew out a general arrangement drawing for a 75 foot boat which was intended to meet the new Admiralty requirement.

Scotty knew that the design of the 60 foot boat had been a 'bloody good guess', and realised that the 'stretching' of the 60 foot hull would be inadequate to meet the emerging requirement for a larger boat. He decided that he would have to recruit additional technical expertise if he were to compete with the threat posed by Vospers. His chance came towards the end of 1936 when George Selman visited Hythe to discuss propeller design with Scott-Paine. Selman had designed the propeller for *Miss Britain III*, and had become one of the country's leading experts on propeller design. At the time he was working with Manganese Bronze but had disagreed with his firm over a proposed collaboration with Stone's, a rival propeller firm, over the design of a new set of propellers for the *Queen Mary*. Selman was recounting his difficulties to Scotty who, with characteristic flair for spotting the right man for the job, asked his visitor to join him as Chief Designer.[2]

Scotty gave Selman a team of thirteen, including Tommy Quelch and Graham Cooksey in the drawing office. Selman soon argued with his new

Boats of the First MTB Flotilla escorting the
Royal Family in a Scott-Paine Admiral's Barge,
for the opening of the National Maritime
Museum, April 27th, 1937.

boss over the best way to design boats as he was a
technician, while Scotty was not a designer in the
technical sense but had an uncanny eye and practical
sense of what would work. He would always trust his
own 'sense' of design rather than the advice of
technical experts, although he never spurned the
carefully thought out proposals of experts such as
George Selman. Selman had been trained in the
design of steel ships but with the expert help of men
such as Steve Biggs, foreman of the secret shop, who
was a mine of information and experience, he learnt
everything there was to learn about the construction
of boats in wood.

On April 27th, 1937, the boats of the 1st flotilla
made their first public appearance when *MTBs 03,
04, 05* and *06* escorted King George VI and Queen
Elizabeth, together with the young Princess
Elizabeth, down the Thames from Westminster to
Greenwich. The occasion was the opening of the new
National Maritime Museum, for which the flotilla

had sailed from Portsmouth. Scott-Paine's pride in
his new boats was complete as he watched the Royal
party board the Hythe-built Admiral's Barge of the
Commander-in-Chief Nore, at Westminster Pier.
Admiral of the Fleet Sir Ernest Chatfield, First Sea
Lord and Chief of the Naval Staff, was with the
Royal party. The new arm of the Royal Navy,
designed and built by Hubert Scott-Paine in the face
of opposition from many quarters, followed the
barge in line astern, past the Tower of London and
under Tower Bridge, down the river to Greenwich.

The traditional Royal river barges, which had
been placed on display in the new museum, had been
replaced with the most modern of the Navy's fast
motor boats. 'The swift relentless machine that has
come onto the scene', wrote *The Times*, 'was impressive in its efficiency and wonderful movement . . .
the modern age of mechanical transport seemed to
have intruded into the traditions of Thames pag-
eantry unheralded and with startling swiftness.' The

river folk of London had no such reservations. Cheering crowds greeted the procession as it sped past the Embankment, banners and flags decorating the offices of County Hall and other public buildings, and all the way down the river. More flags and banners decorated every possible building or vessel, while sirens competed in a relentless and joyful clamour. The river itself was strangely deserted, like a broad highway closed to all vehicles, as the Sovereign, with his entourage of Scott-Paine craft, swept past.[3]

The 1st Flotilla again hit the national headlines when it undertook an epic journey from Portsmouth to Malta under its own power. Despite arguments that the first six boats should be retained in home waters where it would be easier to undertake any modifications that might prove necessary in service, it had been decided, in October 1936, to dispatch the 1st Flotilla to Malta, as soon as it was ready.[4] The Flotilla eventually left for Malta on June 22nd, 1937, accompanied by HMS *Vulcan*, a trawler which, at Scotty's suggestion, had been converted as a tender for use with the 1st Flotilla. The flotilla of little ships called in at Brest, Corunna and Lisbon on the way to Gibraltar, performing well in the Bay of Biscay where there was a Force 4 to 5 wind, and a moderate following sea. The naval coxwains, trained by Scott-Paine, were adept at nursing the craft, easing the speed as the boats ran down the faces of the big waves to avoid plunging the bow into the wave in front. Coming into Gibraltar, the boats had to drive against a Levanter and were forced to making tacks to windward, making port with some difficulty.[5]

The 1st Flotilla, under the command of Lieutenant Commander Sayer, arrived at Malta on July 17th. The long sea journey had been a complete success, although experience in the Mediterranean was to show up the limitations of the 60 foot hull and its machinery. The boats suffered frame damage from the pounding received at high speed in a seaway, particular with the inexpert and enthusiastic handling of the boats in operational circumstances, and there were problems with corrosion of the 'Birmabright' aluminium decks which led to their being replaced with mahogany decks. Each boat of the 1st Flotilla spent seventy-six days refitting and twenty-seven days under repair in Malta Dockyard between January 1938 and March 1939. Notwithstanding the difficulties, the Commander-in-Chief Mediterranean, sent a lengthy signal to the Admiralty in November 1937, detailing the work that these new boats could undertake in attacking enemy harbours and in attacking enemy submarines. Admiral Pound concluded his signal with a request for at least four flotillas of Scott-Paine motor torpedo boats at Malta, with a further four based at Gibraltar.[6]

This enthusiasm for Scotty's boats was not to be found in all quarters. An Admiralty minute of November 16th, 1937, concluded: 'Frankly I do not find the Commander-in-Chief Mediterranean's telegram carries me away to the belief that these MTBs are a vital necessity. I do not wish to obstruct the building of six more but I feel most strongly that we will have to mind our steps with these MTBs.'[7]

Scotty's relationships with the Admiralty were not helped by his continuing insistence that Admiralty policy should reflect his own need to protect the commercial interests of the British Power Boat Company. For some years Scotty's obsession with secrecy had been justified by the Admiralty practice of using his designs as the basis for specifications, issued for competitive tendering. As a result, it had been standard practice at the yard that working drawings were not issued to customers. The Admiralty received few meaningful drawings of the 60 foot MTBs and the so-called machinery drawings were few in number and consisted only of outlines with no dimensions or scales. The drawings were of no use in either design or maintenance, and it was later told that, after the Baedeker air raid on Bath during World War Two, the drawings of Scott-Paine 60-foot MTBs were to be seen in lieu of windows at the home of a naval officer.[8]

The early Admiralty records about the MTBs were vague: 'length about 60 foot, beam about 15 foot, displacement about 18 tons, speed about 35.37 knots'. In fact, under service conditions, displacement was about 20.22 tons and maximum speed 33 knots. Similar problems were encountered at HMS *Vernon* where, in May 1937, the Director of Torpedoes and Mining complained that no detailed drawings of the installation of the torpedo gear were available and that it was not possible to arrange for the manufacture of spare parts. He suggested that a purely naval design should be adopted and that Scott-Paine should be given a one-off payment in recognition of the development work undertaken by the British Power Boat Company in designing the prototype stern discharge system.[9]

In the meantime, Scotty's energetic mind was working on ideas for the expansion of the Admiralty's fast motor boat policy. On October 20th, 1937, he wrote to Admiral M. Tower, Director of Naval Equipment about progress on the experimental boats for minesweeping, anti-submarine work, and the experimental distant-controlled boat for target towing which had just been ordered. The hulls and machinery of the three boats had only just completed preliminary trials, but Scotty urged the

MTB 01 at HMS *Vernon* during torpedo trials,
August, 1938.

adoption of a policy for the purchase of up to two
hundred and fifty boats over the next five years. He
assured the Admiralty that he would be able to fulfil a
commitment based on a long term policy, and that as
he had purchased an additional site of forty acres, he
would be able to turn out one boat per week.[10]

Scotty's vision was not shared by Admiral Tower
who felt that the approach was a commercial attempt
to pre-empt scarce resources in favour of a massive
building programme of boats, for which there was
only a theoretical operational requirement. He
retorted that Scotty's programme was entirely
'imaginary' and that there was no sense in commit-
ting between three and four million pounds to the
construction of boats which were only in the experimental stage. 'All this seems to me to be utter
nonsense and shews the exaggerated view Mr Scott-
Paine seems to have that he assumes that his own
view is shared in official quarters', Tower wrote,
'and he proceeds to spend money right and left in
making preparations for a programme that exists in
his own imagination, e.g. motor torpedo boats, and
now he has actually bought extra land in preparation
for this new programme which is to result from his
experiments. The trouble is that, having spent his
money he then comes down on the Admiralty to

reimburse him directly or indirectly.' Tower went on
to suggest that it should be made quite clear to Scott-
Paine that any expansion of his works would be at his
own risk and that even if the experimental boats were
to be successful, further orders would not be in the
numbers suggested by him. He concluded: 'It is
realised that the sort of reply proposed will not clear
up the position on monopoly, copying by other firms,
etc., but it seems in the highest degree unlikely that
any reply could do so, and the main thing at this stage
seems to be to prevent Mr Scott-Paine from embark-
ing upon the material realisation of his daydreams at
the ultimate expense of the Admiralty.'[11]

Discussions within the Admiralty during 1937
gradually led to the emergence of a motor torpedo
boat policy. With the operational experience of the
1st Flotilla, and with the development of the experimental Scott-Paine motor anti-submarine boat, it
was concluded in November 1937 that future policy
should follow five lines of development:

1. A fast motor anti-submarine boat.
2. A fast motor mine-sweeper.
3. A type of motor torpedo boat suitable for
   specialist operations such as attacks on enemy
   harbours.

Interior of the hull building shop at Hythe,
December 5th, 1936.

4. A type of motor torpedo boat suitable for local defence at ports.
5. A type of 'sea-going' motor torpedo boat suitable for operating in restricted waters such as the Channel and the North Sea, and the Mediterranean.

The first two types were being developed in collaboration with Scott-Paine. Trials with Motor Anti-Submarine Boat *No 1*, powered by two Napier Lion engines, were carried out over three days at the beginning of December 1937 in the area to the south of Portland Bill. A submarine operating at 60 foot, and cruising at 3 knots, was used, in conjunction with a trawler of the First Anti-Submarine Flotilla, which fired charges during the attack. An Asdic dome was fixed below the keel of *MA/SB 1*, and although asdic conditions were poor, the echoes received were good, even up to speeds of up to 30 knots. The trials confirmed the view of the Chief of Naval Staff that these boats might have a valuable operational role, and on January 6th, 1938, the Commander-in-Chief-Portsmouth was informed that a further six motor anti-submarine boats were to be included in the sketch estimates for 1938/39.[12]

A hydrofoil motor torpedo boat under development by Samual White at Cowes was seen to fulfil the third requirement and Scott-Paine's 60 foot motor torpedo boats were seen to fulfil the harbour defence role. The Chief of Naval Staff concluded that the 60 foot MTB was primarily a weapon for weaker naval

powers, but that they would be of great value in local offensive operations at 'ports where we may expect during certain periods of a war to be in a position of general naval inferior strength'. The 1st Flotilla was already operating at Malta in connection with local defence, and two further flotillas had been planned and allocated to Hong Kong and Singapore, and it was suggested that these should be increased to two flotillas of Scott-Paine craft at each port, with further flotillas at Alexandria.[13]

The proposed sea-going MTB was envisaged as having a maximum speed of 45 knots and an endurance of 1,000 miles at 20 knots, carrying a war load of two 21 inch torpedoes. Scott-Paine's 60 foot motor torpedo boat was not seen as fulfilling this requirement and it was concluded that Admiralty policy should be to encourage experimental designs so that a suitable craft would be available for production in times of emergency. Vospers had completed Peter Du Cane's 68 foot private venture motor torpedo boat, and the Admiralty had purchased it in October 30th, 1937 as an experimental sea-going type of MTB, utilising the original provision in the 1937 estimates for the proposed 66 foot British Power Boat craft.[14]

Peter Du Cane was not pleased when he heard that the Admiralty still planned to include nine more of Scott-Paine's MTBs in the 1937 Building Programme, three to complete the Second Flotilla destined for Hong Kong, and six to form the Third Flotilla, to be dispatched to Singapore. He knew that the Vosper boat was superior to the Scott-Paine 60 foot boat both in construction and performance, and he argued strongly against the decision to form further flotillas with what he knew was an inferior, albeit innovative, type. His view was shared by many in the Admiralty where there was a smouldering antagonism between the flamboyant entrepreneur from Hythe and the 'establishment'. There was also a loudly voiced distrust of Scotty on the part of some serving officers of the 'mile-a-minute' boats, fed by the suspicion that some senior officers had been 'mesmerised' by Scott-Paine.[15] The anger, resentment and suspicion then burst into the open in an extraordinary attack on Scott-Paine during the House of Commons debate on the Navy Estimates on March 17th, 1938.

The attack was launched by the Labour Member for Nuneaton, Lieutenant-Commander Reginald Fletcher, an expert on naval affairs and later, as Lord Winster, Minister of Civil Aviation in the post-war Attlee government. Fletcher had been well primed by Scott-Paine's detractors, although his charges were later shown to be either false, or mis-representations of fact.

Fletcher started his attack with contentions that the supplies of fast motor boats to the Royal Air Force and to Imperial Airways had never been put out to competitive tender. 'This Government subsidised firm', he said, referring to Imperial Airways, 'gives contracts to another firm, owned by one of its own directors, without any competition.' He then went on to allege that Scott-Paine, having obtained his first order of Motor Torpedo Boats, was unable to get marine engines of sufficient power and so obtained, from the Air Ministry, a number of Napier Lion aero engines which he then incompletely converted for marine use by fitting reverse gears and water-cooled manifolds, but 'being aero-engines, they are full of ball races and consequently quite unsuitable for the constant load under which marine engines must work . . . I can say from conversations with engineer officers that these engines give trouble.'

At this point in the debate, Scotty's old friend, Admiral Sir Murray Sueter intervened to insist that he had been on one of the boats and that it ran very smoothly with little vibration. Fletcher retorted: 'may I say that I have frequently been taken out in a motor car by a gentleman who wanted to sell it to me, and have had a very fine run indeed.' He went on to refer to the search for a larger, sea-going Motor Torpedo Boat, proclaiming the virtues of Peter Du Cane's boat.

Let me see what other type of British boat is on the market. In 1937 Vospers of Portsmouth, built a comparable boat, only this boat had three 1,000 horse-power Isotta Fraschini engines instead of the three 500 horse-power engines in the Scott-Paine boats. Their maximum speed, light, was 48½ knots, and their maximum speed, service loaded, was 43.7 knots. I believe that this boat was accepted by the Admiralty, but I cannot hear of any more orders having been given for these Vosper boats. Incidentally, if further orders are given, I trust that no foreign mechanics will be employed in connection with the Isotta engines, otherwise they may learn some of the secrets of its hull construction, which are very important. But although Vospers, as I understand, have had no further orders, Mr Scott-Paine has just received an order for nine more of the boats which failed when tried out under service conditions in the Mediterranean.

Old established firms like Thornycrofts and Whites, to whom we owe a great deal of gratitude for their war work, firms of great experience and high reputation, have had no opportunity to tender or to run boats on trial, but Mr Scott-Paine, who has been in the business only since 1927 or 1928 enjoys a virtual monopoly of orders from the Royal Air Force, from Imperial Airways and from the Admiralty. I would like to know if the Admiralty costings branch has investigated the price of £23,000 quoted in the Navy Estimates of 1937 as paid for these boats, I can tell the house this, that Mr Scott-Paine and his boats are a by-word in the boat-building trade, the members of which laugh at this and call this business a racket. They say that 'Mr Scott-Paine must run the Admiralty contracts department.' An officer in charge of the repair and maintenance of these boats has vouched that the engines are unsatisfactory for marine work. Even structurally they give trouble and have a tendency to 'hog'. Engine room artificers who have served in them say the same thing. In fact, you have to get on dry land, and take a train up to the Admiralty before you can find a kind word said for these boats.

Fletcher continued his attack—which, had it not been subject to parliamentary privilege, would have been libellous—with criticisms of the speed of Scott-Paine's boats, claiming that the engines had to be grossly over-revved at 2,600 rpm to achieve the stated 37 knots. The sea-keeping qualities, he claimed, were not good, and the firing mechanism was unsatisfactory. Fletcher then went on with further accusations which suggest that at least one of his informants was a disaffected, and not very knowledgeable, source within the Hythe Yard or the 1st Flotilla.

I want to come to what I think is the most serious part of the whole business. I have spoken about the Napier Lion engines which are fitted in these boats. I can produce evidence that these engines have been bought for from £5 to £10, and yet Mr Scott-Paine has been charging £3,800 for them. It sounds extraordinary but I am willing to produce the evidence for the Ministry. I am told that some of these engines bought by Mr Scott-Paine were painted white and put into some of these boats. They went out to Malta, and, as they gave trouble, spare parts including pistons, had to be ordered from Napiers. When the pistons came it was found that they would not fit as they were too small. Over-sized pistons had to be ordered, and then it was ascertained that the cylinders of these engines had been re-bored. They were not even new when they were put into the boats at the price I have quoted. The brand new engines used in the Vosper boat, which are of 1,000 horse-power instead of 500, are charged at £4,500.

The Vosper boat brought out in May 1937, is a more advanced design. It is 10 knots faster than the Scott-Paine boat; it has a service load of 32 tons, a speed of 44 knots, and carried two 21 inch torpedoes and two ¾ inch automatics. That compares with the Scott-Paine boat with a service load of 20 tons, a speed of 34 knots, two 18 inch torpedoes and four .303 Lewis guns. Yet nine Scott-Paine boats were ordered in February 1938, although the Vosper boat was out in May 1937. The Scott-Paine boats are obsolete before they are even launched. They are costing £29,000 each.

They are held in contempt in the Service. Destroyer officers of experience tell me that they could run down a flotilla of the Scott-Paine boats without opening fire. They say they could run over them and sink each of them on their bows in turn.

I ask the House to note that the Vosper boat appeared in May. In June an effort was made on behalf of the British Power Boat Company to introduce what I can only call a spy into the Vosper works. I dare say that the Minister would like to deny that, but he will have great difficulty in doing it because the police got wind of this, but they thought it was the work of a foreign country. They intercepted telephone messages. One message was 'What about the dough?'. These facts were reported by the police to the Admiralty, and the gentleman, if you may so call him, who was engineering this business and passing the agent into the Vosper works, was interviewed at the Admiralty, and I should very much like to know why he was not prosecuted.[16]

Fletcher's call for an enquiry was widely reported in the press. The works' staff at Hythe gathered together to send a message of support to their employer whom, they felt, was unfairly denigrated, and with whose boats they were proud to be associated. The message, signed by twenty members of Scotty's 'band of faithful fellows' concluded: 'At a time like this we feel that we would again like to express the deep loyalty of all your Works' Staff to yourself and your Company, and we hope the knowledge that all your Works' Staff and employees are wholeheartedly with you may be some small measure of comfort in such trying circumstances.'[17]

CHAPTER 13
Private Ventures

The year 1938 had started well for Scott-Paine with the Royal Navy ordering nine more 60 foot MTBs as part of the 1937 Building Programme.[1] In February, the Air Ministry announced that it was ordering a further seven 64 foot High Speed Launches of the 'RAF 100' Class, and a further twenty-five 37 foot 6 inch seaplane tenders.[3] Scotty had recruited George Selman who, with his enlarged design team, was working on 'PV 70', a totally new 70 foot motor torpedo boat, that Scotty had decided to design and construct as a private venture in response to the threat posed by Vospers. He knew PV 70 would be superior to Du Cane's boat, and was confident that it would be chosen by the Admiralty in preference to his rival's private venture design.

Then, in March 1938, Fletcher had launched his attack in the House of Commons. Scotty was deeply upset by the attack which would have been libellous had it not been protected by parliamentary privilege. He was upset by the lies, and the malicious presentation of half-truths. It particularly distressed him that his detractors saw his motive as commercial greed, for he was intensely patriotic and saw his role as placing his inventive and entrepreneurial genius at the disposal of his country, which was unprepared for a war that he was sure would come. His dedication to his works which he loved 'as a father loves his child', was creating tensions at home; he was becoming more distant from his wife, Brenda, and his children hardly ever saw him. John was later to recall the bitter arguments between his parents at this time, and how he and his younger sister Rosanne would cry in their bedrooms as they listened to the rows downstairs. The attack in the House of Commons also upset John, who had just returned to Worth Preparatory School after a bout of measles, and who then suffered a relapse when he heard the devastating news.[3]

Four days after Fletcher's speech, Scott-Paine suffered another blow. On March 21st, 1938, his mother, who had been ill for some weeks, died at the age of eighty-eight years.[4] Scott-Paine had retained a close affection for his mother and ever since he had joined Pemberton Billing in 1912, he had travelled from Southampton to Shoreham every possible weekend, to visit his family at Dolphin Chambers. He took every opportunity to enjoy the company of his mother who lived with his sister, Katie, Victor and his brother Philip who had been insomniac since his incarceration in a German prisoner-of-war camp during the Great War, joined Scotty for the family weekends. The week-end tea parties, which often included his brother Victor, who by this time was publicity manager for Vickers Aviation, were occasions of great family jollity. Scotty had never lost his boyish enthusiasm for things like pillow fights and jam sandwiches, and one of his favourite party tricks was an impersonation of the comedian Oliver Hardy, of Laurel and Hardy fame, to whom he had more than a passing resemblance.

Scotty's vindication came on April 13th, 1938,

Scott-Paine at the wheel of his yellow Rolls-Royce at Shoreham. His mother is standing at the front of the car with two of his children.

when the First Lord of the Admiralty, Duff Cooper, read a statement in the House of Commons which refuted all the allegations made by Lieutenant-Commander Fletcher, who had clearly been 'put up' by Scott-Paine's competitors or disaffected personnel within the British Power Boat Company or the MTB flotillas. The detailed statement concluded:

It has been asked why the latest order, placed near the end of the financial year 1937, could not have been divided amongst several firms. It is clear from what has been stated [in this statement] that, apart from the desirability of having flotillas homogeneously constituted, no other boat has yet passed out of the experimental stage. While it is only fair that the original designer of this type of boat should have received initial orders proportionate to his enterprise, and to the success of the

design . . . the British Power Boat should not be allowed to consider themselves immune from competition. At the same time, this opportunity must be taken of stating that the Admiralty, which must be largely dependent on the initiative, resource and inventive capacity of private firms, are highly appreciative of those qualities as displayed by the British Power Boat Company; and are gratified that a new company which can supply essential service requirements has thus been started in this country.[5]

By this time, George Selman's work on the design of 'PV 70' was well advanced at Hythe. Selman had introduced a new discipline into the design approach, insisting that most of the trial data at the yard was of no use at all. For instance, the measured mile used by Scotty was based on a short land mile,

Aerial view of the Hythe factory about 1938. Much of the enclosed harbour was reclaimed for additional building sheds during World War Two.

sometimes called a knot for convenience. 'It's one thing to deceive others', he told his employer, 'But you're a bloody fool if you deceive yourself.' Selman argued with Scotty over the best way to design boats, particularly over the use of test tank models for designing the form and the propulsion of boats. He told Scotty that designs should be based on experiments carried out at the test tank at the National Physical Laboratory at Teddington, but Scotty was reluctant to agree. He knew Dr Baker who was in charge of the laboratory, and had himself obtained valuable information about competitors from Dr Baker. 'If I can get anything out of him', Scotty told Selman, I'm damn sure other people can too![6] Scotty was obsessively secretive, but did allow Selman to use a smaller tank owned by Shorts. The tank was too short for accurate results and after further argument, Scotty conceded, and allowed Selman to use the NPL tank, but with the precaution that the notes of speed and resistance in Dr Baker's notebooks could not be scaled without reference to Selman's own notes. Some years later Scotty explained his design process with 'PV 70' when he addressed the Society of Automotive Engineers in Detroit:

We had design after design after design, and models . . . Tanks are all right to measure air resistance of a model or one model against another model, but tanks do not reproduce what goes on in the propeller shaft and instruments, a wheel and a rudder, and it became such a nuisance that I gave it up.

In some areas Scotty's pragmatism complemented Selman's work. For instance, Selman carried out a considerable amount of research into the application of the theory of beams to design wooden laminated structures for the keel and frames, and pioneered the use of 'Aerolite 300', a new urea-formaldehyde adhesive, in boat building. Scotty was sceptical about the use of glues and insisted that copper nails were used to reinforce the bonded structures. His sense of what would work was instinctive and was later justified by later experience. During World War Two, Bishop, the designer of the de Havilland Mosquito aeroplane, visited George Selman at Hythe. He looked at the use of nails to reinforce the glue of the laminated frames and said, 'I wish someone had shown me this before, my aircraft are all falling to pieces.'[7]

In other aspects of the design of 'PV 70', George Selman's calculations were right and Scotty's empiricism was to be proved wrong. For instance, one tank model had a pronounced reverse sheer aft of the wheelhouse, a feature that gave the boat the

distinctive profile of a greyhound in full flight. Scotty was delighted with the look, and announced that this would be the mark of all future Scott-Paine boats, and would distinguish them from boats produced by competitors. Selman insisted that the reduction of the depth of the frames at this point would weaken the hull, but was over-ruled by Scotty. Selman was proved right and all the British Power Boat 70 foot boats were to suffer frame damage in service with the Royal Navy, when they were loaded with additional armaments, for which they had not been designed. The gunwales broke as a result of the stresses arising from the pitching of the boats in a seaway and had to be strengthened with the addition of a timber under the gunwale, exactly where Selman had predicted there would be problems.[8]

The design of 'PV 70' was largely determined by the choice of engines. In February 1938, the Admiralty had offered to lend Scott-Paine three Isotta-Fraschini engines for the project, but Scotty refused, insisting that motor torpedo boat policy must be based on the use of engines manufactured in Great Britain. He was sure that Italy would side with Germany in the event of war, cutting off that source of engine supply. Scott-Paine's experience in the conversion of aero engines for marine purposes was second to none and he knew that the Rolls-Royce Merlin engine which was used by aircraft such as the Vickers-Supermarine Spitfire, was ideal. He travelled to Derby in the early part of 1938 and discussed ideas for a marine conversion of the Merlin engine with the Rolls-Royce engineers. With his experience of the Napier conversion, he was able to provide the Derby engineers with a detailed specification and was able to arrange for suitable ahead and reverse gears to be built to his specifications at the Meadow's Wolverhampton factory. By May, he was able to conclude an agreement with Rolls-Royce for the production of the 'Rolls-Royce-Power-Merlin-Marine-Unit', in which Scotty agreed to the exclusive use of the Merlin engine whenever he had a requirement for an engine of between 1,000 and 1,600 hp: in return, Rolls-Royce agreed to the exclusive use of Scotty's gear boxes in the marine conversion for a period of five years. The agreement also included an undertaking by Rolls-Royce to loan three Merlin engines, suitably modified to Scott-Paine's specifications, and a maintenance engineer to supervise their installation in PV 70, which Scotty had undertaken to construct at his own expense.[9]

Scott-Paine and Peter Du Cane were unanimous in voicing their concern about the supply of engines in the event of war. Du Cane tried to persuade the Admiralty to give Vospers sufficient orders for the Isotta Fraschini engines to enable them to build the

The triple installation of Rolls-Royce Merlin engines in *PV 70*.

engines under license in England, but his entreaties were to no avail. Scotty persuaded both Napiers and Rolls-Royce, together with the merchant bankers Lazard & Co., to come forward with a proposal for a new company to design and build high-speed, light-weight engines for use in motor torpedo boats. Again, the Admiralty declined to guarantee the purchase of sufficient numbers to make the project viable, and the scheme was dropped.

During the summer of 1938, Scott-Paine met with Engineer-Vice Admiral Sir George Preece who had just succeeded Admiral Sir Harold Brown as Engineer-in-Chief. Admiral Brown had been very supportive of Scott-Paine's work in the development of high performance marine engines, but, as soon as they met, Scotty and Sir George Preece developed a mutual and violent antipathy. The meeting was held at the Admiralty in London and Scotty started by expressing his concern that Britain would be left

without a supply of high performance marine engines in the event of war with Germany. He told Sir George all about his agreement with Rolls-Royce, but went on to stress that in the event of war, all the Merlin production of the Derby factory would be required for aircraft. The supply of engines for the Admiralty could only be secured if new manu-facturing capacity were to be developed, and that this could only be done if the Admiralty were to guarantee sufficient orders to make it commercially viable.

Sir George Preece responded with the Admiralty view that the supply of Isotta Fraschini engines would be sufficient for all likely requirements. He went on to tell Scotty that the Admiralty was encouraging a British manufacturer to consider producing a 1,000 hp lightweight diesel engine. He was sure that such an engine could be produced within six months, but Scotty was dumfounded as he

The planked hull of *PV 70* ready for turning over
in the secret shop, summer 1938.

knew that it would be at least two years before such an engine could be produced. The argument became quite heated as Scotty berated the Engineer-in-Chief for his short-sighted policy, which, he reiterated, would have dire consequences for the supply of engines for motor torpedo boats in the event of war. Preece was adamant, but Scotty was to be proved right.[10]

Design work on 'PV 70' was completed by May 1938, when construction started on the hull and engine room mock-ups. The work was carried out in a new Secret Shop amidst the greatest security. The shop was arranged so that the design team were located close to the shop floor, on first floor level. Only those working on the project were allowed into the Secret Shop, and again, Charlie Chiverton kept a book containing the names of those who were allowed in: Stuart Barker was not included on the list, a fact that was to be a cause of friction between him and Selman. Despite the secrecy, there was one major breach of security. One day Bill Sheaff came to

Selman and said, 'Did you see the drawing on the wall down at Hythe?' Selman had not, but went down and saw that someone had drawn a silhouette of 'PV 70', with its distinctive whaleback form, on the wall of a local pub. He returned to the office and got Graham Cooksey to have a general scout around for anything suspicious. Later, Cooksey came back and said: 'You know the drawing office, well there is a bookcase and if you stand on the bookcase . . . you know, they drill holes in corrugated sheet and don't always put bolts through them . . . there's plenty of holes there and you can look down and see the blessed boat we are building!' The spy was identified and soon rooted out of the yard. Later, Scotty came into the drawing office and asked why sacking had been hung from the roof at one end; he was told that it was to reduce draughts in the room![11]

At the same time as the design of 'PV 70' was progressing, improvements were being made in the production techniques of the yard. Since 1927, the mass production of boats had been based on the use

The deck planking being laid on *PV 70* in the
secret shop, summer 1938.

of wooden jigs for the assembly of frames. Each
frame of different dimensions required a separate jig
to facilitate its replication, which meant that the
process of assembly could be quite slow. Jimmy
Wrann, who managed the production side of the
factory, developed an improved system which
utilised one jig for the fabrication of all the frames of a
boat. The jig comprised a metal plate, somewhat
larger than the largest frame of a boat, on which was
marked the lines of boat from tables of offsets
provided by the drawing office. A metal guide was
then fabricated for each point on the keel, the chines
and the gunwale for each frame, and these were then
located on the plate with dowels, designed so that
each guide would locate only at its designated
position. The frame members were cut to the
required shape in the saw mill, with all the necessary
notches for seam battens already in place, and were
then placed against the guides which ensured that
they abutted each other in the right way. The gusset

plates, or biscuits of plywood, would then be placed
over the joints and screwed in place, thereby
completing the frame as a rigid structure. The system
was cheap and accurate. The frames could be turned
out as quickly as the saw mill could produce the
components and, during World War Two, it worked
so effectively that the storage of completed frames
became a serious problem.[12]

PV 70 was a masterpiece, considered by both
George Selman and Scott-Paine to be superior to its
Vosper rival. The length was 70 foot, and the beam
was a remarkable 20 foot; the draught over the
propellers was about 4 foot 4 inches. The hull was of
double diagonal construction both above and below
the chine, and laminated frames were used in places
of maximum stress. It was powered by three Rolls-
Royce Merlin engines, each developing 1,000 hp at
3,000 rpm, and without reduction gearing they gave
the PV boat a maximum speed of 44.4 knots, and a
continuous rating speed of 40.4 knots at about 30

tons displacement. The power/weight ratio of machinery, including reverse gears and auxiliary drives, was 1.9 lb per horse power. The beam was adequate to carry two 21 inch, torpedoes in forward facing tubes, or four 18 inch torpedoes, also with bow discharge. Following aircraft practice, Scott-Paine had developed enclosed power-operated turrets for anti-aircraft machine guns. A sleek, streamlined deckhouse lay above the weather deck, and the boat presenting a smaller profile to enemy gunners than the earlier 60 foot boats. In order to reduce the profile still further, a patent telescopic mast was fitted for signals and the radio aerial. In true Scott-Paine fashion, the accommodation below the deck was well thought out; there was a cabin for two officers and a cabin for one or two Petty Officers and one wireless operator, and there was accommodation for eight crew, with separate heads for officers and ship's company. There was a spacious and well-equipped galley and ward room, and access could be had to any part of the boat without emerging on to the upper deck. Selman estimated that the boat would have an endurance of 1,800 nautical miles at 8 to 10 knots, and that 900 miles at 22 knots could be achieved.[13]

Although Scott-Paine had received an order in August 1938, for five more 60 foot boats, which were to be fitted as motor anti-submarine boats, and which were built as *MA/SBs 2–6* within the 1938 Construction Programme, it was clear that no more 60 foot motor torpedo boats were going to be ordered. Of the orders for seven 70 foot MTBs of the 1938 programme, five were given to Vospers and two to Thornycroft. With the successful launch of *PV 70*, Scott-Paine knew that he had a craft that was better than those built by his competitors, that he had a yard already jigged and tooled for mass production and that he had a monopoly on the supply of the only suitable British built high-performance engines. Scott-Paine also knew that in the event of the Admiralty refusing his new design, there would be no shortage of orders from foreign navies.

CHAPTER 14
'PV 70'

Scott-Paine was to spend about £75,000 on designing and building *PV 70*, and on the development of the Rolls-Royce marine conversion. This expense was a major factor in persuading him to incorporate the British Power Boat Company as a limited liability company. The Memorandum and Articles of Association were signed on June 8th, 1938, and the share capital of £750,000 was all allocated to Scott-Paine or his nominees. Scott-Paine became Chairman and Managing Director of the new company; Stuart Barker became a director and General Manager, while the two other directors were Scotty's secretary, Margaret Dinkledein and Vice-Admiral Sir Geoffrey Blake KCB DSO, who was to be the company's main representative at the Admiralty. By this time, the company employed over one thousand employees, and was the second largest employer in the Southampton area.[1]

Once he had supervised the start of *PV 70*'s construction during May, Scotty put his mind to planning an international campaign aimed at selling the 70 foot motor torpedo boat to foreign naval authorities. He had recently purchased the 176 foot twin triple expansion steam engine yacht, *Sylvana*, which had been built at Troon in 1907 as the *Maid of Honour*, and he decided to undertake a lengthy cruise, accompanied by Bill Sheaff, Margaret Dinkeldein and members of the family. The cruise was planned for the summer of 1938, with the aim of visiting foreign government departments and boat builders, as well as some well earned relaxation.

The first port of call during the cruise was Ostend where Scotty met up with an old friend, Conijn, the owner of a Dutch ship-building firm, Werf Gusto, originally A.F. Smulders of Schiedam. Scotty had first built boats for the Royal Netherlands Navy in 1938, when an order had been placed for a number of 37 foot 6 inch cruisers, powered by two 200 hp engines.[2] These were for use in conjunction with torpedo boats, following practice torpedoes and, as each torpedo's travel was exhausted, marking its position prior to its recovery. The first boat had been completed in July 1938 when it had been delivered by her two-man crew direct to The Hague. Scotty had met Conijn at that time and, anticipating that Holland would remain neutral in the event of war, had discussed the possibility of the Dutch firm becoming the British Power Boat Company's principal agent in Europe. Werf Gusto had built a new yard and was quite capable of mass producing Scott-Paine craft.

The outcome of Scotty's discussions with the Royal Netherlands Navy was a provisional agreement with the Dutch government for the construction of twenty of the new MTBs, for use in the Dutch East Indies, subject to *PV 70* being successful once it had been completed. The first Dutch boat was to be built at Hythe, under the supervision of Lieutenant Colenbrander of the Royal Netherlands Navy, while the rest were to be built under licence by Werf Gusto.[3]

Scotty then took *Sylvana* through the Kiel Canal into the Baltic, en route to visit Denmark, Norway and Sweden. George Selman later recalled that he travelled out to consult with Scott-Paine on details of the design of *PV 70*, while the yacht was moored in the Kiel Canal. Hitler's yacht, and the Belgian Ambassador's yacht were moored nearby, when a new E-Boat came down the canal. Scotty called out to Selman: 'I'll stand one side of the gangway, and you stand the other—Bill, you fetch a camera!' Bill Sheaff fetched a small cine camera and, hidden between the two men, filmed the E-Boat as it passed *Sylvana*.[4]

The British Power boat Company agent in Sweden was K. Hallstrom, an ex-naval officer of high social status. For some two years, Scotty had been supplying Hallstrom with money to mount a publicity campaign in Sweden, an investment that

Scotty's yacht, SY *Sylvana*, at Hythe, 1938.

was to pay dividends. During his visit to Sweden, Scotty visited the Bofors factory and secured a contract for the supply of two 63 foot motor torpedo boats, a smaller version of the 70 foot Private Venture boat, which had been designed by George Selman. Subsequently, four 63 foot motor torpedo boats of the same design were to be ordered by the Norwegian government.[5]

Scott-Paine returned to Hythe to supervise the final stages of the construction of *PV 70*, which was launched on November 6th, 1938. The anticipated sales to the Dutch and Swedish governments were dependent upon the boat's performance being as outstanding as he had led them to believe. *PV 70* behaved faultlessly, so Scotty issued an invitation to a group of Dutch naval officers and constructors to witness trials on Southampton Water. The trials were to take place on November 20th, but the weather was so severe on that day that the *Queen Mary* was unable to berth in Southamptom Docks and was forced to anchor in Cowes Roads.

Notwithstanding, Scotty decided that the rough weather conditions would be ideal to impress his Dutch guests with *PV 70's* performance and sea-

worthiness. George Selman accompanied Scotty on the trip around the Isle of Wight which was to prove a hair-raising experience. He was later to recall:

My God, they were rough weather trials. I reckon there was a 10 foot sea in the Solent and the race off the Needles was like a wall of water . . . I have never seen anything like it. Where was the normal Solent, and the race seemed to stand up. I was pretty busy doing one thing and another, taking readings, and I was aware that we'd got up on this race, but didn't see the transition. I thought to myself, I will see how he comes off it . . . he was that good as a helmsman. Now there was a little skylight a bit open, there was a good deal of spray coming through, and one of these naval constructors (from Holland) called Skelton, dressed in a life suit got a few splashes and said to me, 'Mr Selman, could you lend me a handkerchief for a moment?', and I unthinkingly gave him my handkerchief and he proceeded to wipe his clothes down with my ruddy handkerchief which I thought was a bit much . . . I reckoned the poor devil was as scared as hell . . . he said to me, 'Why

PV 70 at speed during trials, February 1939.

don't you stop him he will smash the boat up in a minute'. The little Admiral after that said 'Thank you Scott-Paine, I think we've seen enough'. But Scott-Paine just grinned benignly at the little Admiral and said, 'Oh, that's all right Admiral, there's lots I can show you yet'. And I knew that Scott-Paine was dead scared stiff because he went red all up the back of his neck. I was standing behind him when he was at the wheel . . . yet he was smiling, you know like this . . .[6]

PV 70's performance was characteristically outstanding and the orders from the Dutch and Swedish governments were quickly confirmed. Scotty then made plans to unveil his new creation to the world's press. A demonstration of *PV 70* was arranged for February 10th, 1939, when the Red Funnel ferry, ss *Medina* was chartered to take the press party out on Southampton Water. It was an ideal platform for the visitors to observe and photograph the boat as it went through its paces with Scott-Paine at the helm. The first run was a head-on approach from a distance of

about two miles, at a speed of about 44 knots. The boat roared past *Medina* towards Southampton, executed a one hundred and eighty degrees turn at full speed and headed back towards the observers. On a second run, Scott-Paine demonstrated the ability of the boat to slow down from over 40 knots to 8 knots in three seconds. This was followed by a demonstration of the boat's ability to accelerate from 10 knots to 40 knots in a mere ten seconds. The silence of a slow approach was equally impressive; at 10 knots, the three Merlin engines were barely audible. Later, the reporters were able to examine the interior. One reporter concluded: 'there can be few craft afloat in which the designer has so cleverly availed himself of every square inch for practical purposes. Steering is made easy by a neatly designed electrical switch which reduces the pull to mere finger-tip control . . . all in, here is a fighting ship evolved upon the principles of a racing motor boat with every surplus projection eliminated and the other officers and crew protected in a very effective manner.

The reporter from *Motor Boat and Yachting* was on board *PV 70* during the demonstration. He was impressed with the lack of noise and vibration, even at speed.

With the engine revolutions at 2,600 rpm, which may be considered as the 'normal maximum' rate, there was little noise and vibration and conversation could be carried out in the wheelhouse without raising the voice. Vibration was absent throughout the whole range of speed and with the port and starboard engines shut down and the centre engine running at a little over 1,000 rpm, giving a speed presumably of about eight knots, we were assured by those on board the *Medina* that it was impossible to hear the machinery until the MTB was within a short distance of them.

The reporter from *Yachting World* was also one of the privileged few on board during the trials. He concluded: 'I could have slept with ease in any of the berths, of course, provided that the weather was not too bad.'[7]

On the very day that Scotty put *PV 70* through its paces on Southampton Water, two men were setting sail from New York on a mission that was to have far reaching consequences for Scott-Paine and the British Power Boat Company. They were Henry R. Sutphen, Executive Vice-President of the Electric Boat Company of Bayonne, New Jersey, and his chief designer, Irwin Chase. Their mission was to see whether the Scott-Paine 70 foot MTB would be suitable for the US Navy. American interest in the development of this type of craft, referred to as Patrol Torpedo (PT) Boats, dated back to December 1936 when Rear Admiral Emory S. Land, Chief of Construction and Repair, suggested the development of experimental torpedo boats. He had been impressed with the developments in Britain and saw a role for this type of boat within the US Navy. Land's recommendation was approved by the Secretary of the Navy on May 7th, 1937, and a year later, Congress approved the expenditure of $15,000,000 for experimental vessels. The expenditure was to be at the discretion of the President of the United States.[8]

In July 1938, the US Navy invited civilian naval designers to submit plans for submarine chasers and motor torpedo boats. One specification was for a motor torpedo boat of between 70 and 80 foot in length, with a trial speed of 40 knots and capable of carrying two 21 inch torpedoes, depth charges and two machine guns. The design contest closed on September 30th, 1938 with twenty-four designs submitted, including thirteen designs for a 70 foot MTB. On March 21st, 1939, Sparkman and Stephens were

The 70 foot motor torpedo boat built for Elco, prior to its shipment to America in September 1939.

announced as the winners of the 70 foot design competition, and two months later a contract was let to Higgins Industries Inc. for the construction of the first of these boats, which had been scaled up to 81 foot by the Bureau of Ships.[9]

However, further developments were to take place and, during January 1939, Henry Sutphen of Elco, who had met George Woods Humphery, discussed Scott-Paine's 70 foot PV design with Charles Edison, the Assistant Secretary of the Navy. The Elco Naval Division of the Electric Boat Company had considerable experience in boat design and mass production, having built over seven hundred 80 foot Motor Launches for British, French and Italian governments during World War One. Sutphen had also learnt much from the development of fast weight-carrying boats used by rum smugglers and coast guards during the prohibition era. The Coast Guard boats, in particular, had shown that properly converted and installed aviation engines could produce spectacular results. He was convinced that, in the event of war, there would be a need for small, fast boats that could go to sea in any weather.

Sutphen decided to enter the PT boat competition. He was aware of the progress made by European navies in the design and development of fast torpedo boats, and decided to examine the possibility of building one of these types under licence as an alternative to developing an American design. In particular, he and Irwin Chase were interested in three British designs. One was the Thornycroft development of the World War One Coastal Motor Boat, then being built for China and the Phillipine Navy; the second was the Vosper motor torpedo boat which was being ordered by the Royal Navy; the third was Scott-Paine's PV boat. Acting on Edison's recommendations, the General Board of the Navy suggested that one of these British boats be obtained as a check against the developments then in hand with American companies. Sutphen discussed the matter with Scotty's representative in New York, George Woods Humphery, and with officials from the Navy Department, who gave an undertaking, that in the event of his purchasing a Scott-Paine boat, the Navy would purchase it as an experimental boat.

Sutphen and Chase decided that *PV 70* was the best available motor torpedo boat. Irwin Chase later wrote: 'All three showed great advances in speed and seaworthiness over anything in the United States and each had its individual points to recommend it. Rough water trials showed that the Scott-Paine model had exceptionally seaworthiness and this feature, with a number of other superior characteristics, made us sure that it could best be adapted to the needs of our Navy.'[10]

Negotiations between Elco and the British Power Boat Company were concluded with an agreement, dated March 16th, 1939, covering the construction of one 70 foot MTB at Hythe, at a cost of £58,250, final payments being dependent upon Scott-Paine obtaining an export licence for the boat. The contract also included an option for Elco to take out a licence for the exclusive right to manufacture the British Power Boat 70 foot MTB in the United States. Sutphen notified the Navy Department of the purchase on March 17th, 1938.[11]

The Admiralty trials of *PV 70* took place in March 1939, in an atmosphere of suspicion and recrimination. Scotty had made the claim that *PV 70* could run at over 40 knots for twenty-four hours without attention. The Admiralty demanded a non-stop twenty-four hour demonstration, whereupon Scotty pointed out that the boat would have to refuel and personnel would need to rest. Eventually, it was agreed that the trial would be carried out in four successive periods of six hours, each on consecutive days. A postwar reviewer later wrote: 'It was alleged, but certainly not proved, that the engines were changed one dark night despite the Admiralty Overseers' seals on the boat house door. The engines being of Rolls-Royce manufacture were doubtless capable of standing up to the exceptional test; a little attention to the installation equipment may have been desirable!'

The trials of *PV 70* were carried out at the same time as those of the Vosper 70 foot boat then under development. The rough weather trials of the two boats were carried out on the same day, *PV 70* in the morning and the Vosper boat in the afternoon. Selman recalled how the Admiralty representative, Captain Morris, got off *PV 70* and walked across to the Vosper boat about 100 yards away: 'Du Cane waved to Scott-Paine, who did not stick his fingers up but frowned at him and turned away. The Vosper boat started up and Scott-Paine said to me, "Shall we go and have a look at them", so I said, "Yes, why not", so we ran alongside for a bit and that caused Morris to write in to the firm objecting to the unsportsmanlike behaviour.'[12]

Admiral Tower was impressed with *PV 70* and agreed to evaluate the Scott-Paine 70 foot boat as a Masbie, agreeing to change the order for *MA/SB 6* from a 60 foot boat to a 70 foot boat powered by three Napier Lion engines. However, the Admiralty decided to standardise on the Vosper boat for the larger sea-going motor torpedo boat. Scott-Paine was furious at the rejection of *PV 70* in favour of the Vosper design, blaming the bad feeling between himself and what he called the 'bowler-hatted brigade' of the Admiralty. Two years later, in May

Torpedo firing experiments with PV 70, July 10th, 1939, with the *Queen Mary* in the background. The oleo struts were found to be unsatisfactory and were later abandoned.

1941, Admiral Tower tried to explain why it was that the Navy had opted for the Vosper MTB. He told Stuart Barker, at a private meeting at the Admiralty, that it was not that *PV 70* was not as good as the Vosper boat. On the contrary, he was quite prepared to believe that it was better than the Vosper boat in a number of important respects. The trouble was that Scotty had designed his boat in secret, along his own lines, whereas Peter Du Cane had designed his boat in conjunction with experts from the various Admiralty departments, who then felt more inclined to favour the boat with which they had been involved.[13]

Scotty's insistence on secrecy, which had served him badly in respect of orders for the Royal Navy, was not a problem in dealing with foreign governments. The largest order for the British Power Boat

Company 70 foot MTB came from the French navy. During his negotiations with the French, Scotty took *PV 70* across the Channel from Southampton to Cherbourg in a dramatic dash designed to impress the French naval authorities. Watching the weather carefully, Scotty chose May 18th for the demonstration, and *PV 70* left Hythe about 3.00 PM, with sixteen people on board. Eighty minutes after passing the Needles, the fort at the eastern end of Cherbourg breakwater came into view. A French Naval launch, trailing a long 'tricolor' behind, came out to meet the speeding MTB. In a dramatic gesture, Scott-Paine dashed past the reception party and roared into the waiting berth in the dockyard basin. The average speed of the journey was 42 knots. As a demonstration of the smoothness of the journey, a glass of water had been placed on the ledge in front of the helmsman, and not a drop was spilt. *The Aeroplane*, in reporting the venture, recalled how Scott-Paine had pioneered the use of flying boats in civil aviation with his flight to Cherbourg in 1918, and later, with the introduction of the Sea Eagle on the Channel Islands and Cherbourg routes.[14]

The return trip was made the following day. Despite a confused swell during the first part of the trip, the time to the Needles was eight-seven and a half minutes. The company's foreign sales representative, Frank Bishop, had suggested that the glass of water trick was tried again, but Scott-Paine retorted, 'Look, its all right to risk Providence once but only a bloody fool would repeat it!' The French were impressed with the cross-Channel dash and ordered eighteen boats, designated *VTB 23* to *40*, for proposed bases at Cherbourg and Lorient, and Saigon in French Indo-China. French archives record that the financial provision was made from the Supplementary Budget of March 4th, 1939, and that the contract with the British Power Boat Company was signed on July 3rd, 1939. It appears that at least one of the hulls was started before the contract was signed, as Admiralty records note that *VTB 23* was laid down on May 31st, 1939.[15]

Scott-Paine was desperately concerned to secure the supply of engines for his foreign contracts and for any boats that might have been built by Elco in the event of their exercising their option to build the 70 foot boats under license. The outlook was optimistic for further foreign orders as negotiations got underway with Canadian Vickers for a license to construct his boats in Canada, and as preliminary discussions took place with the Cockatoo Boat Company of Sydney for a license to build in Australia.

The search for an alternative supply of engines for the hoped-for American contract led George Woods Humphery to make contact with Mr Platt, the Paris representative of the American Packard company. Platt came to England and met Woods Humphery in secret on May 25th. He was told that an English boat building company was interested in purchasing one hundred engines, and that the enquiry was discreet so as to avoid offending certain British engine manufacturers. Platt informed Woods Humphery that Packard had done no serious selling of engines since 1930, but that it could develop a 1,200 hp machine of the sort that had been used by Gar Wood for racing. Woods Humphery then requested technical information comparing the engine with the Rolls-Royce and Napier engines, and discussed the possibility of the British Power Boat Company being the agents for Packard marine engines in the British Empire.

M. N. Gilman, the Engineering Vice President of Packard, wrote to Scott-Paine on June 30th, with the information that Packard had received authority from the US Navy to export their new 'V' form, 12-cylinder supercharged marine engine for export. He attached a detailed specification of the 3M-2500 engine which was in limited production for the US Navy, for installation in their experimental PT boats. Assuming an order for one hundred engines, he reported that deliveries could be started five months after the date of a contract, and would continue at the rate of three engines per week.

Woods Humphery then travelled to America and met Gilman and Packard's Chief Engineer, George Brodie. The meeting, which took place on July 18th in Detroit, started badly as Scott-Paine had instructed Gilman to communicate only with him personally, in two plain envelopes marked Private and Personal, and Woods Humphery had no written authority to change the arrangement. The matter was finally resolved and Woods Humphery reported that Packard were confident that they would obtain the required 1,200 hp, and that it would be a suitable alternative to the Rolls-Royce Merlin engine. Discussions between Woods Humphery and Gilman continued through August while tests on the engine continued. Packard quoted a price of $25,000 per engine for sixty engines, or $23,000 per engine for one hundred. However, the US Navy had ordered only seven experimental units, and it became clear that Packard would require a substantial order if the engine were to be put into production.[16]

During his visit to America, Woods Humphery set up an American company to represent Scotty's interests in the United States. The company was incorporated as The Marine Engineering Labs Inc., of 100 West 10th Street, City of Wilmington, Delaware, the directors being Hubert Scott-Paine, as Vice-President, Margaret Dinkeldein as Secretary, George Woods Humphery, as President, and Cyril Hyde ('Cy') Condon, Scott-Paine's American lawyer. A letter to the Company from the British Power Boat Company, dated November 20th, 1939, states that in the event of Elco taking out its licence to construct the 70 foot boats, then Elco would pay the British Power Boat Company five per cent of the proceeds from the sale of the boats for engineering expertise, and that, because of hostilities, the Marine Engineering Labs would provide this expertise for five per cent compensation. The Company was re-incorporated as the Marine Design and Engineering Development Corporation on December 8th, 1939.[17]

Although most of Scott-Paine's energies were being directed towards selling the 70 foot boat, the civilian market still represented a substantial busi-

106

ness. In August 1938, The British Power Boat Company launched *Kalan*, a luxury cruiser built for Lord Strathcona and Mount Royal. The hull of *Kalan*, intended for use off the west coast of Scotland, was exactly the same as that of the 60 foot MTBs, and the yacht was powered by two Napier Sea Lion engines, finished in spotless white enamel. The accommodation included crews quarters forward, a captain's cabin on the port side, a well-appointed galley opposite and a large dining saloon. There was also a well-appointed deck saloon aft of the control cabin. In typical Hythe fashion, the attention to detail and the luxury of the fittings were of the highest standard.[18]

July 8th, 1939 was a red letter day at Hythe. Sir Kingsley Wood, Secretary of State for Air, visited the Air Training School at Hamble, RAF Calshot and the British Power Boat Company. After inspecting an Imperial Airways Ensign airliner undergoing modifications at Hamble, the Secretary of State embarked on *Kittihawk*, a 37 foot 6 inch

Power 'Sea Coach' and transferred offshore onto a 70 foot MTB, where he was introduced to Scott-Paine and Vice-Admiral Sir Geoffrey Blake. The VIP party was then shown the boat's capabilities, a demonstration that concluded with the MTB coming into a berth at Hythe at speed, so that when Sir Kingsley Wood emerged from below the deck, he was amazed to discover himself in a boatshed. On landing he was presented to Stuart Barker, Margaret Dinkeldein and the company secretary, Maurice Wright. Whilst touring the factory he also met Flight Sergeant Bradbury who had worked with Aircraftman Shaw on the first RAF boats and who was by then the Air Ministry Inspector at Hythe. Before he left for Calshot, the apprentices at the factory presented the visitor with a scale model of the Rolls-Royce Power Merlin marine engine.

That evening, Scotty and his fellow directors attended a dinner in the works canteen as guests of the foremen and works staff of the factory. The dinner was not only to celebrate the visit of Sir

Scott-Paine and his staff at Hythe, about 1938.

Kingsley Wood; it was to mark the opening of the canteen which had been constructed at the personal expense of Scott-Paine. The guests included Lieutenant Colenbrander of Werf Gusto, Commander de Booy of the Royal Netherlands Navy, Wilson Hammil of Meadows, P.T.S. Yelland of the Warships Production Superintendents Department of the Admiralty and Flight Sergeant Bradbury. Mr V.W.F. Meager, foreman of the metal shop was chairman of the dinner and proposed a toast to the health of Scott-Paine. 'I think you will all agree', he proclaimed amidst shouts of approval, 'that in Mr Scott-Paine we have an employer and leader who is, without question one of the best.' Scotty replied, telling the company that Sir Kingsley Wood had paid them all a compliment by saying that it was one of the finest factories he had ever visited, and that he had never seen a more united body of work people. 'His words pleased me more than I can tell', Scotty went on, 'because I do feel that in the twelve years of our existence we have created something more than a mere factory, we have got together a grand team of men. The Chairman referred to me as a good employer. It is quite an easy matter to be a good employer when you have got together a grand team of men.'[19]

CHAPTER 15
The Outbreak of War

As the crisis in Europe deepened during August 1939, Scott-Paine met with his fellow directors to discuss how the production of boats and engines could be secured in the event of war. Scotty called a Board Meeting and, as he sat in the saloon of *Sylvana* with Margaret Dinkeldein, Stuart Barker and Sir Geoffrey Blake, he outlined his plans.

'My duty', he told his colleagues, 'is to go to America to obtain by some means or other, supplies of engines. Napiers have most patriotically placed the whole of their manufacturing drawings in my hands with a free hand to do as I like, and, of course, to safeguard their interests as far as possible.' He went on to say that the Director of Supplies at the Air Ministry had agreed to the purchase of both engines and machine tools to the extent of some £15,000,000, but that Sir George Preece had again insisted that there was no need to secure an alternative supply of engines for the Admiralty from America. Scotty went on: "I have pooled my resources and have obtained a bank chit from the National Provincial Bank advising J. P. Morgan & Co in New York that I am good for half a million pounds sterling. This is a very heavy burden of responsibility to bear, but the Admiralty have no money or way of giving me credit. This, therefore, is the only course open to me. I must underline that this mission is strictly confidential, but if I can order sufficient engines on our own account, for both the Elco boats and our own foreign orders, I can set up manufacturing capacity that will be of use once the Admiralty brigade have realised their folly!'[1]

Scotty went on to insist that the immediate priority was to get the Elco boat across the Atlantic, and that securing a large order from the United States Navy was essential for the development of a suitable motor torpedo boat engine. Scotty was also concerned to set up a partnership with Elco for the production of Scott-Paine type boats, so that there would be an alternative supply of boats for the British Admiralty, in the event of the Hythe yard being bombed. The finishing touches were being put to the Elco boat at that moment, and hectic arrangements were being made for the loading of the 70 foot vessel as deck cargo on an American freighter, the ss *President Roosevelt*, which was in Southampton Docks preparing to cross to New York.

War plans for Hythe were then discussed. It was agreed that Sir Geoffrey Blake would remain in charge of the company as Deputy Chairman, and that Stuart Barker would be in sole charge of the factory. Plans were discussed for a shadow factory at Poole, about thirty miles to the west of Southampton. A site had been selected and negotiations had been started with a view to purchase, and it was agreed that an approach would be made to the Admiralty for funds to undertake the construction of the necessary sheds, slips and workshops. Training of skilled personnel was a major concern and Scotty agreed that the nearby Marchwood House should be purchased as a training centre for women. He had employed large numbers of women at Supermarine during the previous war and was sure that with training, women could again replace the men who would be called away to fight. He was also concerned about the ability of the Royal Navy to train personnel in the use of high speed craft, and urged Sir Geoffrey Blake to resurrect a scheme that he had put forward some years earlier, for the establishment of a training flotilla based at Hythe. The scheme had been rejected despite the support of officers such as Captain Mark Wardlaw, who had been Chief of Staff to the Commander-in-Chief Portsmouth.[2]

As soon as the conference had ended, Scotty dictated letters to Margaret Dinkeldein with instructions for Stuart Barker. He wanted to ensure that the Hythe yard maintained his own policy of secret development of new types and that the yard should under no circumstances build craft designed by other firms. Hythe was an élite yard, and he was going to keep it that way. He was aware that Barker and Maurice Wright, the company secretary, would be put under pressure to disclose details of the company's finances to the Admiralty cost department and he instructed Barker that under no circumstances was he to disclose the balance sheets of the company while he was abroad.[3]

Scotty announced that he would sail to America with Margaret Dinkeldein and his son John. He suggested that Elizabeth should join Brenda and his youngest daughter, Rosanne, who were living in Rhodesia, having visited that country in 1938. By this time, Joyce was married and living in Rome, but Scotty urged her to travel to America as soon as possible.

The floating crane in Southampton Docks lifted the Elco boat onto the deck of the ss *President Roosevelt*, which left with its precious cargo at the end of August. Scotty arranged for cases of technical drawings to be dispatched to the States, and, at the last minute, gathering together a small amount of baggage in his Rolls-Royce Phantom III, he boarded the *Aquitania* with Margaret and John on what was to be its final sailing before the outbreak of war.

The crossing to New York was one of the most unpleasant trips that Scotty had ever undertaken. The anxiety surrounding his mission was such that he never slept more than one hour at a time. He had arranged that neither his name, nor those of John and Margaret were published on the passenger list that he was sure would be scrutinised by Nazi agents. The tension was made worse by the fact that no lights were allowed at night in any cabins or public rooms, for the blackout had to be complete to avoid attracting the attention of enemy submarines.

The party was thankful when the *Aquitania* arrived in New York on Saturday, September 16th, 1939. Scotty was met at the quayside by George Woods Humphery, and a few minutes later Henry Sutphen arrived, relieved that Scotty had made it across the Atlantic. The party had some difficulty in avoiding the crowd of newspaper men, but Sutphen had arranged for the customs authorities to give Scotty priority clearance. Scotty's Rolls-Royce was quickly off loaded and soon a convoy was speeding on the 160-mile journey to New London, Connecticut. The baggage was carried in a spare car brought by Henry Sutphen who travelled with Scotty and John in the Rolls, while Margaret Dinkeldein travelled with Woods Humphery. They had lunch at George Woods Humphery's house, and by mid-afternoon Scotty was in conference with Henry Sutphen and Irwin Chase at the Mohican Hotel, New London.[4]

The ss *President Roosevelt* had arrived in New York with its precious cargo on September 5th. In fact, the Elco boat almost failed to make the crossing as the ship had met hurricane force winds during the crossing and the Captain had just been about to cut the boat free to reduce the windage of the deck cargo when the weather moderated and the order was not implemented. Scotty's men who had travelled with the boat had had a most unpleasant crossing, but, thanks to the skilful loading and packing carried out in Southampton, the boat itself was not damaged. As soon as it arrived in New York, the boat, by then designated *PT 9*, was transferred by a floating crane onto a lighter and shipped to New London where preliminary trials were to be carried out.[5]

PT 9 was taken out for her first trials on the morning of Sunday, September 17th. Scotty carried out a thorough survey before running the engines, and was satisfied that the Works had turned out an excellent job. He later wrote to Barker, congratulating him and the men at Hythe:

> please accept and extend to the men concerned how pleased and gratified I was and also to be able to say that the boat, its detail and finish has received nothing but the highest praise, not only from our American associates but from those other people who have been over the boat as well.

Throughout the Sunday and the following Monday, trials continued, with modifications being made to air intakes and propellers. A speed of 47.7 knots was achieved on the Sunday, much to the delight of Irwin Chase, who clocked the record-breaking run. The following day, Henry Sutphen brought Secretary of the Navy Charles Edison to New London in a friend's yacht. Scotty met Edison on board for an 8.00 o'clock breakfast, and then transferred the party on board *PT 9*. The day was spent with Edison who, as he left at 5.00 o'clock that evening, told Scotty to hold himself ready at 'train-time notice' to travel to Washington to explain personally all his ideas on motor torpedo boats to the President of the United States.

While he was with Edison, Scotty outlined his mission to obtain a source of engines for use at home. There were two lines of enquiry in hand. For some months he had been in discussion with the engine manufacturers, Allison, through Sutphen, and there had been the approach to Packard through George Woods Humphery. Scott-Paine was quite candid with both the American parties, explaining that it was in all their interests to co-operate in the development of a suitable 1,000 hp engine so that the initial costs of manufacture could be spread as widely as

PT 9 on trials at New London, September 1939.

possible. It was also important, Scotty went on, to ensure that the price was not increased through competitive purchase of engines. It was agreed that the US Navy would not purchase engines directly, but would do so through Henry Sutphen, who would then ensure that engines were also available to meet any future British requirements.[6]

Within days of his arrival in America, Scotty had set in train much of what he had set out to do. He had been told informally that the US Navy was likely to purchase twenty-five of his boats through Elco, and it seemed that the stage had been set for detailed technical and commercial talks with Packard about the production of an engine. On September 20th, he then travelled by train to Montreal to discuss the building of 64 foot and 37 foot 6 inch boats under license for the Canadian government. He met with an old friend Harry Greening who 'knows Canada politically and commercially inside out and who has considerable personal knowledge of Detroit and the Packard factory'. While he was in Canada, Scotty also met Admiral Sir Percy Addison and Sir James Rae of the British Treasury, who had also travelled on the *Aquitania* as the nucleus of a British purchasing mission.[7]

Scotty arrived in Detroit on Saturday 23rd, having

travelled overnight by train with Margaret Dinkeldein. At 9.00 o'clock, he strode into the Packard conference room, full of energy despite the gruelling timetable of the previous week. He was introduced to the President of Packard, G. M. Gilman, and the Vice-President, Engineering, Colonel J. G. Vincent and their Head of Engineering, George Brodie. Gilman told Scotty that Packard had an order for seven engines from the US Navy, and had developed a suitable unit by modifying the engine that Gar Wood had used when he had raced against Scotty in 1933. The engines were being produced by hand, and Gilman made it quite clear that he would need a large order if they were to be put into production. He then astounded Scotty by announcing that he had received an enquiry from the British Admiralty for the purchase of four of these engines. Scotty was horrified, as competitive bidding for engines by the Admiralty could put in jeopardy the immediate supply of engines for the Elco boats.[8]

With his many years' experience of marinised aero engines, Scotty knew that the Packard unit was ideal as soon as he had inspected it in the workshops. He knew that it would need several important modifications and he suggested to Gilman that a marine unit could be based on the use of the British Power Boat

Company gear box, in the same way as he had done with Rolls-Royce. Scotty was pleased with the morning's work and took a train back to Hamilton, Ontario, to arrange for John to attend the top Canadian school, Ridley College at nearby St Catherine's, and where he again conferred with Harry Greening. He arrived back at New London on the 25th, when he learnt that Sutphen and Chase had been asked to provide a firm quotation for twenty-five boats for the US Navy. Colonel Vincent and Brodie travelled to New London on September 27th, to examine the Merlin installation in *PT 9*, and the next day, Gilman and Henry Sutphen arrived to discuss the installation of the Packard engine with Scotty's gearbox.[9]

Scotty was delighted. It was clear that the US Navy order would require one hundred engines, added to which he could order a hundred on his own account to complete his French contract, and he had received an enquiry from Werf Gusto for a further seventy engines. It was enough to get Packard into production and to negotiate a favourable price. A conference was held in the Mohican Hotel; Gilman and Colonel Vincent were there representing Packard. Sutphen and Chase were there representing Elco, and Scotty was accompanied by George Woods Humphery and Margaret Dinkeldein.

As Scotty looked across the room, he knew that this was his chance to fulfil his mission for Sir Reginald Henderson and the Air Ministry. He knew that Gilman would only go into production if there was a large enough order to warrant the modifications to the M-2500 engine that Scotty had requested. However, he knew that the order from the US Navy had not been confirmed and that the demand for Packard engines for his French and Dutch contracts was only based on an assumption that the Merlins would not be available. He was on his own, but he was used to taking calculated risks and, presenting his bankers' letters, he told Gilman that he would place an order for one hundred and twenty engines. The atmosphere eased and detailed discussions started on the rate of delivery, the supply of gear boxes from Meadows in England and the price of the engine. A week earlier Gilman had quoted $27,000 per engine, but Scotty managed to knock this down to $19,500.

The agreement was made and Scotty immediately set to work with Packard's engineers to design modifications to the M-2500 engine. These included the adoption of Scott-Paine's patented assembly rails, as used with the Merlin installation, the adoption of magneto ignition, changes to the water jacket and crankcase material, and the redesign of the crankshaft and connecting rods. The Packard method of supercharging was replaced with the method Scotty

had developed with the Merlin, and modifications were made to the induction pipes and cylinder blocks. Discussions also took place with Mr Nebstedt of the Joe Reverse Gear Company on the supply of suitable ahead and reverse gears for use in boats built for the US Navy.[10]

Meanwhile, another problem presented itself. The drawings that Scotty had brought over with *PT 9* were far from complete. There was no general arrangement drawing, no electrical drawings, insufficient machinery drawings and no drawings of fittings such as the propeller brackets, water scoops, petrol tanks, cooling gear or petrol and oil tanks. The collection included some drawings from 57 foot and 64 foot boats, and an embarrassed Scott-Paine found that Elco did not have anything like the information it needed to put the boat into production. Scotty wrote at once to Barker asking for drawings to be made and sent out, and for men such as Steve Biggs to be sent out with details of the manufacturing arrangements. 'It is most important', he wrote, 'that he should be familiar with as much of the new scheme of mill manufacturing of timber and bring with him particulars of the frame jogging machine and the arrangement for jigging it. They have asked me particularly how we fashion the chines and the gunwale and I could not remember.'[11]

Scott-Paine's position with Packard was then put in jeopardy with the arrival of news that the Dutch government had been able to bring diplomatic pressure to bear to obtain the release of Rolls-Royce Merlin engines. But Scotty had hardly had the time to digest this when he received a summons to the White House in Washington. The meeting with President Roosevelt took place on October 3rd, and Scotty was delighted with the warm and enthusiastic reception he received. The President had a personal interest in the development of motor torpedo boats and he used the occasion to confirm the order for twenty-five boats from Elco.

The ordeal of the last four weeks had been exhausting and the pace was to continue relentlessly. Scotty, suffering from exhaustion, was having some health problems. Margaret Dinkeldein wrote to Stuart Barker:

> Of course he is working himself to death and I am dreadfully afraid he is going to have some kind of breakdown, if he is not very careful. His eyes and ears are very much worse and he can't even find time to go and have them seen to.[12]

Scotty had achieved what he set out to do, although much work remained to ensure that the production of boats and engines could proceed smoothly. On October 9th, he wrote home:

Therefore, to sum this up again, by March/April of next year I shall have established a power plant and we shall be in production with boats and if the British Admiralty wants one or the other, there is no doubt in my own mind we can supply them with any quantity they require . . . Neither one nor the other is costing the British Admiralty anything, but in passing I do not mind telling you that it is taking a pretty heavy toll of me, which of course in the circumstances does not matter.

Advertisement featuring the 70 foot Scott-Paine MTB in service with the United States Navy.

CHAPTER 16
Elco and Packard

Wartime conditions meant that reports of what was happening at Hythe were taking several weeks to cross the Atlantic. The first news since his arrival in America reached Scotty at the Mohican Hotel on October 15th, as he got back from yet another trip to Canada. There was no shortage of work at Hythe which was employing one thousand five hundred men, more than it had ever done before. The Admiralty had ordered thirty-three 70 foot boats, fitted with Napier Lion engines, to be completed as Motor Anti-Submarine Boats, *MA/SBs 7 to 39*. The order had been placed on September 4th, just before

Scotty's departure, as part of the War Emergency Programme. Work was also progressing on the French motor torpedo boats, referred to as the '10th Flotilla', and the 63 foot boats for the Swedish and Norwegian governments were still under construction.[1]

The Hythe Yard was beginning to look a mess with air raid shelters and dug outs under construction, and with the installation of army huts and guns on the mole. Work had been made difficult when the roof lights of the sheds had been blacked out as an air raid precaution. It was to be some time before

MA/SB 6, the prototype 70 foot Masbie, powered by Napier Lion engines, ordered by the Admiralty in the summer of 1939.

114

moveable shutters were installed and until then day shifts had to work in artificial light. During September, Barker had completed the purchase of Marchwood Park for £2,500, the total cost of the purchase and conversion as a residential training centre being estimated at £8,000. He had appointed Mrs Grace, 'a young woman of thirtyish who has been well known to my wife for some years, a games mistress and good disciplinarian', as the Principal of the centre. The Admiralty refused to provide funds for the establishment of a second factory at Poole, stating that it was unlikely to want more than the thirty-three boats already ordered. The scheme would have cost £125,000, so Barker had decided to abandon the proposal for the time being. Scotty complained that if he had remained in England he would have built the second factory notwithstanding the Admiralty view, and he at once wrote back, criticising his manager for not proceeding with the plan on his own account: 'It is the means whereby I could keep you all employed after a bomb raid.'[2]

Admiral Tower was concerned that the Hythe yard would not be able to cope with the sudden rush of orders. He asked Barker to allow existing contracts for 35 foot and 45 foot boats to be diverted to the boat building firm of Groves and Gutteridge, rather than the British Power Boat Company sub-contracting the work. Barker felt that to agree to this would assist relationships between Hythe and the Admiralty, and told Scotty that he had concurred with the scheme. He also considered options for increasing the manufacturing capacity of the company; he looked at the possibility of purchasing an additional yard such as the Lymington Boat Yard, but in October, he had given instructions for some land reclamation at Hythe so that additional sheds could be put up.

Scotty's request for drawings of the 70 foot boat placed an additional strain on the factory. Barker knew that the drawing office had diagrammatic layouts of the engine room but, as he wrote to Scotty, 'a correct drawing is quite a piece of draughtsmanship and something that we have never previously

The drawing office at Hythe which was rapidly expanded to provide drawings required for the construction of 70 foot MTBs in America.

done at all . . . we never make accurate dimensional drawings of exhaust pipes, at least not in a way in which they can be fabricated from the drawing. This is usually done by templates or jigs.' Barker promised Scotty that the work would be put in hand, and by January 1940, an additional sixty draughtsmen had been employed. However, Barker had greater difficulty in finding volunteers to travel to America to help with the production of the Elco boats. Steve Biggs declined the invitation, as did Norman Jeans and Reg Holley who were not willing to leave their families in danger.[3]

Several of Scotty's launches, including a 'Sea Lord' and a 'Sea Emperor', and a boat called *Soonah* destroyed two weeks later in a Calor gas explosion, were taken over by the Board of Trade upon the outbreak of war. Scotty's yacht *Sylvana* was requisitioned on November 2nd and taken to White's Yard on the River Itchen for conversion to a mine layer. A barrage balloon company was established in the grounds of 'The Cliff' and a request was received for one of Scotty's Rolls-Royce cars to be used as a works ambulance. 'Do not agree Grey Rolls being turned into an ambulance,' Scotty wrote, 'the body and refitting would cost more than buying a complete outfit. If Grey Rolls wanted nationally O. K.'[4]

Barker's news from Hythe cheered Scott-Paine as he continued his marathon tour around the United States and Canada. On October 18th, he was again in Detroit, working on details of the crankshaft for the new Packard engine. From there he travelled with Margaret Dinkeldein to St Catherine's to visit John who was settling happily at Ridley College. They then went by night train to Ottawa to visit Admiral Nelles of the Royal Canadian Navy, 'who is an absolutely No. 1 grand fellow'. At 3.00 o'clock that afternoon, Scotty went on to Montreal where George Woods Humphery had come from New York to spend the whole of the next day with Canadian Vickers.

For some two years, Scotty had been discussing the production of boats for the Royal Canadian Air Force. These boats were now urgently required along with quantities of the 37 foot 6 inch general service launch, and Scotty had held lengthy discussions with Canadian Vickers who had the capacity to produce the boats under licence. During the visit, Scotty and Woods Humphery met the Canadian Vickers Chief Engineer, Mr Wardell, and looked over a disused steel frame building that was ideal for conversion to a boat factory. They discussed the layout and the requirements for sawmills and other facilities, which Scotty, from his years of experience, knew were essential in a modern mass production unit, turning out high performance wooden motor

boats. He told Wardell that skilled men were travelling over from England and would soon arrive to help in the setting up of the new plant.[5]

Before leaving Montreal, Scotty called on Air Marshal Sir Christopher Courtney, still suffering ill health following his injury in an aeroplane crash, who had travelled from Britain to Canada to pursue the RAF's requirement for aircraft. Both he and Woods Humphery were old friends of Courtney, who was interested to hear of their mission to build engines and boats in America, and the progress Scotty had made in respect of boats for the Canadian Air Force. Scotty asked Courtney to use his best efforts to obtain the release of a 64 foot boat and a 40 foot armoured target boat from the RAF, so that these could be used to set up production in Canada.

The following day, Scotty travelled to Boston, arriving there at 8.00 o'clock in the morning and leaving at 6.00 o'clock in the evening to travel overnight to New London where he met up with Packard's engineer, Brodie. *PT 9* continued to impress the American navy officials; Commander Robert Carney, one of the inspecting officers, later reported to Secretary of the Navy, Edison:

> The weather conditions afforded an opportunity to see the boat in almost every condition of sea, and she was handled and manoeuvred without reservation or without attempt to spare either boat or personnel and under all conditions of course, wind, sea, and speed, the boat performed amazingly well . . . as a sea boat *PT 9* has my unqualified approval and I have such confidence in the boat after observing her in rough water that I would not hesitate to take her anywhere under any conditions.
>
> I started out on the trials frankly sceptical about the claims I have heard for this boat during the past year, and I asked for every condition which I thought might bring out the weaknesses in the boat's performance; Mr Scott-Paine was more than glad to go anywhere at any speed or on any course that I requested, and on the run from Watch Hill to Race Light he handled the boat more roughly than was necessary to demonstrate the qualities of the boat.[6]

The rough weather trials took place on November 1st. Scotty took the boat out into the Atlantic from Montauk Point, New York, into seas that were twenty-three feet high, or more. The boat took them in its stride and performed outstandingly. One of the party was a naval architect who had been with President Roosevelt when he had been Secretary to the Navy during the Great War. He told Scott-Paine

116

that he was 'frankly and utterly amazed with the performance of the boat as to say it would be quite impossible for him to draft a report on what he had seen, as nobody would believe it.' He went on to congratulate Scotty, saying that the British designer 'would undoubtedly rank as being the greatest Marine Engineer and Naval Constructor of the era since the steam boat superceded the sailing boat.' The ex-naval architect was L. Y. (Larry) Spear of Elco, who later wrote to Henry Sutphen:

Some information reached me today which I think will be interesting to you and Chase and SP. You will recall that on the last rough water of *PT 9*, a high speed coastguard boat went along. The coastguard boat is now in one of the local yards for repairs. The man inspecting the repair job for the Coast Guard said that he was on the CG boat on the run referred to. He confirms that the fact was the CG boat was smothered in water when *PT 9* was riding high and dry and running away from them quite easily, also that the double planking of the CG boat was split during the run for a distance of 30 ft from the bows.[7]

The news that Werf Gusto had been able to secure a supply of Merlin engines had been a setback in Scotty's negotiations with Packard. Two weeks after the meeting at the Mohican Hotel, he had written to Gilman with the news:[8]

This has totally altered the picture, and I feel it only prudent not to go any further with commitments from myself until there is some clear explanation from home. When I left home my intention was to purchase engines to carry on with my own Dutch contract where boats are being built to my design under licence in Holland, the same thing for France, and as I told you the Rolls engine was not only not available for this purpose but it was made clear that it was not available for any other purpose, other than for aviation at home.

In the meantime, Gilman had approached Rear Admiral Tower, Director of Naval Equipment and Assistant Controller, and Rear Admiral Fraser, who had become Controller of the Navy and Third Sea Lord, following the untimely death of Reginald Henderson. However, Tower, whilst interested in obtaining details of the engine and its price, replied by cable on 14th October to the effect that the Admiralty had no immediate requirements.[9]

There was much hard bargaining between Gilman and Scott-Paine who wanted sole rights over the sale of the engines in Europe, the Colonies and the Dominions. He had been annoyed at Gilman's direct approach to the Admiralty, and complained that Packard agents were contacting foreign governments direct. This, he told Gilman, was contrary to the spirit of discussions that had taken place between them. Gilman wrote back on December 19th, pointing out that there was no formal selling agreement as yet, and arguing that Scott-Paine's modifications of the Packard engine did not include anything that his own engineers could not have worked out, and that, as the modifications were made to enable the engines to fit the 70 foot boat, the advantages were Scott-Paine's who did not therefore have to modify the boat to fit the engines.

On the same day, December 19th, Scott-Paine met Gilman at the Packard Headquarters in Detroit to thrash out a provisional agreement for the production of the 4M-2500 marine engine that was to substitute for the Rolls-Royce Merlin in the Elco boats. With the knowledge that Elco had received an order for the construction of 70 foot boats for the US Navy, Scotty placed a firm order for one hundred engines, and at the same time, concluding an agreement for the British Power Boat Company to become the sole agent for the sale of the engine in the British Empire. The agreement gave the British Power Boat Company a ten per cent commission on the sale price of the engine, and there was provision for the agency to be transferred to Werf Gusto in the event of the war coming to an early conclusion and Scott-Paine's exclusive agreement with Rolls-Royce becoming effective again. The basic price of the engine was to be $21,500, plus the ten per cent commission.[10]

Scotty told Gilman that, in view of the currency situation arising from hostilities, he would ask the British Power Boat Company to withhold from claiming any commission on engines sold direct to government departments in Great Britain or the Empire, for the period of the war. However, he did insist on a two and a half per cent commission from Packard to cover his expenses in the United States and as some recognition of the development work over many years which had contributed to the successful development of the 4M-2500 engine.[11]

On December 1st, Scott-Paine and Woods Humphery signed a license agreement with Elco for the exclusive right to manufacture the Scott-Paine motor torpedo boat. Scotty received a payment of $17,000 in respect of his engineering expertise, while his Marine Design and Engineering Development Corporation were to receive five per cent of Elco's proceeds from the sale of the boats. Elco received its own contract from the Navy Department on December 7th, 1939 for the construction of eleven

Scott-Paine boats of Squadron 1 in New York
Harbour.

motor torpedo boats of Scott-Paine design, to be
designated *PT 10* to *20* and twelve motor submarine
chasers of identical design, to be known as *PTC 1* to
12.[12]

Scotty's success in selling his boats to the United
States Navy through Elco was not universally welcomed in America. 'The vested trade interests', he
wrote to Blake, 'has howled like a pack of wolves . . .
there is also some difficulty between Elco and the US
Navy as their opposite number to Holt seems badly
slighted as his own designs for experimental jobs has
not been taken on.'[13] In January 1940, representatives of the American Motor Boat Association met
in New York to consider sending a protest against the
way in which the Navy had awarded the contract to
Elco without competitive bidding. George W.
Rappleyea of Higgins Boat Industries of New
Orleans, was particularly incensed and personally
attacked Charles Edison for the way in which he had
placed a contract for the construction of Scott-Paine
type boats. He told the *New York Times* over the
telephone: 'The Navy has spent more than $100,000
a year ago in awarding prizes for four different types
of small American-designed torpedo boats and has
now turned about and ordered boats built on a secret
British design. I want a congressional investigation
into it.'[14]

Charles Edison responded, pointing out that
expenditure out of the $15,000,000 for experimental
craft was at the discretion of the President and he was
not required to go to competitive tenders. The decision to go ahead with building the Scott-Paine boats
before all the American designs had been built and
evaluated was based on a need to have boats for training purposes, until it could be ascertained whether
the American boats would be better.

With the benefit of Scott-Paine's extensive experience of the mass production of hard chine boats, the
construction of the new Elco plant at Bayonne, New
Jersey, was well under way by January 1940. The
latest machine tools were adopted and within a
short period of time a work force of two thousand
employees was working a three-shift system with
production through twenty-four hours a day on four
assembly lines. The parent Elco company at Groton,
with its experience in the construction of submarines, undertook the construction of components
such as torpedo tubes.

Production started at the end of January with a
view to delivering the first complete boats in May or
June. Prior to receiving the Elco order, Scotty had
arranged during the previous November for the
dispatch of all the necessary templates, jigs and scribe
boards to assist in the building of the American

118

boats. At the beginning of January, Scotty was joined by several technical assistants from Hythe, including Leonard Munn, Weeks and George Pengelley. However, problems arose when the jigs and other material disappeared, only to turn up at Halifax, and when Elco complained that the drawings, which had been shipped over on the ss *Statira* were found to be either inaccurate or insufficient in detail. The drawings referred to at least three different boats, none of them exactly matching *PT 9*. In order to facilitate the construction of the new boats, the Navy Department then granted Elco a delay in delivering *PT 9* so that it could be used as a working model, from which a new set of drawings could be made. To strengthen his case to retain *PT 9*, Sutphen argued that Elco would not hand over *PT 9* to run in competition with other experimental PT boats in the hands of an inexperienced 'green' crew. He insisted that he would cancel the contract for further boats, and dispatch *PT 9* as a demonstration boat, possibly in South America, rather than damage his commercial interests by placing *PT 9* in the hands of an untrained personnel. In the event, *PT 9* was not delivered to the Navy until June 17th, 1940.[15]

On January 15th, 1940, Scotty wrote to his old friend Bill Sheaff from New York, about his success since leaving Hythe for the United States:

I was so pleased and so very glad to get your letter from home. How I envied reading of your Christmas, how I very much liked hearing all the kind messages you sent to me from all sides. It's grand to hear that all the boys kind of remember. You all seem a long way away—and me away from it all. Twenty thousand times a day I wonder what's to do—what's going on—whether the show is being held together—or if its running wild and going to the devil. Write and tell me how the factory is. I don't want any backchat—whether the show is being run well. How many times I wished I made you come out here. Old Man Yank blows and storms, and talk about carrying sail and apart from causing so much waste of time, at times I have to sit down and really have a laugh. Why William, I can lick 'em at any angle. You would have got the best laugh out of that. Just think of it, three months from the time I landed here, I landed an order for 5 million dollars and got the Yanks to build a yard costing 700,000 dollars and so will get into production over here without costing the British a dime. Of course you don't want to talk about it, but it's a grand job, perhaps the best I've ever done—and certainly William, I've worked harder and longer hours that I can remember. I've moved around a lot—8,000 miles in the first nine weeks . . .[16]

CHAPTER 17
1940—The Storm Breaks

Both Scotty and Margaret Dinkeldein were delighted to receive a Christmas telegram with greetings from the employees at Hythe. 'We are definitely homesick,' Margaret Dinkeldein wrote to Stuart Barker, 'I don't think I should mind blackouts, rationing (this of course wouldn't worry me because I am always dieting), just to be home and see you all in the Works again.'

For tax reasons, Scotty had decided to settle in Connecticut and had set up his new home, Smythe House, in Shore Road, Greenwich. The bitter cold of the American winter brought with it news from home that made him sad and angry. His old enemies in the Admiralty had again told Sir Geoffrey Blake that they had no requirement for 70 foot boats of Scott-Paine design from America. On February 21st, 1940, a secret cable was sent to Scott-Paine:

My Lords appreciate the work that has been carried out by your company and are glad to observe that as a result there is now a possible alternative source of supply of these craft. At the present time, however, my Lords do not require to order motor torpedo boats in the USA, although this matter will be reconsidered should the necessity arise.[1]

'Actually I can't believe it', Scotty wrote to Admiral Blake:

'There must be a reason but it has shaken me very badly because it disturbs my own belief. Talk about being heart-sick, foot sore and weary, that is to put it mildly! But I still believe that the 70 ft boat with A/S gear and depth charges makes the finest submarine destroying units there are in existence . . . I believe ultimately it will be wanted.'

He went on to say that 'the only thing I can do is to sit back and laugh at the whole situation, because no prophet ever prophesied more accurately than I have done during these last five years. If you take it step by step it unfolds itself as a perfectly accurate picture . . . and everyone sat snugly in their chairs and left for their offices every day thinking that [what] they had was all sufficient, no matter how I argued and talked . . . the prize fool of the lot, and I hope by God, he reads this, Sir George Preece, Engineering Chief of the Navy, turned it down with sarcasm.'[2]

Scotty was also having considerable problems at Bayonne over the construction of the first 70 foot PT boats and had been told by Sutphen that Elco might want a revision of their contract because of the insufficiency and inaccuracy of the available drawings. Scotty became angry with the 'procrastinations and delays', and the 'intrigues' between Elco and the Bureau of Ships which were worse than anything he had experienced with the Admiralty at home. 'There is no doubt in my own mind that the opposite number to Holt, who has been responsible for designing their own job, feels that he has been badly slighted . . . I wish I had never come near this country nor the people in it.'[3]

Back in England, Vice-Admiral Blake again wrote to the Admiralty, informing their Lordships that Scott-Paine had carried out Admiral Henderson's wishes and was in a position to proceed with orders for both engines and boats. Again the Admiralty refused, stating that in view of the foreign currency situation, it intended to continue with the Isotta Fraschini engine, and had no requirement for additional boats. A dispirited Scotty replied, 'I am not feeling inclined to take a personal risk at all . . . I suppose that it is because I am not feeling kindly disposed towards anyone that I can say that.' He went on to complain that he was out of touch and that he 'felt a little hurt as I love my Factory more than a

PT 10, the first Elco built 70 foot MTB.

mother loves her children', and that only the need for him to see the first Elco boat working 'to avoid his prestige being badly interfered with', was stopping him from coming home.[4]

Matters in Canada were no better, with continual delays over the placing of a contract for the boats that were to be constructed by Canadian Vickers. Both Scotty and Woods Humphery travelled to Canada during February to be met with stone-walling and a 'great deal of goings-on which I do not pretend to have fathomed'. One visit to D.B. Carswell, Director of Shipbuilding at the Munitions and Supply Board, then brought a ray of hope. It was becoming clear that the 40 foot armoured target boats would be required, and that the Royal Canadian Air Force and the Royal Canadian Navy might be interested in the 70 foot boat, powered by two Packards, instead of the 64 foot boats that had been the subject of so much discussion. Scotty immediately wrote to Barker with instructions to ship *PV 70* to Canada as a matter of urgency so that it could be used as a model for production by Canadian Vickers. He suggested that the Rolls-Royce engines could be returned to Derby where they could be reconditioned for use by the Admiralty, and he gave

instructions for the latest modified wheelhouse, anti-submarine gear and other features to be fitted to *PV 70* before shipment. Barker was horrified as the boat's electrics had been stripped out to provide parts for the French contract, and he replied that it would take at least three months to get the boat ready for shipment, even assuming that a ship could be found to carry the cargo.

Hopeful that he would at last obtain an order for boats from the Canadian government, and that his arrangement with Canadian Vickers would at last bear fruit, Scotty went with John and Margaret to Bermuda for a short break at the end of March. He returned to New York to a bombshell in the form of a telegram from Stuart Barker, then on holiday at Fowey in Cornwall. Barker wrote: 'Ladycross reverting original contemplated position.' The message, referring to Sir Geoffrey Blake's address at Ladycross Cottage in the New Forest, told him that his trusted colleague had taken up an appointment at the Admiralty.[5]

Vice-Admiral Sir Geoffrey Blake had been asked by the First Sea Lord and by Winston Churchill, to take up an appointment as a Lord Commissioner of the Admiralty and Assistant Chief of Naval Staff, and had resigned his position on the board of the British Power Boat Company. Scotty had come to value Blake's influence in the Admiralty. For instance, Blake had written in January 1940: 'We are now regarded as quite good boys by the Admiralty, during such times as these there must be 100% cooperation. The old Napier has come into its own again and another 150 are to be ordered, together with a separate order for the 70's.' Scotty wrote back: 'Now what I want you to do is to consolidate our position with your old service. I repeat that if it is me and my personality which are at fault, I am willing to resign or do anything else that might be in the company's interest.'[6]

The management of the Hythe yard in his absence was causing Scotty considerable concern as he wrote to Stuart Barker with an overview of the situation at the beginning of April. 'With the movement of G.B. I feel that I have left you inadequately supported with the worries and troubles that must always be associated with our business . . . Actually his leaving at short notice and without any warning to me was simply dreadful. Actually it worked almost as quickly as death, and, in my own mind, in almost the same

way.' He went on to suggest George Wilkinson as Joint Managing Director and Chief Engineer, or Sir Eric Fullerton, who was Commander-in-Chief, Plymouth when the first Admirals' barge had been ordered in 1936. In the event it was his old friend Wilson Hamill who became Deputy Chairman and who was to provide Stuart Barker with considerable personal support in the troubled times that lay ahead.

By the middle of April, the Elco plant had been completed at a cost of $800,000, the first hull was planked and four others were in frame. The Packard engine was promising to be highly successful, and both the Canadian Royal Navy and the Canadian Royal Air Force had indicated that they would order 70 foot boats. Canadian Vickers then told Scott-Paine that it would no longer be in a position to build these boats for Scott-Paine in view of the huge orders that it had in hand for ships and aeroplanes. By now Scotty had recovered from his winter ill health and he announced that he would establish a new company, Scott-Paine Canada Limited, and build a factory to fulfil the orders. He wrote enthusiastically to Stuart Barker, outlining his plans and discussing ways in which Hythe and the Canadian factory could colla-

60 foot boats at Felixstowe in 1940, including *MTB 18* in the foreground.

borate, concluding: 'Get over here as soon as you can.' Scotty asked Barker to restrict circulation of information about the Canadian enterprise and the plan to ship *PV 70*, as 'V's [Vosper's] agents are doing their old, old business; i.e. while I go plowing the furrow, they simply wait until it is plowed and then seek to take the benefit of my labour, and if it is possible to keep this water-tight as long as possible, it might delay some of their chicanery . . . the position is really appalling for any decently minded person to have to contend with.'[7]

Stuart Barker flew out to America via The Azores during April, bearing news of all that had happened at Hythe over the six months since Scotty had left. Scotty was particularly interested to hear news of the boats of his 1st Flotilla which had returned from Malta earlier in the year. Barker went down to see them at Felixstowe, where he had noted that they were in a 'dickens of a state', and were having to contend with old Victorian steam cranes for the delicate job of loading torpedoes. The 1st Flotilla and the 3rd Flotilla, destined for Singapore, had been at Malta when war broke out in September 1939, and in November, both flotillas had been ordered back to Portsmouth. Nine boats had proceeded to Marseilles under their own power, while three were freighted to the French port. Most of the older boats, *MTBs 01 to 06* were suffering from hull damage and the passage from Bizerte to Ajaccio in the teeth of the Mistral proved too much for *MTB 06*, under the command of Commander (Harpy) Lloyd. The hull leaked so badly that the level of water in the engine room rose until the engines were covered. The boat sank lower and lower until it was abandoned and taken in tow by destroyer HMS *Dainty*. The situation was hopeless and *06* was then deliberately sunk by ramming. The rest of the 60 foot boats finally made it back to England after a 'splendid and hair-raising trip through the

MA/SB 15 and *16* under construction at Hythe. *MA/SB 15* is being completed as a motor gun boat with a Rolls-Royce gun on the after deck.

French canals, with bent props and all sorts of other damage to boats and persons.'[8]

Barker was able to tell Scotty that the first French boat had been completed and had been over to Cherbourg for torpedo trials. The boat had reached 44 knots, fully loaded. The next two French boats were in the process of undertaking yard trials. Both the Norwegian and the Swedish boats were nearly completed, although it was not clear whether the Admiralty would be taking them over or not. The 63 foot boat had proved exceptionally successful and a version powered by Napier Lion engines had been under development since the early part of the year. During January, Beauforte-Greenwood had persuaded the Air Ministry to accept the 63 foot boat in place of the four-year old 64 foot type, and had ordered the change about half-way through the completion of his last order for 64 foot boats, *HSL 116 to 121*. Known as the 'Whaleback', these were to prove to be the most popular Air Sea Rescue craft of World War Two. He had at first intended to experiment with Merlin engines in the 64 foot *HSL 116* to increase its performance, for a similar, Merlin-engined 64 foot boat was under construction for the South African Government during January. The trials of the South African boat were undertaken on January 23rd, 1940, but the view was that the Merlin engine was not suitable for the boat to carry out the intended dual role of towing and rescue work in South Africa. The outcome was that Barker had received a firm contract from the South African government for nine 63 foot Air Liaison Craft, powered by the Napier Lion engine.[9]

The Napier Lion 70 foot boats, ordered as motor anti-submarine boats at the outbreak of war, were proving to be a problem. They were achieving a speed of 34 knots, or 26.6 knots when fully laden with twelve depth charges, but trials at HMS *Osprey* were suggesting that they would be less successful than the 60 foot *MA/SBs 1 to 5* that were then operating within the fixed anti-submarine loops at Portland and Dover. The problem appeared to be associated with propeller noises interfering with the Asdic reception, but in view of the long running dispute with Scott-Paine over patent rights in respect of the Asdic gear, HMS *Osprey* refused to collaborate with George Selman on overcoming the problem. It was not until Admiral Blake had intervened personally that any co-operation was forthcoming.[10]

Despite the enormous pressure of work at the Factory, George Selman had been able to carry on with some experimental work. He had designed a 41 foot 6 inch boat with similar lines to the 63 foot boat and the Admiralty was expressing some interest in it. He had also developed the novel *Queen Gull* in

response to a War Office requirement for a fast, manoeuvrable target boat to be used by the Coast Branch of the Royal Artillery in training crews of 6 pounder and 12 pounder coastal guns. The *Queen Gull* was a 12 foot 6 inch hard-chine boat, of ply and double diagonal plank construction, powered by a Ford 10 'C' engine with direct drive to a two-bladed propeller. The boat was designed to be radio-controlled, running at speeds of up to 22 knots at a mean range of 2,500 yards. In the event of the target being hit, it was unlikely to sink as it was designed with twelve watertight compartments, and was filled with bouyancy chambers filled with 'Onazote'. The radio equipment was being developed by Victor Bull in association with Rediffusion. Three prototypes had been built and tested, as a result of which an agreement was signed with the War Office for the provision of one hundred 'Jinking Target Boats', on May 20th, 1940.[11]

Scotty was also pleased to hear that the Marchwood Training Centre was working out successfully and had awarded diplomas to its first trainees during a 'school speech-day' event in December 1939. The workshops at Marchwood were producing components for the 16 foot Admiralty dingy and it was proposed that the entire construction would eventually be carried out by the trainees. Despite the training of women workers there was still a shortfall of skilled workers and Barker told Scotty that he should be employing three hundred men more than he was able to recruit.

While Stuart Barker was with Scotty, planning the construction of a factory in Canada, the war situation in Europe changed dramatically as the Germans invaded Belgium and Holland during the early hours of May 10th, 1940. Faced with the possibility of German forces on the Channel coast, Admiral Tower telephoned Frank Bishop at Hythe enquiring about the possibility of ordering boats from Elco. At the same time, Tower asked for a confidential enquiry to be made in America about the possibility of the boats then under construction for the US Navy being made available to the Admiralty. Scotty knew that the supply of boats would be controlled by the ability of Packard to produce engines and immediately cabled Blake at the Admiralty:

Reluctant communicate you direct but factory cabled new requirement for 70 under urgent consideration therefore my duty acquaint you and your colleagues of engine supply stop there is only one engine here suitable and available stop if any boats contemplated now or in future it is essential to secure engine production by immediate order as this is controlling factor stop engine manufacturers tiring of many abortive enquiries and declared to Barker and me in Detroit yesterday will accept first order for any equipment that will occupy their plant whether this or other type engines or any other class of equipment stop fear their government will absorb their capacity stop they will only negotiate seriously on basis of firm order stop this matter most serious and urgent stop because of services rendered their government believe am in advantageous position to serve admiralty in this matter stop recommend ordering 500 units regards Scott-Paine.[12]

The next day Scotty wrote a long letter to Frank Bishop at Hythe, urging him to take up the matter of engine supplies with Craven Ellis, Member of Parliament for Southampton. The letter concluded:

To sum up all this word picture, unless the British Admiralty secure a source of supply of engines from Packards, it will automatically lose the only source of supply there is. I found this one and created it, I cannot do another. There is no other source of supply open to us in the whole length and breadth of the World. If this is wanted now or in the near future or even the far future some action must be taken *at once*. Someone must be strong enough and fearless enough to over ride the cumbersome and obsolete machinery within the Admiralty itself that prevents this sensible action being taken and in my opinion apart from the sense of it, it is of such national importance as to demand that any lengths should be run to obtain this essential action now. This is my definite opinion. I will stand behind it and back it. It is no use asking for favours, it is no use holding out possibilities, it has got to be a firm order with money deposited or else they will 'miss the bus.'

As far as I am concerned I can do nothing more. I am here to do everything I can do to help. No two people could be on more friendly terms that Packard and I. They have redesigned their engine to meet my requirements. It is the best of its kind in the world. I am sure they would give the Allies the best price deal they could. They can give immediate deliveries. I have advised them and everyone at home that there is no question of commission or profit for the factory at Hythe. What more can a man do? Except give up in despair.[13]

Frank Bishop and Maurice Wright went to see

Admiral Tower to press the need for an immediate order for Packards to ensure the continued production of the engine. They were told that the Admiralty intended to rely upon the 500 hp Hall-Scott engine in the event of the Isotta Fraschini engines becoming unavailable. Scotty was distraught at this news that was cabled to him on May 21st. The following day he dispatched a further appeal to Admiral Blake, urging the immediate order of five hundred or one thousand 70 foot boats to patrol the North Sea, and again pointing out that Packard was threatening to cease production of the 4M-2500 engine unless substantial orders were forthcoming. It was a hard hitting letter, ending with the plea: 'We have no time to waste. I am doing all I can to get the 24 boats building for the United States Navy diverted to you at home. It is no use saying God help us, if we don't help ourselves. Can't I be given some instructions to get to work?' Scotty took the desperate step of sending a copy of his letter to the Prime Minister, Winston Churchill, to whom he wrote:

I am enclosing a letter herewith, the original of which I have sent to Vice Admiral Sir Geoffrey Blake, who until recently was my colleague on the board of my Company, the British Power Boat Co. of Hythe, Southampton.

You may remember that at the commencement of the last World War, you and Murray Sueter gave me a great deal of encouragement for building flying boats for the RNAS, when I owned the Supermarine Aviation Works.

For many years I have been trying to get the Admiralty to act with these new inventions of mine, the only man who showed any kind of foresight and indeed who was responsible for the Royal Navy having any of these boats at all, was the late Third Sea Lord, Sir Reginald Henderson.

In my opinion we have no time to lose. As every other pioneer, I have been cordially disliked and my efforts frustrated by every Department in the Admiralty and yet other foreign Admiralties, even the American Navy Department have not hesitated to adopt my products and accept this new Arm.

As the result of our efforts there is a new and the most up to date shadow factory available for your use. It is in full production, can take on any quantity of Motor Torpedo or Anti-Submarine Boats and start deliveries in four months. This has been done at no expense to the British Admiralty.[14]

CHAPTER 18
The Canadian Power Boat Company

Scott-Paine's appeal to the Prime Minister, Winston Churchill, did little to improve relationships between the Admiralty and the British Power Boat Company. Admiral Blake telephoned Frank Bishop as soon as he had received the letter, expressing his annoyance and requesting that an urgent cable be sent to Scotty telling him to take no further action until requested to do so by the Admiralty. 'Such letters', Blake complained, 'do very little good at the present time and if a little more control could be exercised over your correspondence, it would be appreciated.' He pointed out that the letter had been circulated to most of the departments in the Admiralty and that it was 'prejudicial to the negotiations which were still underway'. Maurice Wright wrote to Scotty on June 7th with the news that the letter had caused a 'first class row', and that . . .

> G.B. would not tell me what view the P.M. had taken of the matter, so one can only assume that it probably was not favourable to the Authorities at 'A'. However, it has had the effect of putting up their back against us and so I thought it advisable to send Brown to see T. personally and to endeavour to clarify the position, along with all the telegrams that had passed between us. His reception by T. was a particularly stormy one and merely resulted in his reiterating that they had taken all the action they considered necessary and that, in their own time, they would order such boats as were required.[1]

But the appeal did not go unheard. On May 31st, Tower telephoned Frank Bishop at Hythe to tell him unofficially that he had again approached the Treasury and thought that he would get authority to purchase fifty or one hundred engines. This was followed by a letter from Blake who replied to Scotty on June 6th that the letter to Churchill had been sent to the Deputy Controller with a request for details of action to be taken. Blake complained that he found this embarrassing in view of his present situation, but he assured Scotty that the position was in hand and that the history of his endeavours was well appreciated. Tower got clearance to order one hundred engines, but the only confirmation Scotty had that some action had been taken was a report in the American newspapers on June 7th that a contract worth four million dollars for high speed marine engines had been awarded to the Packard Motor Company by the British Purchasing Commission in New York.

The deteriorating situation at home pursuaded Scotty that the construction of a factory in Canada was a matter of utmost urgency. He told Stuart Barker that he was going to stay in Canada, orders or no orders. 'This is how I see the position', he said, as they drove up to Montreal in the Rolls. 'Hythe must run itself, and my job as I see it is to stop here, keep the whole of this side working, raising the efficiency as high as I know how, and when the time does arise, I shall be in a position to make deliveries that will not be available in any other part of the world. If the demand never arises, I shall lose whatever money I invest in the Canadian factory—that I know; but I shall look upon it as being the best part that I can play in this fight that we are having with the German people.'[2]

The scheme that Scotty had in mind was greater than anything he had started before either with Supermarine or the British Power Boat Company. The factory was going to be the most modern and efficient boat building plant in the world, completing 70 foot boats for the Canadians and capable of mass producing hulls fitted with Packard engines, for shipment to England where they could be fitted with torpedo tubes, electrics, propellers and other fittings. He was going to share the work with Hythe and he insisted that Barker should be a director of the new company. Despite the fact that it suffered the disadvantage of becoming iced-up in winter, Scotty had selected Montreal as the site for the new factory as it was well placed for the supply of labour and raw materials.

The new company was registered on May 11th, 1940 as the Canadian Power Boat Company, and a small design office was established in the Dominion Square Building, Montreal. Hubert Scott-Paine was the President of the Canadian Power Boat Company and George Woods Humphery was the Vice-President; the Secretary-Treasurer was a Canadian national, J.R. Ralphs and the directors were Margaret Dinkeldein and J. Edouard Labelle KC, Chairman of Canadian Vickers, and Stuart Barker.[3]

The availability of engines was the key to the Canadian Power Boat Company being able to undertake the production of boats for Canada, and although tenders were not to be submitted until June, supplies from Packard were secured on May 18th, when Scotty persuaded D.B. Carswell, Director of Shipbuilding at the Canadian Munitions and Supply Board to order seventy-two engines in anticipation of the proposed 70 foot boat construction programme.[4]

On May 23rd, Maurice Wright confirmed from Hythe that he had made arrangements for the transfer of £40,000 from Scott-Paine's No 4 account for the construction of the Canadian factory, and that a further transfer of £20,000 would be made in September 1940. Sir Geoffrey Blake had promised to use his influence with the Bank of England and the High Commissioner for Canada to secure the necessary authority in view of the government restrictions on the transfer of American and Canadian dollars. Scotty also requested the loan of skilled personnel and the immediate shipment of a 40 foot armoured target boat and *PV 70* for use as models in setting up production in Canada. Wright reported that arrangements had been made for the shipment of jigs and templates for the 70 foot boat, and that passport applications, exit permits, military releases and Admiralty permissions were in hand for the staff who were going to help set up the new factory.[5] Amongst the volunteers who sailed in July were R.E. Freemantle, a test engineer; Peter Ayling, a Scheduling and Progress Clerk; George Hall, a draughtsman in George Selman's team; Parker, from the Machine shop; W. Langford, a sheet metal worker; and two of the best hull builders, J.E. Weeks and George Pengelly. The Works Manager at Montreal was A.L. Hall.

Scott-Paine's instructions for *PV 70* and a 40 foot armoured target boat to be shipped to Canada for experimental and development purposes were passed to Admiral Tower for his approval. This was forthcoming and, although Hadfield of Sheffield were unable to supply the armoured deck for the target boat, the craft was shipped on the ss *Beaverdale* in the first week of June with a plywood mock-up of the armour. There was some difficulty in arranging the shipment of *PV 70* as shipping companies had been instructed to turn around in port in the shortest possible time; this made it difficult to arrange for the modifications to derricks, winches and other equipment that would be necessary to stow *PV 70* as deck cargo on most ships. Eventually the boat left Southampton on June 12th as deck cargo on the ss *Ville D'Arlon*, a Belgian ship which had been in Southampton for repairs to bomb damage sustained at Le Havre. Three days later, Wright wrote to Scotty:

> . . . our arrangements went ahead rapidly with Harland and Wolff to build the platform on the ship, ourselves having to supply the timber (which of course had to be requisitioned from the Control Board), and to make all the arrangements with the Export Board, Customs Authorities, shippers, etc., etc. The dispatch of the Elco boat last year was child's play compared with this, but eventually we managed to get all the formalities concluded and the boat was towed over by us to the floating crane, lifted on board, packed, etc., and is now on its way to New York.[6]

PV 70 was consigned 'in bond for Canada' to Elco, where Scotty hoped to install Packard engines. In the event of that not being possible, plans were put in hand for the boat to be towed via the system of rivers and canals that linked New York and Montreal. The boat arrived in New York on 24th June and was taken by Elco to Bayonne. Scotty wrote to Barker:

> I must say how surprised and pleased we all are at the grand and splendid job the factory have made of her. I don't think that anything has happened in the factory since we first started it that has given me so much acute satisfaction nor has anything been brought home so clearly, what a capable lot of men we have gradually turned all those fellows into whom we have been able to give promotion to and bring in their various spheres of life . . . I do want you to see that everyone is posted with our gratitude and to say how much we appreciate what was done.[7]

PV 70 was towed to Montreal by the Davie Transportation Company of Beaverhall, Montreal. The necessary permissions were secured, and *PV 70* was made ready with a crew of four of Scott-Paine's men who were to accompany it during the journey. A storm beset the convoy while it was crossing the one hundred and eighteen miles of Lake Champlain, the wind tearing away the protective wooden crating around the wheelhouse. The journey through the Richelieu lock system was a delicate operation as there was less than twelve inches clearance on each side as it passed the lock gates. However, *PV 70* arrived in Montreal on July 16th where it was placed in store in the Montreal Harbour Commissioner's drydock. The 40 foot armoured target boat had arrived almost three weeks earlier on June 24th.[8]

During June, Scotty submitted tenders to the Department of Munitions and Supply for six 70 foot high-speed launches and six armoured target boats for the Royal Canadian Air Force, and twelve 70 foot motor torpedo boats for the Royal Canadian Navy. The tenders were accepted on July 18th, two days after the arrival of *PV 70* in Montreal. On June 15th, Maurice Wright wrote to Scott-Paine with the information that the Dutch government, which had lost the torpedo boats under construction by Werf Gusto to the German invaders, had enquired about the construction of eight motor torpedo boats in Canada for direct shipment to the Dutch East Indies. Scott-Paine replied, quoting a price of (Canadian) $130,000 plus (American) $62,400 for twin-engined boats, including torpedo tubes, gun emplacements and depth charge gear. The price of a three-engined boat was (Canadian) $133,000 plus (American) $86,000. On July 22nd, an order for eight three-engined boats for the Royal Netherlands Navy was received, a further eight being ordered on December 28th, 1940.[9]

Having secured the Canadian and Dutch orders for boats, Scotty rapidly drew up plans for what was to be the most modern and efficient plant for the mass production of wooden boats. A site for the factory had been selected and purchased at 4000 St Patrick Street, on the south side of the Lachine Canal. The site had a small basin, although it was derelict and silted up. Work started immediately on reclaiming the site and on erecting a temporary timber shed that was to be used as a training shop for local labour. The main factory building was to be steel framed but on July 29th, information was received that there would be a twenty-two week delivery period for the structural steel. The timetable for the building of the boats could not accommodate such a delay so Scotty immediately set about re-designing the factory with the consultant engineers, Messrs T. Pringle & Co. of Montreal, so that it could be constructed in reinforced concrete. At this point speed was critical so

that the structure could be erected before the onset of winter precluded the pouring of concrete.

Nine months of war had not only caused a shortage of materials, but the rapid expansion of the aircraft industry meant that there was a crippling shortage of skilled labour. Scotty's answer to this was to recruit Captain Beauforte-Greenwood, who had resigned from the Air Ministry to join the British Power Boat Company earlier that summer. Scotty asked him to join the Canadian Power Boat Company as Factory Superintendent, and he arrived in Montreal during August. Scotty wrote to Barker:

> I found B. G. a very improved man. I really think that you should have kept him. I can imagine that he would have been of the greatest help to you; anyway the trip will do him good. I have put him to work and give him plenty of responsibility. The experience will be of the very greatest use to him and at a later date should you want him back, I am sure he would be willing to join you again. In the meantime I know exactly what it feels like to be in your position without help or assistance from an older man. I can remember my own experiences very well.[10]

The recruitment of labour was Beauforte-Greenwood's first priority; advertisements were placed in newspapers and visits were made to boatbuilders which had been listed as unsuitable for naval work. There was no ready supply of men skilled in modern woodworking techniques so he travelled to the East Coast where, from Cape Breton to the Bay of Fundy, through Moncton and Nova Scotia, he interviewed fishermen who built and repaired their own fishing boats in the winter, and fished in the summer. Men who were willing to come to Montreal were guaranteed a year's work if found to be satisfactory. The training shop soon had willing, though raw recruits, as Scotty later wrote to his brother Victor,

> Capt. B-G did a job bringing in some 50 men who knew wooden ships and fishing vessels and dory building, smelt of the sea and chewed 'bacca—couldn't have asked for much more, but boy, heavy handed. Well, how anything ever survived being sawn in half, how any screw wasn't twisted double, how anything anywhere survived their first shock assault can never be explained—it took me the first week clearing up and only a detailed elevation of my soul kept me from buying a revolver and calmly and deliberately shooting the whole 50. It ironed itself out, I took all their tools away, the same gear as old Brackley had or any of Stow's shipbuilders of our youth—same

men—same gear, looked and smelt the same—same thumbs, square, wide and very strong, steel rules marked in ⅛" finest reading, with brass joints, and the ends all worn away where they had been used to scratch into suspected places to uncover hidden sorrows. With a few new tools, no saws, no hammers, we've started them into a new and troublesome existence. 'I call this stroking a piece of lumber' says one, 'making models easier' says another, and so we are gradually making headway, but so many times and so many relapses that I often wonder why we ever started so much worry.[11]

A wooden temporary shop was opened in August 31st and work started on training the new recruits, making frames and planks and bulkheads. The problems of training adze-swinging boat builders

continued and on April 3rd, 1941, Scotty had to send a memorandum to the works office pointing out that at the mill a man was seen drilling holes in biscuits, forcing the tool through and splintering the rest of the cut. He pointed out that rough, wide pitch saws and hammer and chisels are quite unsuitable and pleaded for the men to be made more 'three ply conscious'.[12]

On August 30th, the Company received a request from the Canadian government for the urgent delivery of *PV 70* as Canadian Motor Torpedo Boat *No 1*. The launching basin was successfully restored to working condition by early September, whereupon *PV 70* was brought round from her storage place and trainees started converting the engine room to accommodate two Packard engines. While this work was proceeding, Beauforte-Greenwood travelled around Canada and the United States to secure the purchase of machine tools which were in

The Canadian Power Boat company's temporary building shed known as 'The Ark', October 2nd, 1940.

short supply. He visited Ontario, the New England States, Ohio, Wisconsin, New York, Illinois and Indiana, meeting with the Presidents of supplying companies who promised to deliver before the planned opening date of the factory in December. Scotty wrote to Victor Scott-Paine:

How we obtained machine tools is a story itself—unobtainable, delivery one year, etc. and the cost, well just double what the tool would cost in England. We bought the best we could, never more than one tool from one shop and then pleaded the urgency of it to complete the operation of one special job, sent men down to pal with the man in the shop and another to urge with the President—there was only one required out of their vast output and the urgency meant so much to us, telephone calls, cables, and when the machine shop was finished there was the machinery, another miracle so it was said.[13]

The main contract for the construction of the factory was awarded to the Atlas Construction Company of Montreal. The main features of the plant were a boiler house, and a wood store with controlled heating which led direct to the saw mill equipped with the most modern high speed cutting tools. Finished parts from the mill could thus flow in two directions, planks to the lofty hull shops, while smaller pieces could go via a lift to the wood assembly shop floor, located above the saw mill. Beyond the sawmill were the quarantine and inward and outward stores from which material could flow through a wide corridor to assembly stores which ran the whole length of the factory, feeding to the engine shop, the electric shop, the throttle and fitting shop, the armament and torpedo shop, the machine shop, the sheet metal and the coppersmiths shops. Material could also be taken direct to the main assembly shops which ran parallel to the smaller shops. It was planned that a hull constructed in the hull shop would be picked up by a monorail system and placed in the assembly shop in its own cradle, where it would be served by the assembly stores until it was finished, and ready for launching into the basin via large sliding doors. On the second floor of the factory were offices and the drawing office, and a large modern cafeteria was provided for the employees.[14]

Despite the onset of the bitter Canadian winter, construction on the plant continued and by December 5th, it was possible to occupy the timber shop, saw mill and stores. Temporary heating had been arranged by linking into the contractor's boilers during November, but on December 11th, the main heating plant, designed to run off waste wood from

the factory, was completed and the Dominion Square office was closed. The first keel was 'laid down' for a 70 foot boat on December 16th and keels of three other boats followed within fifteen days. By the time that the factory was occupied, the training shop, known as 'The Ark' to the employees, had produced three sets of frames and had trained thirty hull builders. About two hundred and ten employees were on the payroll, including a number of women. Scott-Paine had experience in employing women workers at Supermarine during the Great War, and Margaret Dinkeldein undertook the task of recruiting and training women employees, as Scott-Paine recorded:

We are pioneering women workers in factory life . . . the women side of the question is highly interesting. There is no background to work on and our main trouble is getting the young women to realize they are not in here for a lark, nor to attract the attention of the males with whom they are working. Psychologically, from observation, the men are not interested and these women are gradually getting the hang of things. Naturally when the first fifty are at work most of our difficulties will be over. M.D. has shouldered pretty nearly all of this burden, and on top of this has coaxed an office staff out of very comfortable well located city offices and business, to our factory which is in the city but on the outskirts, and rather difficult to get to and from. She is continually losing girls, but generally speaking the office staff is as high quality of girls as I have had anywhere. The stenographers and women clerks, who were at a premium long before we started (and indeed we couldn't pay a cent more than is customary) we

Women workers at the Montreal factory.

130

had to take our chances on their being enthusiastic enough to be interested in a new business and see a future in it. This, in many ways, will gradually eliminate the scatterbrain, which is all to the good.[15]

Margaret Dinkeldein also ran the canteen which was operated by the St Dunstan Institute for the Blind which ran canteens in various factories. The Institute did not aim to make a commercial profit, but aimed merely to cover their expenses and to find employment for one or more blind person within the canteen.

PV 70 was launched on November 16th in freezing temperatures. It had been a race against time, as Scotty wrote to Barker:

If you can imagine, temporary buildings, canvas screens, heavy snow, below zero weather, French Canadians not understanding English and Weeks, Pengelly and Freemantle worked out and completely fatigued, and I think that I was averaging frequently thirty hours at a stretch and well over eighteen hours a day for the rest of the time and virtually really doing much of the work myself. That gives you some idea of the picture; so much to do over again as to be heartbreaking to a degree and then, during the last week, to watch the ice film making over the water and knowing that in any one forty hours the ice would make sufficiently to ruin the whole of the project.[16]

The first yard trials of *CMTB 1* were run on November 17th in a snow storm with less than a quarter of a mile visibility, and with two petrol stoves inside the wheelhouse to melt the snow and the ice from the windows. On their return to the works the crew found that almost one ton of ice had formed in horizontal icicles where the fresh water spray had been blown onto the weather side of the boat, and that all the hatches were frozen solid. The next day a big end failed in one of the engines which had to be replaced prior to the acceptance trials on the next

day. Scotty and his men worked all night:

. . . we got the new engine in at quarter past three in the morning, and such were the conditions that oil pipes, coolers, tanks, etc., I took out and cleaned myself for fear of any loose metal being in them, and made up every pipe joint on the engine myself, to make quite sure that this important job was done properly. Freemantle I had sent home, and the new men, of course, could not be trusted. At eight o'clock that morning we were up together and at ten o'clock had run the engines.

The Trial Board arrived at eleven o'clock and the boat was taken down the locks to the St Lawrence River where a fifty-mile run, with full war load, was undertaken. The boat performed magnificently, but further problems emerged when the boat was hauled out of the water on the following day and it was discovered that the 'P' brackets, which had been cast in Canada, had failed. Scotty wrote to Barker:

. . . so we had to cast and start machining while I actually saw the ice forming on the water. We worked all the day and all that night and all the following day, which took us into Friday, and we were all together somewhere about mid-day on Friday, all feeling a little limp and tired. I took the boat out in the canal and ran it to prove and test everything and after three-quarters of an hour, brought her in again where we refuelled with 2400 gallons . . . we got out of the canal on the Friday night, with thin ice scrunching and got underway the next morning at 7:47 and then made the fastest time on the St. Lawrence that had ever been made since man used it.[17]

As Scotty triumphantly took his old *PV 70* up the St Lawrence River, the war in Europe seemed far away. He little knew that his works at Hythe had just suffered its first damage in the air raids that, a week later, were to culminate in the virtual destruction of Southampton.

CHAPTER 19
The Boats go to War

Stuart Barker returned to the United Kingdom in June, sailing to Liverpool in an Atlantic convoy. He arrived at Hythe to find that much had happened while he had been with Scott-Paine. Production had continued unabated and during the last week of May the factory had delivered six large boats including the 64 foot *HSL 120* for the Air Ministry, two French motor torpedo boats, *VTB 25* and *26*, two anti-submarine boats, *MA/SB 8* and *9*, and one of the two Swedish boats. The second Swedish boat was delivered during the following week, and one of the Norwegian boats shortly after that. The factory was working twelve hours a day, seven days a week, although 'in the interests of the health and the efficiency of employees, it was arranged that everyone should have a weekend, from noon on Saturday to Monday morning, once a month'.[1]

The factory was also kept busy with boats coming back for repairs, including those damaged in action with the enemy. One of these was *TM 51*, the 70 foot boat built at Hythe for the Dutch, which had been 'unofficially transferred' by Lieutenant Colenbrander to the Royal Netherlands Navy. The British government had informed the Netherlands government that the boat was to be requisitioned for the Royal Navy, but the Dutch crew at Hythe had other ideas. Permission was obtained for trials to be completed, whereupon *TM 51*, under the command of Lieutenant-Commander O. de Booy, left Hythe with a full load of fuel. The boat took off in an easterly direction. The 'trials' ended with the arrival of the boat at a Dutch port where it joined the Royal Netherlands Navy. On May 10th, the Germans invaded Holland and *TM 51* happened to be in Rotterdam, under the command of Lieutenant J. van Staveren, when a force of parachutists was dropped to take bridges over the River Maas. The motor torpedo boat played a dramatic part in the Maasbruggen battle as it defended the bridges with

its machine guns, receiving damage from bullets and shells, and a near-miss of a bomb from an attacking aircraft. However, the engines remained serviceable and, when the position became hopeless, van

TM 51, the 70 foot MTB built at Hythe for the Royal Netherlands Navy and which later became *MGB 46*.

132

Staveren brought the boat back to Hythe. *TM 51* was repaired and subsequently entered service with the Royal Navy as *MGB 46*.[2]

The French boats, *VTB 23* and *VTB 24*, made a dramatic departure for the war on May 17th, after several hectic days of preparation. Scotty had wished with all his heart that he could have been there when he had read the letter that Frank Bishop had written to Stuart Barker in America on May 24th:

I think the most interesting events from our point of view have been the spectacular departure, in a great hurry, of the first two '10th' boats, with Pepin and Troadec. We managed to get an enormous amount of stuff into them in the last 24 hours hectic work, Mr Wells doing marvels in this connection. The boats did not go away looking as one would have wished them to look but the appearance went by the board in favour of fighting efficiency. The actual moment of departure was incredibly funny as, when Pepin [Pepin-LeHalleur] started up his engine, a smoke float went up at the same moment blotting the whole factory out for about 1/4 hour. That having been dealt with (you can imagine the panic with Pepin's

compatriots) Troadec shoved of and waved good-bye. Abeck and Lawson leapt on board in great excitement and at that psychological moment Troadec remembered that he had not switched his telegraphs on. He immediately switched them on and, as he had already put them to ahead, the engine room, naturally, obeyed. The next few moments were about as funny as I have seen in this yard. Abeck ran about on the deck of the boat waving his arms and shouting like a madman, whilst Lawson endeavoured to leap into a dinghy, which raced alongside, with the boat going about 15 or 16 knots. If I observed things correctly, Lawson succeeded in dropping his boots in the drink in his efforts but both were eventually rescued.[3]

St John Beaumont went with the crew of *VTB 23*, to supervise the removal of the torpedo tubes, depth charges and the A/S gear batteries, and the installation of additional armaments. Over the next few days the war situation at Cherbourg deteriorated, with regular air raids taking place at night. The port was full of refugees and on May 25th, St John Beaumont wrote: 'last evening I went to the civil port

VTB 23, the first of the 70 foot boats built by Hythe for the French Navy, prior to its delivery in April/May 1940.

and saw thousand upon thousand of these poor Dutch, Belgian and French people disembarking from trawlers, fishing smacks and cargo boats.' Operation DYNAMO for the evacuation at Dunkirk started the following day, May 26th, and the French VTBs joined the armada of eight hundred and sixty vessels that was to rescue one hundred and twenty thousand men from the beaches. Very little news about their exploits reached Cherbourg, other than a report that the two boats had performed excellently but were both out of commission due to war damage and were in an English port on May 30th. On May 30th, *VTB 25* and *26* left Hythe for Cherbourg. Armour was added to give protection to the engine rooms, while St John Beaumont checked the engines and attempted to instruct the inexperienced engine room crews. The two boats left Cherbourg on Sunday, 2nd June. St John Beaumont commented:

I do not know how the Bendix springs stood up to their attempts at starting up . . . if there is any failure on these two boats, due to Bendix pinion failure, cooling, fuel pressure, reverse gear, etc, I am afraid I must report that it will be largely due to the inexperience of the crew and possibly the stupidity of the French Navy who have two fully trained men here, Coiffier and Bernard (both well trained on our boats) who they could have sent.

On June 18th, the German army entered Cherbourg and the VTB base was blown up. St John Beaumont and his wife left the port on the last ship to get away to England. Looking over the rail of the railway steamer, *St Briac*, he saw the torpedo tubes of *VTB 23* and *24* floating in the harbour. It was a bitter end of months of strenuous effort.[4]

Five British Power Boat Company boats took part in the evacuation of Dunkirk. *MTB 16* and *MTB 100*, which had been built as Motor Minesweeper *MMS 51* in the 1936 Programme, shared the honours with three Masbies, *MA/SB 6*, *7* and *10*. On May 30th, Churchill sent a telegram to Lord Gort instructing him to hand over command of the British Expeditionary Force and to return home once his force was reduced to the equivalent of three divisions. 'It would be a needless triumph', wrote Churchill, 'to the enemy to capture you when only a small force remained under your orders.' The honour of bringing back Lord Gort fell to Lieutenant W. G. (Bill) Everitt, Commanding Officer of *MA/SB 6*.[5]

Admiral Tower, Controller of Naval Equipment, visited Hythe during a weekend leave in June and Barker was delighted to pass on to Scotty the news that the Admiral had expressed considerable plea-

sure at the work being carried out at the yard, and that the British Power Boat Company was the only yard keeping to its production schedules.

The unsuccessful trials of the prototype 70 foot Masbie, *MA/SB 6*, had led to the consideration of the 63 foot hull, with Napier Lion engines, as a more suitable boat for anti-submarine work. The yard trials of the 63 foot boat under construction for South Africa were carried out during May 1940, and these confirmed the possibility that the smaller hull was better suited to the installation of three Napier Lion engines than the 70 foot hull. The results were raised at a meeting held in Room 24 at the Admiralty on May 23rd, to discuss the programme of delivery of the 70 foot boats which had fallen behind, largely due to the Admiralty reluctance to allow the cost of weekend working in the £18,000 price for the boats. Wright suggested to Admiral Tower and E. C. Jubb of the Contracts Department that some of the proposed 70 foot boats could be built as 63 foot Masbies, subject to trials which were to be carried out in early June to determine whether the boats would meet the requirements of HMS *Osprey*. He went on to reveal that a change over to the new type of boat would not cause any delay to deliveries as the factory had anticipated this possibility by leaving out one of the bulkheads in the hulls under construction for South Africa, so that in the event of the type being satisfactory, these boats could be completed as Masbies at the same time as the last of the 70 foot types.[6]

The experimental 63 foot boat underwent official trials in Southampton Water on June 25th, 1940. The results were satisfactory and it was decided that the new type should replace the production of the 70 foot boats. Maurice Wright wrote to the Admiralty at Bath on July 6th:

We have the honour to acknowledge receipt of your letter dated 3rd July, 1940 and note the decision that MA/S boats are to be built as 63 ft types in lieu of the 70 ft boats which were ordered in September 1939. We would respectfully inform you that we have arranged that the change in boat sizes shall be made from the 16th boat onward, being Motor A/S Boat No. 22, which will cause the least dislocation in production. We would inform you that the matter has been discussed with representatives of HMS *Osprey*.

The price of the 63 foot anti-submarine boats had been the subject of some acrimonious correspondence with Admiral Tower during May, but on May 31st, Wright informed Scott-Paine that a price had been agreed for the 63 foot high speed launches

134

HSL 122, one of the first 63 foot 'Whalebacks'
built at Hythe for the Air Ministry.

under construction for the Air Ministry. 'We have
just learned from the Ad that they accept a price of
£23,200 for these boats including engines', he wrote,
'which should stand us in good stead when coming
down to a settlement of the 63′ A/S Boat, which is
bound to come along very shortly now as soon as
trials have been carried out on the first S.A. boat
next month.'[7]

The first trials of the experimental *Queen Gull* took
place on June 11th, soon after Barker's return. Ten
senior officers came to Hythe including Admiral
Boddie, Colonel Redman, Colonel Barrie, Major
Cole and five other majors. Scotty did not know
whether to laugh or cry when he heard what had
happened that day. The visitors gathered in the
Board Room for an initial briefing, where they were
told of problems with the radio transmitter. The first
problem had come when the War Office representatives had suddenly found it necessary to alter the
operating wavelength of the transmitter some days
earlier. However, Victor Bull had worked day and

night to overcome the resultant difficulties and was
ready to test the equipment the day before the trials.
He was installing his aerial and transmitter on the
bandstand on the end of the north jetty, when he
accidentally kicked the chair on which the transmitter had been placed, with the result that it fell into
the water. It took half an hour to recover the equipment, and Bull spent the rest of the day trying to dry
it out with an air compressor and a blow lamp. It was
to no avail, and the assembled VIPs were told that
the radio-controlled trials could not take place. They
were understanding and joked that the transmitter
would indeed be worth purchasing if it could be made
to work after such an accident. Notwithstanding, an
impressive demonstration was carried out for the
visitors. Tommy Quelch squeezed into the boat and
drove it at 22.8 knots, demonstrating its manoeuvrability. Later, George Selman demonstrated the fact
that the boat could not sink by towing a hull, without
its engines and radio equipment, underwater. The
day was a perfect mid-summer day, at the end of

Marchwood Park, purchased in late 1940 as a
training centre for women workers at Hythe.

which the visitors expressed their pleasure and left for
London on the 4.20 PM train from Southampton.[8]

Two schemes were considered for the production
of the 'Queen Gulls'. The first was to contract out the
hull construction to the Dauntless Company. The
alternative was to build the hulls at Marchwood Park
which was by then well-established as a training
centre, capable of producing small boats. It was
decided to concentrate much of the 'Queen Gull'
production at Marchwood House, which continued
to produce the target boats until 1943 when the house
was taken over as a re-habilitation centre for airmen
who had suffered burns and had undergone the then
revolutionary treatment of plastic surgery.

As soon as Barker had left for home, Scotty
resumed his bombardment of the Admiralty with
cables and letters, urging the immediate purchase of
70 foot boats from America or Canada, saying that
hundreds of them in the North Sea could clear the
area of enemy submarines and shipping. In fact, he

was right in realising that Admiral Tower's search
for additional boats had been made all the more
urgent with the capture of Channel ports by the
Germans. During the first week of June, Scotty was
asked to assist in discussions with the US Navy about
the transfer of the 70 foot Elco boats to the British
government.

At the time that the first Elco boat, *PT 10*, was
being delivered, the Chief of the Bureau of Ordnance
had recommended an increase in the size of the boats
to accommodate four 21 inch torpedoes. A stretched
77 foot Elco PT boat was proposed, and the US Navy
was happy to agree with the request to transfer the 70
foot boats to Great Britain, as this would facilitate the
standardisation of the 21 inch torpedo which was to
be carried on the larger boat. It was also recognised
that the delayed production of the Packard engine
was causing a potential bottleneck, and that, by re-
ordering and accepting deferred deliveries, the
production facilities of both hulls and of engines

could be expanded. The Navy Department also argued that no appreciable amount of time would be lost as it could undertake competitive tests on the various PT boats designs during the six months it would take to construct replacement Elco boats, and that this would enable it to 'determine an ultimate type for mass production'.[9]

Scotty threw his weight behind the proposal and offered his expertise in preparing the Elco boats for service with the Royal Navy. The proposed release of the Elco boats was announced by Louis Compton, Acting Secretary of the Navy, at a stormy executive meeting of the Senate Naval Affairs Committee on Friday, June 14th. The following Monday, Irwin Chase contacted Scotty in Ottawa, asking him to return immediately as Elco had at last received an official enquiry from the British Purchasing Commission about boats for the British government. Scotty drove back overnight in the Rolls-Royce, arriving at 10.00 o'clock the next morning. Two days later, *The New York Times* reported that Senator Walsh, Chairman of the Senate Naval Committee had complained that the transfer of the PT boats was a 'grievous wrong'. Stephen T. Early, the White House Secretary, defended the Navy position, re-iterating that the United States would benefit by letting the British have the boats as it would obtain an expansion of plant for the production of both hulls and engines at no cost to the United States, and a subsequent production of a boat capable of carrying the 21 inch torpedo.[10]

American isolationists were delighted when the President cancelled the proposed transfer on the advice of Robert H. Jackson, the Attorney General, who ruled that the sale of an armed vessel to a belligerent power would be in violation of a law passed in 1917. Senator D. Worth, Democrat of Idaho, jubilantly declared that 'the New Deal was backing down in its programme of aid to the Allies'. On June 26th, Arthur Purvis, the Chairman of the British Purchasing Commission in New York reported to Churchill that President Roosevelt had stopped the deal and that the decision also prevented the proposed sale of destroyers to Britain. Almost another year was to pass before the twenty-three Elco boats, and *PT 9*, built at Hythe, were eventually transferred to Britain under the provisions of the Lend-Lease Bill, which was signed by President Roosevelt on March 11th, 1941.[11]

In fact, the actual wartime operational requirements that Admiral Tower was anxious to fulfil, were turning out to be very different from those that Scotty had anticipated before the war. Admiral Blake wrote to Scott-Paine as much as he could get past the censors:

the situation is quite different to what we both imagined it would be. Neither MTB or A/S boats have had any targets. All the movement of German ships are carried out by day along the coast under cover of fighter protection, and any surface craft who tries to attack gets dive bombed—so far as submarines are concerned they avoid the narrow waters entirely and work out between 18 degrees and 25 degrees west, which is too far out for our craft.[12]

Blake told Scotty that the anti-submarine boats had been converted to deal with the German E Boats that 'prowl around at night'. The Rolls-Royce Merlin powered boats that had been ordered by the French, Dutch, Norwegian and Swedish governments were being converted into motor gun boats with the addition of armour and the installation of a 2 pounder Rolls-Royce gun on the after deck. The conversion of these boats was at first thought to be a temporary expedient as P. M. F. Cooper, Director of Anti-Submarine Warfare, issued an instruction on August 12th that asdic sets would not be required in *MA/SB 40* to *46* (the Dutch, Swedish and Norwegian boats) or in *MA/SB 50* to *67* (the French boats) 'until

MGB 59, originally built for the French Navy at Hythe.

the boats are no longer needed as motor gun boats'.[13] In the event, the boats were to continue in this new role, and the motor gun boat was to join motor torpedo boat and the motor launch as one of the three principal weapons of Coastal Forces. In November 1940, Rear-Admiral Piers K. Kekewich was appointed as Rear-Admiral Coastal Forces to co-ordinate the maintenance, improvement and future construction of motor gun boats, motor torpedo boats and motor launches. Seven of the converted British Power Boat MA/SBs were formed into the 6th Motor Gun Boat Flotilla at Fowey in December 1940, although it was not until February 1941 that the boats were officially designated Motor Gun Boats.

The use of the British Power Boat Company Masbies and French MTBs as gun boats during 1940 placed strains upon the 70 foot and 63 foot hulls for which they had never been designed. In common with the Vosper boats, the hulls suffered structural failures arising from the considerable stresses that arose from the use of the boats at high speed in bad sea conditions. The fitting of heavy armaments on the after deck of the Masbies made the situation worse; fractures occurred in the frames and longi-tudinals and the gunwale tended to part from the frames just aft of the deck house. The structural problems were eventually solved by fitting longitu-dinal stiffeners, aft of the wheelhouse, to most of the 70 foot boats. But the operational experience with the

Masbies as gun boats led Admiral Tower to ask Selman if he could design a boat specifically for use as a gun boat to counter the E-Boat threat. In November, Barker told Scotty that Selman had been asked to design the new boat, adding: 'For obvious reasons I cannot explain any further as to what this new design is . . . and I rather think there is going to be some strong objection to my letting the drawings come over to you.'[14]

On November 17th, 1940, a single bomb fell on the Hythe factory, severely damaging Scotty's personal yacht store in which several of his racing boats had been stored. *Miss Britain III* had been moved to Downton, near Salisbury and so escaped destruction, and a Sea Eagle flying boat which Scotty had been storing as a relic of his past, survived, having been taken to the Denham film studios to star in a film on the Schneider Trophy and Spitfire stories. Even if he had known of the damage, Scotty would not have been able to give the matter much attention as he was pre-occupied with the problem of delivering *PV 70*, by then designated Canadian Motor Torpedo Boat *No 1*, to Halifax before the onset of winter closed the navigation into Montreal.

The delivery of *CMTB 1* was to be an incredible story of courage and endurance. It left Montreal on November 23rd under the command of Lieutenant Garrard RCNVR, with Scott-Paine on board. It made the trip to Quebec in four hours, a faster time than the express train. Scotty left the boat at Quebec to

70 foot Motor Gun Boats at Hythe, late 1940.
MGB 50 in the foreground was built as *VTB 23* for the French Navy.

138

travel to New York and the boat continued on what was to be an adventurous journey to Halifax. On November 24th, *CMTB 1* left Quebec for Rimouski where arrangements had been made for the boat to refuel. The weather was deteriorating and, as *CMTB 1* reached Rimouski, heavy snowstorms were setting in; the temperature was fourteen degrees below zero and ice was making fast. The intention was to make the five hundred-mile trip to Shediac in one stage the next day, but the weather got worse and the boat put into Matane with three inches of ice over the entire deck and superstructure. The life lines on the fore-deck were about six inches in diameter with a coating of ice. Gale force winds prevented the journey being continued the following day, but on the morning of Wednesday, November 27th, Lieutenant Garrard decided that the weather had moderated enough for an attempt to be made on the journey down the Gaspe coast. The engines were warmed up at 9.45 AM, and half an hour later *CMTB 1* left Matane. It

was fine and clear with the wind Force 4, with a moderate sea, and Cape Gaspe was passed at 3.09 PM. Garrard decided to take advantage of the weather to make a run for Shediac, New Brunswick. The course was set to pass inside Bonaventure Island, and passing three miles east of the Richibucto Head Light, to clear the shoals and banks extending from the West Point of Prince Edward Island. The course would then take the boat through the Northumberland Straights to Shediac Harbour.

Snow started to fall about 6.30, about one hour after dark. The speed was slowed to 28 knots as the snow became heavier. By 7.30, Garrard's dead reckoning placed the boat to within 13 miles of the Richibucto Head Light, but visibility was down to about half a mile and speed was reduced yet again. There was no sign of the light and at 7.43 one of the crew shouted 'Stop her, hard a port!' A snow covered beach was looming through the blizzard, about fifty yards ahead. The Cox'n mistook the order and

Canadian *MTB 1*, built as *PV 70* at Hythe, stranded near Richibucto Light, Halifax, November 1940.

turned to the starboard whereupon Garrard grabbed the wheel, closed the throttles and put the engines into reverse. But it was too late, and *CMTB 1* grounded, without any shock at all. All hands were mustered on the after deck and attempts were made to hold the after end off the beach, but to no avail as the wind and surf drove the boat further ashore. Despite the appalling weather, the crew struggled to transfer spare petrol stored in drums in the after compartment onto the fore deck, but no progress was made in shifting the boat and, as the hull was not making any water, it was decided to sit tight for the night and to attempt a refloating in the morning.

It was later discovered that the failure of the Richibucto Head Light was due to the lighthouse keeper falling from his bicycle on his way to attend to his charge; he was found frozen to death at the bottom of a precipice the following morning. Meanwhile, the crew on the boat suffered from the intense cold: food and heat soon ran out and attempts to contact Halifax by radio raised no reply. With daylight it became clear that the boat had grounded on a sand bar, and that land was about two miles away. It was realised that the boat could not be refloated without a tow, so Freemantle, together with Lieutenant S. McComb were sent to scout out the island. A small dingy was found near an abandoned lobsterman's hut and it was decided that the two men should try for what appeared to be the mainland. Disaster overtook the pair when the one good oar was lost, and the dingy floated with the wind and tide. At 6.30PM, the crew in *CMTB 1* saw a flashlight 'S.O.S.' from the helpless dingy. The wind was reaching gale force as the dingy crew signalled that they could not last the night in their present position. At 11.30 at night, in desperation the two men plunged through the slush ice and water and waded ashore onto the island they had been making for. They ran through the deep snow and sand towards a light which turned out to be in a building occupied by Thomas Hebert who tended the range lights at the entrance of the harbour.

The following morning, Friday, 29th November, the wind had driven out the water between the two

Canadian *MTB 1* at Halifax, Nova Scotia, December 1940.

islands and a party from *CMTB 1* was able to join up with Freemantle and McComb, and that afternoon a schooner took a group into Richibucto where news of the accident was passed to the naval authorities in Montreal. On the Saturday morning the group returned to the stranded motor torpedo boat in the company of an officer of the Royal Canadian Mounted Police with orders to abandon ship. A Captain Featherstone of the Maritime Salvage Commission was to be sent from Halifax to take charge of the salvage operation. A blizzard blew all Sunday and the following Monday as discussions took place on how to rescue the stranded boat. Featherstone advised the Admiralty that the boat would have to be chocked up and left on the sands with a scratch crew for the winter. However, Scotty's engineers on board telephoned their boss with the opinion that the boat could be re-floated, and eventually orders were received that the salvage was to proceed at all costs. On Wednesday, December 4th, the temperature was nineteen degrees below zero as work started on digging a trench to enable the underwater gear to be removed. The work was completed by the Friday when Captain Featherstone came out to the boat for the first time, with the news that the Department of Transport's ice-breaker, SS *Montcalm*, was on its way from Charlottetown to the stranded MTB. Early on Friday morning it was realised that the *Montcalm* did not have suitable towing gear and the ship departed for Cape Tormentine where it was to pick up a new six-inch manila line.

At a quarter past two on the afternoon of Sunday, December 8th, *Montcalm* started towing the boat off the sandbank. Half an hour later, the MTB had been moved eighty feet toward the water when the line broke. The line broke again when the boat was only thirty-five feet from the water, but, the following morning, the boat was re-floated, and was found to be watertight. The *Montcalm* then proceeded to tow the MTB to Charlottetown, but during the night a full gale arose, with high seas running and ice forming, and the ship was forced to put into the lee of Price Edward Island. The boat continually overran her tow, but the crew managed to fend her off from the sides of the ice-breaker. Eventually, the tow arrived at the Charlottetown Navy Dock where repairs were made to damaged cleats on the deck. On December 10th, the tow continued, but again gale force winds caused problems. Part of the samson post gave way, but by chance the line fouled one of the propellers that had been lashed to the deck and held for two-and-half hours. In this way the boat arrived at Port Hawkesbury where a gunboat took over from the *Montcalm* which refused to face the appalling weather any longer. On December 12th, HMCS *Fleurdelis* proceeded to tow *CMTB 1*, and despite further snow and gale force winds, the 70 foot PV boat arrived in Halifax on December 17th.[15]

CHAPTER 20
Reports from Hythe

The strain of getting the Canadian Power Boat Company factory into operation took its toll on Scott-Paine's health. For some time he had been suffering from what he referred to as 'pinny pains in my tummy', and in February 1941, he spent a week in the Royal Victoria Hospital, Montreal, having a thorough check-up. As well as the strain of work, Scotty was showing the effect of years of motor boat racing. He wrote to his brother Victor, 'a new process of X-Ray showed that many years ago I had broken my back and have fractured it twice more . . . enough to make any twenty men have aching backs the expert said.' The doctors advised twelve weeks rest, and a careful diet to deal with digestion problems and high blood pressure. 'I got dressed', Scotty wrote, 'and went back to the factory rejoicing—in other words I feel fine.'[1]

Scott-Paine's energy remained undiminished. He dictated a long letter to Stuart Barker from his bed, detailing at great length a scheme for towing 70 foot anti-submarine boats behind ships of the Atlantic convoys so that they could be released and track enemy submarines.

'If the convoy is attacked our boat or boats standing at '2 minutes' call would start their engines and let go their towing gear and if fitted with A/S gear which worked as efficiently as our original gear 3 years ago, could find the submarine and it could never get away. We could wireless its position and stay with it day and night to the extent of our fuel, which is ten days continuous speeding at 8/10 knots (a 24 hour day) say 7 days to be on the conservative side. Visualise what this means. Actually it means that no submarine would dare to attack because it would know that it would be destroyed. You will see that I am entirely discounting the possibility of our boat destroying it with its own depth charges'.[2]

Five hulls were turned over at the Montreal Factory by the end of February. Scotty's aim of being able to produce a boat a week was becoming a reality. 'Well, H.V.', he wrote to Victor, 'the job's done and well done.' He continued:

The best you ever saw, the best place for men to work in Canada or anywhere else. Now, the big job is to get the workmanship as I want it. The office staff we continually change—it's now pretty good—I might be tempted to say very good; draughtsmen are non-existent. We have two architects—a drains engineer—a bank clerk who thought he liked drawings—two full grown boys who did well at drawing at school—an old timer returned for the duration—a fitter turned draughtsman, or nearly turned, and an outside foreman engineer who was a draughtsman who lost his last job for shocking the Boss (I hope he doesn't try it on me); an English woman with no money so is back to work again; another old woman back for the duration, and six girls, now actually all good tracers up to a point! But I'm back at the old game, a big black-board, chalk up everything full size in the shop and the pencil pusher makes the drawings from that—all modifications that way too. You'll see by this that it's a grand game of sharing everything in front of you.

The British Labour Member of Parliament, Sir Walter Citrine visited the Canadian Power Boat factory on January 20th, 1941. He was clearly impressed with what he saw as he went around the workshops with Dunlop Palmer, the Works Manager and Edouard Labelle:

Mr Scott-Paine, who is the head of this concern evidently believes in first-class layout and modern equipment. This shop was spacious and magnificently equipped with some of the finest machine tools I have seen. The hulls of the boats were built completely of wood and naturally one expected to find a good deal of sawdust kicking about. Quite the contrary. The sawmill was a model of cleanliness.

Wages for skilled men were approximately 75 cents (3s.) per hour. Every department was self-contained as far as possible, but I didn't like the wire grilles round every one of them. One had to gain admittance through a narrow door which was always kept closed. It gave one a feeling of being caged, and on enquiring as to the reason I was told that it is mainly to prevent workpeople from strolling about. Lavatories were attached to each department and they were first-class. Smoking was not allowed and the Manager said that whilst this is right enough in the woodworking sections, it is a source of grievance that the men cannot smoke elsewhere. Scott-Paine had one of his works burned down, and he doesn't want to have that happen again.[3]

Scott-Paine then met Sir Walter Citrine in Washington on January 30th, and arrangements were made for him to visit the Bayonne factory. Sutphen and Scott-Paine showed the visitor around the works, expanding on the possible use of the anti-submarine boats to accompany Atlantic convoys. Citrine concluded:

Sutphen knows what he is talking about in such matters, and has had long experience in building submarines . . . I was convincd that these very fast craft can be put to far better service by the British Admiralty that they are at present.

In the meantime, Scotty had become frustrated with Barker's reports which told him little of value about what was going on at Hythe. While Barker had been in America, Maurice Wright, the Company Secretary at Hythe, had sent detailed reports of work in hand, negotiations with the Admiralty and the financial situation of the company, but in January 1941, Scotty complained to Barker:

Wright says that three of his letters, some reports and Board Meeting Minutes have been returned to him, and have been refused to let go forward. He does not say whether this is the Censor, or whether it is you, but if it is you, I should like you to explain exactly what you mean by it.

Barker tried to explain:

It is quite probable that you have not quite understood the position which has arisen between last June and now, or how the whole atmosphere has changed. One of the reasons is, of course, that shortly after I returned we got into that trouble with the Censor and it has been impossible to give you a true and clear picture of not only the physical side of our difficulties, but the changing psychological factor.

Admiral Tower read all the correspondence between Scott-Paine and the British Power Boat Company and he took the trouble to send a hand-written letter of support to Barker, congratulating him on what he was achieving in difficult circumstances.[4]

Scotty began to get the feel for a problem at Hythe, which was beginning to affect the whole of the management at the yard, and which was centred around a major conflict between Stuart Barker and Maurice Wright. In September, 1940, Stuart Barker, backed by Wilson Hamill, had summoned Maurice Wright to a meeting in London to clear the air. Even George Selman had handed in his notice and Admiral Tower had visited Hythe to try to sort things out. The pressure of wartime conditions and the immense amount of work at the yard was putting Barker, who was unable to share his problems with Scotty, under considerable strain. Matters were made worse for Scotty by the imposition of censorship of letters which prevented him getting useful information.

Barker's greatest challenge came in October, 1940, when the Admiralty decided to proceed with a shadow British Power Boat Factory. Before the war, Scotty had purchased a large site at Marchwood, near Southampton, but when Admiral Tower raised the matter of a second factory, Barker concluded that it was too vulnerable to bombing and resurrected the 1938 scheme to build at Poole, Dorset, about thirty miles west of Southampton. No 2 Factory, as it became known, comprised three adjacent sites, the largest being big enough to construct an assembly building of eighteen berths. Barker had tried to recruit Flight Lieutenant Jinman as manager of the yard, but in February, 1941, he wrote to Scotty with the news that Sergeant Bradbury, who had worked with T. E. Shaw on the first seaplane tenders for the RAF, and who had joined the staff at Hythe in 1940, was to take charge of the new factory. After months of negotiation, it was agreed that the Admiralty would pay for the construction of the yard, that the British Power Boat Company would manage it on a 'profit and loss' basis, and that the company would have an option to purchase the yard at the end of the war.[5]

Scotty was concerned that he was not personally

MGB 36, ordered as a 63 foot MA/SB in 1940
and later used for special operations.

involved in the project, and was aggravated by the
fact that what information he did receive arrived at
least three months after decisions had been made.
'Must give you definite instructions,' Scotty cabled
angrily, 'surely you cannot imagine you have [the]
right to embark [on] such matters without consulting
me.' On the other hand, Barker was not able to
consult, sending a cable in reply, '[it is] very difficult
for many reasons to keep you fully informed'. The
first work at the Poole factory was the replacement of
Napier Lion engines in the 70 foot motor gun boats
with the Packard engines which were beginning to
arrive in England in substantial quantities. On June
25th, 1941, Barker wrote to Scotty:

Bradbury got his first Brodie re-engined boat out
absolutely first class. He went through the whole
of the preliminary trials and full power trials
without finding a leak in the engine room, an
electrical defect, or in fact any kind of fault

whatever, something we have never been able to
do here, and it wasn't luck—it was because I have
concentrated on picking a first class bunch and
kept their enthusiasm up to the highest pitch.[6]

Details of George Selman's development work at
Hythe were equally difficult to pass on to Scott-
Paine. In January, Barker wrote: 'We have some
most interesting jobs on hand, which I am afraid I
cannot tell you about at all. There is one thing so
secret that I daren't even hint at what it is.' The most
urgent development work was the design of a
purpose-built motor gun boat to counter the E-Boat
threat. These had been requested by Admiral Tower
following the operational experience of the 70 foot
gun boats. Scotty was not convinced that Selman had
the ability to design a new boat without the benefit of
his experience. 'Selman. I confirm that I cannot
possibly agree to any major design being contemplated [unless] I have been able to fully investigate

A 20 mm Oerlikon gun mounted on the stern of
a 70 foot Scott-Paine motor gun boat in the
British coastal forces.

same', he instructed, 'being quite sure no one should
accept the responsibility other than myself . . . I
think it is fantastic and little short of utter stupidity to
meddle with the design of this boat, without at least
having enquired from me, its designer, what should
or should not be done, but I quite understand you are
not your own master.'[7]

In fact, George Selman's design was to be a
masterpiece, and the most successful boat ever
produced by the British Power Boat Company. The
design had been worked out in conjunction with
Lieutenant Commander Robert ('Hitch') Hichens
DSO DSC RNVR, the most celebrated motor gun boat
commander of the war, whose exploits with the 6th
Motor Gun Boat Flotilla at Fowey in February 1941
were to earn the motor gun boats the sobriquet 'the
Spitfires of coastal forces'. In his discussions with
Selman he enthused about the thrills and dangers of
taking a 70 foot MGB to sea in a gale:

We were all inexperienced and the height of the
sea was hard to judge. On we sped until,
suddenly, we reached the top of the first big swell.
It was a breath-taking sensation as we dropped
off it; the boats fell so sharply that men were left
two feet in the air. The sickening drop as you left
your stomach behind, the shuddering bang as the
forepart of the boat hit the hollow of the wave.

We had none of us done this before. We were all
pretty startled. Automatically throttles were
brought down and the unit slowly pulled itself
together at about 20 knots. In one case the harm
was already done. Whitehead's boat dropped
further and further back, her lamp beginning to
speak:

'Coxswain's back severely damaged; returning
to harbour for immediate medical attention.'

The poor man was coming down to earth, so to
speak, had missed his footing and injured his back

severely. He was in hospital for many months . . .
The wind had risen to almost gale force, at least 7
or 8; with the effect of the race on the sea, there
were some very sharp and, for us, large waves.
We jumped through them like porpoises, at one
moment entirely hidden from each other by the
crest of a wave or by solid sheets of spray, at
another exposed to view well down to the under
belly of the ship, with a third of the boat's keel
forward clear of the water, like a large fish leaping
from a wave. It was an exhilarating and satisfying
experience. Slowly, as we plunged and thrust
across West Bay, my admiration for the sea qualities of these little boats grew and grew.[8]

The design of the new gun boat was started in
December 1940. The team at Hythe worked night
and day on the project and numerous tank
experiments were undertaken, as details of hull,
machinery and armaments were worked out, and in
February, 1941, the general arrangements were
approved by the Admiralty. The gun boat was 71 feet

6 inches long overall, with a beam of 20 feet 7 inches,
a depth of 10 feet 7 inches, and a displacement of
about 46 tons. The hull lines were similar to those of
the original 70 foot hull, but it was structurally much
stronger. The hollow back profile of the deck, which
had worried Selman when the PV boat had been
built, was eliminated and the deck given a hogged
sheer. Experience had shown that the stresses produced in a wooden planning hull travelling at speeds
of up to 40 knots in bad sea conditions are considerably greater than had ever been anticipated.
Selman designed his new hull to withstand the longitudinal stresses by dividing the lower part of the hull
with six fore and aft girders, built like steel plate
girders, having strong top and bottom members of
cross braced mahogany, connected with mahogany
struts and bonded by ply webs. Additional fore and
aft strength was provided by constructing the hull
below the chine of three layers of planks set at forty-
five degrees, the middle layer being set fore and aft.
   When he had heard that Selman intended to
mount a 40 mm gun on the fore deck of the new gun

MGB 77, the 71 foot 6 inch motor gun boat
commanded by Lt Commander Hichens.

boat, Scotty had written, 'In anything like broken weather, much less a moderate condition of sea, it will in my opinion be impossible for men to work with this installation. A worse place could not have been chosen for it. I note that it is said that you can do nothing about it . . . which I question. Having lifted the chine and put this weight there you will have a deeper rising and trimming hull. The whole thing is I think a pity.' Selman had solved the problem of the recoil of the forward-mounted gun by dividing the forward part of the boat into three by two longitudinal bulkheads so that the deck and bottom of the boat were connected.

Selman designed the gun boat to be powered by three Packard 1,200 hp supercharged engines, the wing engines driving through Vee drives. The five petrol tanks, containing 2,600 Imperial gallons, were situated immediately below the chart room.

Accommodation comprised a forecastle, a galley, a cabin for two officers on the port side and a cabin for four officers on the starboard side, plus a crew's and an officer's lavatory. The intended armament for the boat was one Vickers 40 mm automatic on the foredeck and a twin 20 mm Oerlikon situated in a turret on the centreline, just aft of the wheelhouse. In addition, there was to be two stripped Lewis guns, a star shell gun and a Holman Projector.

The predicted speed, with a full load of ammunition, fresh water and petrol, and a complement of fourteen men, was 42 or 43 knots. The range at 20 knots was estimated to be 1,000 sea miles, decreasing to 760 sea miles at 30 knots. The boat was designed to travel at 30 to 36 knots in Sea 3 or 4, and at 20 to 24 knots in Sea 5 to 6.[9]

The final design was presented to the Admiralty at a conference held at Bath where W. J. Holt, Chief

The 70 foot Elco/Scott-Paine PT boats during their cruise in the Caribbean in 1941.

Constructor of the Naval Construction Department, said that he did not like the proposed boat, and that in his opinion it was not strong enough to operate in a sea of more that force 2 or 3. A disappointed Selman quietly rolled up his drawings, whereupon Admiral Tower intervened, saying that, as Director of Naval Equipment, this was the boat he wanted and was going to have. Subsequently, ninety-six of George Selman's 71 foot 6 inch motor gun boats were built, and the type was recognised as the most successful of the 'short' boats of coastal forces, and the only one that showed no structural defects, despite exceptionally hard use.[10]

The experiences of the motor gun boats in the English Channel and the North Sea were not far removed from those of Squadron 2 of the United States, comprising the Hythe built *PT 9* and the first batch of Elco boats, *PT 10* to *19*. The Squadron undertook a cruise to the West Indies in December 1940, where they met exceptionally heavy weather, running through fifteen to eighteen foot waves at high speed for as long as fourteen hours at a stretch. The boats suffered frame damage of the type then being experienced by Hitch's MGBs in British Waters. Scotty wrote about the adventures to Barker:

I think I have told you their operations off Florida in the Gulf Stream and their running at such high speeds as to show their propeller shafts pretty nearly off every wave, and they had cracked frames on all boats with the exception of four on the port side in the officers' quarters. The four boats that were undamaged had the best skippers, which shows I suppose to some extent handling comes into it . . . the enthusiasm of the crews was immense, they lost all sight of their tender and I heard yesterday that she had been knocked about so much she had to go back to the mainland and that the Flotilla had gone back many hundred of miles to pick her up. They had another amusing incident by one of their boats making the acquaintance of an unheard of coral reef at some peculiarly high part of that particular job's performance. The results were most illuminating. She managed to run more than a hundred yards on it. The crew managed to remove it themselves . . . everyone at Washington seems to be more than pleased with the results.[11]

CHAPTER 21
Lend Lease and the Plywood Derbies

'The United States is completely electrified', Scotty wrote on the passing of the Lend Lease Bill in March 1941. The year-old decision to transfer the 70 foot boats built by Elco for the United States Navy to the Royal Navy could now be implemented. At the end of March 1941, Squadron 2 of the United States Navy was ordered to return to New York so that most of its boats could be transferred to the British. *PT 9*, together with *PTs 10* to *15* were transferred during April, while *PTs 16* to *19* were transferred during July 1941. The delay in transferring the latter boats was to facilitate their use in training personnel

PT 20, the prototype 77 foot Scott-Paine/Elco MTB, designed to carry four 21 inch torpedoes.

pending delivery of the larger 77 foot Elco boats. The United States Motor Boat Submarine Chaser Squadron 1 was commissioned in February 1941, but while the Squadron was fitting out in New York, it was agreed that the boats would be transferred to the Royal Navy as motor gun boats, *MGB 82* to *93*. *PTCs 5* to *12* were transferred on April 4th, 1941. *PTCs 1* to *4* went to Key West, Florida, where they were fitted with experimental Asdic gear, but just as the 70 foot Masbies were unsuccessful due to propeller noise, so the Elco boats failed to locate submarines during trials, and were transferred to the Royal Navy on July 15th.[1]

The conversion of the Elco boats for British use was undertaken at Bayonne under Hubert Scott-Paine's direction. The Admiralty appointed Commander Garnett and a warrant officer shipwright to be resident at Elco, and it was much to Scott-Paine's amusement that Garnett had been at the Legation in China when the British Power Boat Company had supplied armoured boats for the Chinese Customs. Scotty wrote to Barker with another coincidence: 'the Engineer R.C.N. who is resident with us at Montreal was the engineer in the Chinese Customs who accepted the launches. What a small world this is.' One of Scotty's recruits from Hythe, Len Munn, was detailed to assist in the re-fitting of the boats, but work soon came to a halt as a representative of the Admiralty, Mr McClogherie, until recently superior to Holt at the DNC, insisted on a number of expensive and time consuming modifications. The delays over the re-fitting of the Elco boats continued to frustrate Scotty who wrote on July 31st:

Three service Officers have just arrived from home. Some of them had something to do with bringing the first Elco boats down from where they landed to where they had to go. They had nothing but the highest praise for them from everything including the engine installations, etc., and were dumbfounded when visiting Bayonne to see the number of articles that are there, stalled because of changes and appalled when they knew that we could have delivered the whole lot by the end of last May if the requirements for these changes had not come through from the authorities concerned. Can you believe it, we are receiving instructions to throw out first-class electrical cooking gear and replace them by old paraffin stoves which have caused more casualties by fire than anything else in the world. We have had instructions to throw out the refrigerating gear and ice box, for what reason, no-one can possibly understand. They have received no instructions for three months on how to rubberise

tanks, the same thing regarding instructions for turrets, and the modifications to the tubes (which are completely unnecessary) . . . unless something is done these things will be here for goodness knows how many more weeks or months.[2]

Scotty travelled to Ridley College to see John and told him of his troubles. John Scott-Paine later recalled some of the arguments with the Admiralty over the modification of the Elco boats.

The bowler hat technicians of the British Admiralty were the true enemies, they were enemies even during the war . . . they wanted hammocks for the seamen to sleep in rather than the built-in bunks, that were part of the bracing for the deck . . . My father put his foot down and said either you get the fixed bunks, well, you've got to have the fixed bunks. Letters went back and forth, the US Navy was getting pretty browned off saying, what are these English doing, what is wrong with them?. Don't they want to win the war. Finally the Admiralty sent over two bowler-hats to New York, and there was a ship loaded with two PT boats the day they were supposed to arrive, and these two bowlerhats were going to go down to the ship and stop it. My father met them; he never would tell the story of what happened, except that he thought they might be hungry and he bought them dinner. If you ask me I think he got them drunk, they never got to the ship.[3]

The release of the Elco 70 foot boats had been made possible by the development of the 'stretched' 77 foot version which could carry four of the US standard 21 inch torpedoes. The Bureau of Ships was still undecided whether the Scott-Paine/Elco design should be the basis of all future PT boat production, particularly as the British Admiralty view was to support the experimental Higgins design. Scotty wrote:

They [the Bureau of Ships] thought here they must be wrong in their own judgement in going on ordering ours and as I have reported to you before, it came to a point when very nearly the whole of these affairs which I have created to be of benefit to the A at home, by their own action, were very nearly forced out of existence. The A's representatives were also in favour of Higgin's articles which had a very great bearing on the US outlook as well.[4]

On May 19th, 1941 a meeting was held between officers of the PT boat Squadrons, the Chief of Naval

150

Operations, the Bureau of Ships and other departments to discuss the future of PT boats in the light of the operational experience in the West Indies and Florida. The conference recommended that comparative trials of the different experimental and production PTs should be held to determine the model for future production. Admiral Stark, Chief of Naval Operations wrote:

> It is apparent that a considerable divergence of opinion exists among the various offices of the Navy Department and among officers of Motor Torpedo Squadrons as to the suitability of various types of Motor Torpedo Boats which have been acquired, or are now being built. In order to crystallize as far as possible, opinion as to the suitability of these various types of Motor Boats and to establish criteria for future contracts, it is desired that the Board of Inspection and Survey conduct comparative service test.[5]

The trials, which included an open sea run of 190 miles, later known as the 'Plywood Derbies', were held off New London between July 21st and 24th, 1941. Four Elco 77 foot boats took part; the

prototype *PT 20*, fitted with special propellers and additional strengthening to the hull, and Elco *PTs 26, 31* and *33*. The other competitors were *PT 6*, an 81 foot Higgins boat powered by three Packard engines; *PT 8*, built with an 81 foot aluminium hull by the Philadelphia Naval Yard; *PT 69*, a 72 foot Huckins boat powered by four Packard engines, *PT 70*, a new 76 foot boat constructed by Higgins, powered by three Packard engines, and a 70 foot boat constructed for the British Admiralty by Higgins, and powered by three Hall-Scott engines.

Leonard Munn, Scott-Paine's representative at Elco prepared the Elco boats at Bayonne prior to the trials. He was instructed to slip *PT 20* and to fit the propellers that he considered to be most suitable. He later recalled discussing the trials with the cox'n of the boat who explained his strategy for the sea race: 'When the signal to start is given I shall push the throttles wide upon and keep them there until we return to base.' To Len Munn's surprise, a directive was then issued that no boat with him as a member of the crew would be admissable as an official entry. Clearly the opposition was rattled, but Scotty said: 'Don't worry, accept it as a compliment and go aboard the observation boat.' *PT 26* had developed

Start of the trial known as the 'Plywood Derby' with the Scott-Paine Elco *PT 20* in the lead.

cracks during the initial trials and had been detailed to serve as the observation boat. Len Munn went on:

The starting signal came, a roar of exhausts following instantly, and the coxswain who told me his strategy was to immediately push the throttle wide open evidently did just that. The boat literally leapt ahead like a greyhound and took all the competitors by surprise and within seconds almost, had established a considerable lead. The second and third boats following him at the start were the other Elco entries and the whole pack headed out to sea on the set course. Not wanting to confuse the issue we waited until they were out of sight, and knew where they could be intercepted by taking a short cut through the Islands. On route we caught up with a United States Navy destroyer evidently with official observers on board. As we came alongside she was making 40 knots. By riding up her tremendous bow wave we could see right over her deck. We increased our speed to approximately 45 knots and soon lost sight of her. We headed in the direction of Nantucket, no Elco boat was in sight, but we did pick up the American designed boats, and were able to photograph them . . . Eventually we saw in the distance coming towards us on the homeward leg the first of the Elco boats. Within minutes the second boat appeared followed by number three. We turned about and followed them back to New London. The results were confirmed; Elco took the first three places at an average speed, as close as it could be calculated, of over 42 knots.[6]

Since the Elco boats were the only entries with complete ordnance, the other boats had been ballasted to the required weight. Mr Higgins contended that this placed his boats at a disadvantage, and that the deck failure of *PT 70* in the race was due to the loading of weights on the deck in order to compensate for armament which had not been allowed for in the design. In order to acquire more data, a second 'Plywood Derby' was arranged for August 11th and 12th. The weather was bad with heavy cross swells prevailing, but again the Elco entry, *PT 21*, won the Derby.

As a result of the data available from the trials, it was decided once again to increase the size of the standard PT boat. A design conference was called which resulted in a specification for PT boats in which 'the hull shall be the hard chine stepless bottom type with lines formed with a view to minimizing stress on the hull and fatigue of crew under all conditions and to assure a suitable platform for torpedo

and gun fire. The lines shall also be formed to insure easy manoeuvring of the boat and a small turning circle at full speed and ability to change direction quickly. The sides shall flare outwards from chine to gunwale.' The specification records the permanent influence of Scott-Paine on all subsequent PT boat design which eventually standardised on an 80 foot Elco boat and a 78 foot Higgins boat.[7]

Scott-Paine's main concern in the spring of 1941 was to secure further orders for the Montreal factory. He was distressed that, despite his initiative in constructing a factory capable of producing a boat a week, Admiral Tower would not place an order for boats with the Canadian Power Boat Company. Scott-Paine was quite open in blaming the British Admiralty for turning the Canadian authorities against him. He wrote to Admiral Blake, complaining that the factory had been boycotted and that no officers from any of the British purchasing missions had ever visited the facilities; 'Admiral Nelles returned from his visit to the Admiralty in London in September 1941, cancelled his orders and has done no work with us since.'

Early in May, Scotty learnt that the Admiralty had decided to arrange for the construction of Vosper motor torpedo boats in the United States by the Annapolis Boat Company. On hearing the news, Scotty wrote to Barker:

We are again going through a very bitter period. Here is all the work that we have done in getting these two factories started, overcoming our material difficulties, training our men, etc. etc., and all the acknowledgement we are getting from the people at home is for them to insist upon a major change to a Vosper type of boat to be built which everyone knows, has not one feature that is better than ours. It is slower, has less range and carries less load. I am informed on good authority.

Confusion is rampant everywhere. The building of his boats is entirely another promise as are their forecast of deliveries. The firm is putting up new buildings, the drawings are not reliable, and it is said, must be completely remade. They are, of course, touting Irwin's men, draftsmen and responsible people, quite a number of whom they have already cajoled away. All the work that we have done to get immediate deliveries is being thrown away, for what purpose, goodness only knows. And yet, in your letter to which I have just replied, you tell me that you are advising and helping Mackie's own firm and doing electrical and pipe work for V's and giving them information regarding progress and processing. All I can say is that it is almost beyond human nature to put up with it.

Virtually, I think we have become the laughing stock of Washington. I also found out that the new V which is supposed to go into construction here has not yet been passed out your end. Irwin also tells me that it has been modified again so as to more closely resemble the characteristics of our own design.[8]

Scotty and Elco both made urgent representations to Sir Clive Baillieu at the British Embassy in Washington. Scotty wrote to Barker:

Our main point in seeing Sir Clive was the appalling position of both Bayonne and Montreal being completely short of work and yet a policy of letting these two places die out and supporting a new programme for V boats necessitated the building of a new factory, new priorities, taking our men, etc., seems so inconsistent with a reasonable war policy that we had no other option.

Scotty went on to say that he had told Sir Clive that as one of the heaviest individual tax payers in England, he felt that he was entitled to at least an explanation. Stuart Barker attempted to provide some insight into the Admiralty policy that appeared so meaningless to Scott-Paine. He and Admiral Tower had been developing a close relationship and, as Barker explained on June 5th:

We have almost got to the stage that you and R. H. [Admiral Reginald Henderson] did, but with one very important difference, that he is very careful to explain that he cannot move outside recognised machinery . . . he expresses to me the outlook of the combined Departments, his weighing up of a situation—which I may say is done in the most able manner—makes it perfectly clear to me what he is getting at and why he is telling me.

Barker then went on to make it quite clear that Scott-Paine would not get clearance to travel back to Britain, to 'upset the apple cart and start raising a lot of questions in various places.' Barker continued:

There was a good deal of background reverting perhaps, to the past, which I can't possibly put down here, it would take too long; but he said that he quite realised there were a lot of difficulties that I was experiencing, and a great deal of back-chat against the Company from a number of Departments, and all I could do was to try and

wear it down. He said the real reason, and I think you will understand this perfectly, was that you and R. H. used to do so much together, and that R. H. did them in the most unorthodox manner possible. My friend [i.e. Admiral Tower], without wishing to speak ill of the dead, blamed him for it. If he had lived and carried on it might have been different, but there is no doubt about it, he upset a very great number of people who still remember this, and as you are still alive and the Company is, the reflection is still coming back on us.

Barker's conversation with Admiral Tower then turned to the choice of the Vosper boat as the standard MTB for the Royal Navy:

Now dealing with another aspect of your letter, you mention that this man states that it is the 'V' job that is going down over this side. My friend tells me that that is the case. Bear in mind, please, that he is merely the mouthpiece, but he informed me that the considered opinion is that our boat was designed entirely on our own lines and not in any way in conjunction with the Departments that might have been consulted. This, of course, I realize is perfectly true. They came down and saw it, but they saw it after it was designed and built. You must realise that I am taking the summing up of the position, not individuals. The other people [i.e. Vosper] consulted considerably before they built, and all these Departments like this sort of thing; apart from any other reason at all they are much more inclined to favour it because of that. That is why there is this 'hic-boo' going on your side that our people would like the other type of boat.

Barker's letter continued in a conciliatory vein:

[Tower] said he was grateful, and knew that the consensus of opinion in the Admiralty would be appreciative of your efforts in getting this Packard engine into production and helping on the design but whilst I am being perfectly frank in this matter I must say that he went on to remark that he didn't quite understand your attitude, expressed in one or two ways, that you have been left out of this type of thing. He said that he had ample evidence to prove that you were drawing a commission of 1¼% on the Packard price, and bearing in mind the number of engines that had been ordered, he thought you had been treated pretty well. He was careful to say that he had no objection at all, and thought it was reasonable that you should get something out of it; the only thing he didn't like was the implication, several times, that you had said you would never make a penny out of anything that was produced that side for here. I might just as well tell you this in this letter. If it is incorrect I think we ought to know, but that is the official view taken this side. Your help in getting the Elco boats away is appreciated but the feeling is that you are doing this in conjunction with your associates and that it is all part of your commercial transactions with them.[9]

Barker's feud with Maurice Wright continued as a bitter fight throughout the summer of 1941. Despite this, when Admiral Tower heard that Scotty had submitted a request for Barker to visit America, he refused and made it clear to Barker that, as Director of Naval Equipment, he was not willing to deal with anyone but Barker. Tower amplified:

I regard the rest of the people at Hythe, able as

they may be, as a pack of children compared with you, and I know perfectly well that if you took your guiding hand off this Company even for a few days, as your absence in America obviously would entail, in a different way from your going away for a few days holiday, the same kind of chaos might ensue as you know and I know perfectly well did ensue during your visit to America last year.

Barker was confident that things were going in his favour at Hythe and was pleased at the praise that was heaped on both Hythe and Marchwood when Peter Du Cane and Admiral Sir Philip Chetwode visited the yard in May. 'There is no question in my mind,' he wrote, 'that they were quite embarrassed at the extent of our business there.'

The amount of work on hand at Hythe and Poole during June 1941 was indeed impressive. Barker had seventeen of Selman's new 41 foot 6 inch boats on order, nine of which were laid down; sixteen boats

ST 360, one of the first 41 foot 6 inch seaplane tenders built in 1941 for air-sea rescue duties.

The 70 foot boats of the 6th Flotilla commanded by the renowned Lt Commander Hichens who worked closely with the British Power Boat Company on improving motor gun boats.

were being converted to Packard engines, thirteen of what he called the '33 Class', referring to the order for thirty-three 70 foot Masbies in September 1939, were under construction, eleven 63 foot High Speed Launches were under construction for the Royal Air Force, and the hull of the prototype 71 foot 6 inch motor gunboat was well on the way to completion. In addition, there were numerous small craft such as the 12 foot 6 inch 'Sea Gulls' and 16 foot Admiralty launches in various states of completion around the yard. Admiral Tower was well pleased and wrote a rare personal letter to Scotty:

I should like you to know that Mr Barker is doing excellent work. He has many difficulties to cope with, many of which must be difficult for you in America to understand, but he puts his back into the job and without him, your Company at Hythe

would not be doing anything like the work for the Country that it is.[10]

In the meantime, Scotty had failed to obtain orders for further boats to keep the Canadian Power Boat Company busy. The last order had been the confirmation, on December 28th, 1940, that a second batch of eight 70 foot motor torpedo boats was to be built for the Royal Netherlands Navy. But work in the factory proceeded at a remarkable rate on the boats in hand; the first hull was turned over during January 1941; five hulls were turned over during February; three 70 foot hulls and one 40 foot hull were turned over during March, and by July 28th, nineteen hulls had been turned over. By the summer, the factory had 490 employees, and by October 1st, the hulls of thirty-nine boats had been almost completed: six 70 foot boats for the Royal Canadian

Air Force, eleven 70 foot boats for the Royal Canadian Navy, sixteen 70 foot boats for the Royal Netherlands Navy and six 40 foot Armoured Target Boats for the Royal Canadian Air Force.

The operational experience with the 70 foot boats constructed by Elco led to several modifications in the design of the Canadian boats. Additional laminated frames forward of 34 bulkhead were fitted, and the hull shape was also modified with the sheer raised aft of the wheelhouse, additional intermediate timbers were inserted in the bottom, gunwales were enlarged, fittings were made stronger throughout the hull, and plywood decks were later introduced to improve longitudinal strength.[11]

Wartime shortages of materials also forced Scott-Paine to redesign details of the Canadian boats. For instance, the gun turrets of *PV 70* were built of aluminium, but a shortage of metal led to the adoption of a laminated timber construction, integral with the wheelhouse. Throughout the summer of 1941, considerable efforts were made to chase up supplies of castings, thrust bearings, torpedo tubes, glands for the anti-submarine gear and V-drives. Particular difficulty was experienced in obtaining armour plate for the Armoured Target Boats from the International Harvester Company. Supplies were eventually forthcoming after pressure had been brought to bear on various government deparments, and just as the fabrication was almost complete, the Royal Canadian Air Force notified the company on July 7th, that work on the armour plate was to be stopped as it had been decided to use the boats for towing targets rather than as armoured targets.

On May 16th, Scott-Paine telephoned Admiral Nelles and told him that the first boat was to be launched the next day. He was in a jubilant mood as the search for additional boats to send to Britain under lend lease had raised hopes that the Canadian Power Boat Factory at Montreal might be used to build Elco type boats for shipment across the Atlantic.

Two weeks later, Scotty attended a Works Conference at Elco's plant at Bayonne on June 2nd, to plan the transfer of the 70 foot Elco boats to the Royal Navy. The capture of Crete by the Germans was discussed along with the operational requirements for motor torpedo boats and motor gun boats in the Mediterranean. Scotty wrote to Barker:

the indecision and apparent lack of requirement of our articles has affected the outlook here and it was within an ace of being totally discontinued. However, last week the matter was settled and their great potential value recognised and a

programme is being embarked upon that would delight you [which], at the same time, visualises the way this new invention should be treated.[12]

Following the fall of Crete, the Admiralty enquired about the possibility of obtaining some of the motor torpedo boats then under construction for the Royal Canadian Navy by the Canadian Power Boat Company. As the need for motor torpedo boats in Canadian waters was deemed to have passed with the development of the submarine war in the North Atlantic, the Canadian Government agreed to the transfer of all twelve of the MTBs, and on September 9th, 1941, Scott-Paine was notified by Admiral A. H. Walker that the boats would be taken over by the British Admiralty Technical Mission.[13]

With the continuing difficulties in the delivery of components and the modifications required by the British Admiralty Technical Mission, it soon became obvious to Scott-Paine that he would not be able to complete and deliver the Royal Canadian Navy and Royal Netherlands Navy contracts before the freeze-up of the Lachine Canal in early November. The only way to get the boats clear of Montreal before the winter was to move them south before the close of navigation and complete the boats at a yard in the United States.

Scotty inspected almost every ship and boat yard between New London and New York and eventually chose Greenwich where Marine Design and Engineering Development Corporation had its main office. Greenwich had advantageous tax laws, an ideal harbour, with good rail connections and, while having a good supply of labour, was uninfluenced by the New York Trade Unions. Fortuitously, the Greenwich Shipyard at 648 Steamboat Road was closed down as all of its domestic work had been curtailed by the war, and, with only a few weeks to go before the onset of winter, Scotty concluded a five-month agreement with the yard for the completion of his Canadian boats as well as the repair of American PT boats.[14]

Agreements were reached with the British Admiralty Technical Mission to transfer the twelve MTBs, and with the Dutch to transfer six of their boats so that they could be made ready for shipment to the Dutch West Indies. Two crews were arranged in conjunction with the service departments and the inland waterway route through the Richelieu Canal and Lake Champlain was explored by Scotty who personally took the Dutch boat *TM 23* from Montreal to Greenwich on October 23rd. In spite of bad weather, the trip was completed without any trouble in twenty-five hours running time. However, what at first appeared as if it were to be a simple

Royal Canadian Navy MTB nearing completion
at Montreal, May 22nd, 1941.

operation, turned out to require a feat of organisation as great as anything Scotty had undertaken
before. At the heart of the problem was the network
of red tape required by the US Customs, the US
Immigration officials and the New York State
Department of Canals and Waterways.

On the following day, October 24th, 1941, the first
flotilla of four MTBs for the British Admiralty Technical Mission, Nos *332*, *333*, *335* and *336*, were
commissioned and set out for Greenwich with Royal
Canadian Navy crews. On October 27th, Scotty
received word that the flotilla was in difficulties due
to bad weather: *335* and *336* had damaged their
underwater gear, while *332* was hard aground on a
reef in Lake Champlain off Point au Fer. *MTB 332*
was none other than *PV 70* whose adventurous
history already included a stormy crossing of Lake
Champlain in the summer of 1940 and the dramatic
stranding off Richibucto as *CMTB 1* in the winter of
1940. Despite a shortage of men, the Montreal
factory sent out a salvage team, led by Beauforte-
Greenwood, to remove the engines and torpedo
tubes and to construct a coffer dam around the
damaged bows. The boat was got off the reef by 1st

November and was safely towed to Greenwich for
repairs. It was a remarkable tribute to *PV 70* that,
despite this second mishap in her career, she went on
to give several years service with the Royal Navy
and, subsequently, the Royal Air Force in India.

Meanwhile, as the operation moved into its second
week, the factory was in daily contact with the
Weather Observatory at McGill University in
Montreal, and as the weather deteriorated, plans for
the movement of the boats were modified. As there
was an extra week of clear water at St Johns, Quebec,
after the beginning of the freeze-up at Montreal, it
was decided to move boats there as a precautionary
measure. Arrangements were made with the Cusoms
authorities at St Johns for the mooring of the boats
under armed guard while Canadian Power Boat
employees did last minute jobs fitting parts and
painting. When some four or five boats had been
collected at St Johns, they were transferred to Troy,
New York, where they were left under the armed
guard of the New York State Police. *TM 24* arrived
at Troy on November 1st and *TM 25* arrived on the
3rd, and thence was taken direct to Greenwich. By
this time, it was realised that four of the Royal Navy

70 foot boat built for the Royal Canadian Navy,
leaving Montreal on December 1st, 1941.

MTBs would be unable to proceed under their own
power and arrangements were put in hand for towing
by the Davie Transport Tug Company. The local
Naval Service Headquarters provided four ratings to
handle *MTB 340* through the locks and canals as it
left Montreal on November 1st. The tow was
concluded successfully and on November 4th the
four ratings returned to Montreal and joined *MTB
341* as it left the factory under tow. Soon after it left
the Lachine Canal, the Naval Service Headquarters
withdrew their ratings and a scratch crew of four
Nova Scotians from the factory was put together.
The men, all with considerable boating experience
were rushed through immigration formalities and
overtook the tow below St Johns where they replaced
the Naval crew.

*MTB*s *337, 338* and *339* were commissioned on
November 5th and set off under their own power
with Royal Canadian Navy crews. With the benefit

of a local pilot for the trip across Lake Champlain,
the boats made a rapid trip direct to Greenwich.
Early the next day, Scotty left St Johns at the helm of
TM 22, arriving at Greenwich during the afternoon.
MTB 342 left Montreal under tow on November 8th,
but a substitute crew had to be put together as the
experienced tow crew had failed to return from
Greenwich in time for the departure. When they did
arrive, they were rushed by car to St Johns where
they picked up *MTB 342*. Three days later, on
November 11th, the two remaining Dutch boats,
TM 26 and *TM 27* left Montreal under the command
of the Canadian Power Boat pilot, James Yeaman
and Captain Thomson of the Royal Canadian Navy
respectively. They made the trip to Greenwich
without difficulty. *TM 24* was still lying at Troy, but
left for Greenwich on November 15th with Scotty at
the helm.

The last of the four motor torpedo boats to leave

158

The British Admiralty Technical Mission boats
at the Greenwich Boatyard, January 23rd, 1942.

the factory under tow left Montreal on November
13th. Slush ice covered the basin by the Lachine
Canal the very next day, and, on November 26th,
the Department of Canals officially announced that
the navigation was closed for the winter. The
movement of the six boats for the Royal Netherlands

and the twelve boats for the British Admiralty
Technical Mission was a triumph. In addition to this
feat, six 70 foot High Speed Launches and one 40
foot target towing boat were completed and handed
over to Royal Canadian Air Force crews for delivery
to Halifax by November 12th.[15]

CHAPTER 22
Turning of the Tide

Scott-Paine decided to act on what appeared to be a crisis at Hythe. Stuart Barker had long realised that he needed help in the management of the yard and had even asked Sir Geoffrey Blake to return from the Admiralty. Blake was unable to obtain permission and, in October 1941, Scotty cabled an old friend, Colonel Frank Searle, who had been a fellow director on the board of Imperial Airways, asking him to take up the role of Deputy Chairman, with Wilson Hamill remaining as Acting Chairman. The decision coincided with a sudden breakdown in Stuart Barker's health. He had been attending the official trial of the *Queen Gull*, when he collapsed with exhaustion and overwork. He was sent on compulsory sick leave, taking a little cottage by the 'Jolly Sailor' pub at Bursledon, a village on the River Hamble, about three miles east of Southampton, and well away from the bombing.

Scotty wrote to his General Manager:

I was so very sorry to hear of your nervous smash! That's just the way it goes, such a pity. How are you? I hope and know Marjorie will insist that this time, at all events, you make a proper recovery, no patching, a proper job. Just relax, you have all of us, your friends, a new one in Col Searle, who can take the load off your job . . . We all want a rested and vigorous SNB.[1]

As he recovered at Bursledon, Barker wrote again to Scott-Paine, reflecting over the difficulties of communication by letter that often took three months to cross the Atlantic:

As I go thorugh my files, I find that you do not answer the tone of my letters, and in fact you seem to ignore them completely. I often wonder how you look at my letters your end. Do you open them yourself, glance through them to see if they

contain anything important, and thereafter park them on one side, or does someone read them through and then give you the gist of what they think they should . . . do you realise how angry I can be when I think about all this and how you have left me in this position.[2]

Before the letter reached Scotty, the motor torpedo boats that he had developed for the United States Navy were to be thrown into the centre of the world stage. On December 7th, 1941, Japanese aeroplanes attacked Pearl Harbor, where PT Boat Squadron 1, commanded by Lieutenant Commander William C. Specht was based. By this time, there were three PT boat Squadrons; Squadron 2 was at the New York Navy Yard and No 3, comprising six of the new 77 foot Elco boats, was in the Philippines at Manila Bay. The part played in the defence of the Philippines by the PT Boats, commanded by Lieutenant John D. Bulkeley, and the evacuation of General MacArthur in *PT 41*, was to become a legend in the history of the United States Navy. President Roosevelt's faith in Scott-Paine's boats had been repaid and when Lieutenant Bulkeley returned to the United States he brought with him a verbal message from General MacArthur for delivery to the President, the Secretary of War, the Secretary of the Navy, the Commander in Chief US Fleet and Chief of Naval Operations:[3]

Motor torpedo boats should be the basis of a separate branch of the service for specialists, and who must have confidence in their own weapons.

These boats can be used effectively for coastal defence 200 miles or 300 miles offshore, in the Philippine Islands, straits, narrows and potential blocks.

There is no other location such as the Philippine

Islands and the islands south of the Philippines where they can be so effectively used.

With enough of this type of craft, hostile Japanese shipping could be kept from invading an island or continent, and kept 200 to 300 miles offshore.

I want 100 or more MTBs of your type with the improvements which have been developed since the outbreak of war. Two hundred boats if possible with the tenders, spare parts, and equipment necessary for them within 8 months.

In the event, between December 7th, 1941, and the end of the war, the United States Navy gave contracts for the building of 754 PT Boats. The popular publication of the exploits of Squadron 3 in *They Were Expendable*, which appeared later in 1942, was the pinnacle of Scott-Paine's adventurous career. His vision of a motor torpedo boat had become a reality, thanks to the foresight of the Presi-

dent of the United States, the engineering expertise of Elco and the courage of the young men who fought with them in often impossible situations.[4]

But the tide of Scotty's fortunes was about to turn. Whilst the United States Navy was building up its PT Boat fleet, his association with Elco was coming to an end. A bitter row developed between him and the Bureau of Ships which insisted that Scotty had no claim on the 80 foot PT boat, which had been decided upon as the standard PT following the Plywood Derbies. Scotty was outraged: 'My associate company, the Electric Boat Company', he complained to the Minister of Munitions in Canada, 'has been ordered to carry out a certain policy whereby they broke off relationships with us as they no longer wish to be associated with a vessel of British design. They lengthened our 77 ft boat by a few feet, raised its chine line and altered the slope of its bow, trying to alter its individuality and make it possible to designate it as an American designed vessel.' His old

A Canadian Power Boat Company 70 foot boat
transferred to the Royal Navy.

friend Henry Sutphen was sympathetic to Scotty's point of view, but would not agree to his claim that he should be paid a commission on the sale of the new Elco boats. He told Scotty that his claim was outrageous, for although the 80 foot boat, with its hardchine form and Packard engines had many Scott-Paine features incorporated into its design, it owed as much to Elco's development work as it did to Scotty's original design. The final break in relations came when Scotty arrived at the Bayonne works in his Rolls-Royce, only to be told by the gateman that he was not allowed to enter the factory.[5]

Scotty continued his battle to obtain work for the Canadian Power Boat Company. The British Admiralty Technical Mission boats and the Royal Netherlands Navy boats that had been transferred to Greenwich were being altered for service in the West Indies, while the remainder of the 1940 orders were being completed at Montreal. A journalist, George W. Sutton Jnr, accompanied the trial of one of the Royal Netherlands Navy motor torpedo boats on the St Lawrence River:

The trip I took on the St Lawrence in one of these boats was an eye-opener. With some foreign naval officers aboard with their engineering officials, mechanics and seamen, as well as Scott-Paine's own crew and young Ed Gregory of Detroit, Packard inspecting engineer, we started at slow speed down the river. Before we returned we had been half way to Quebec and back, almost 150 miles, running for various periods at various speeds for the official observance of the foreign accepting engineers . . . So smoothly did the three great white-painted Packards function and so harmoniously did her hull form embrace the water that there was no sensation of excessive speed, no vibration and, even with almost thirty people a vessel intended for a crew of eight or nine, there was no feeling of crowding.

We got one moment of excitement to show us partially what the boat could do in turbulent water. A big freighter was coming up the river at a narrow and shallow spot at 14 knots, throwing huge bow waves and stern waves. Scott-Paine had

Canadian *S-09* in August 1941. The boat was built at Hythe in 1939, and became *PT 9* before transfer under Lend-Lease.

162

to steer, without reducing speed because of trial conditions, directly into the bow waves within ten or fifteen feet of the ship. The bow went high up as she leaped from the dead smooth water to that first wave with a concussion that almost tore my uppers from their moorings. But she never faltered and in a few seconds we had cut safely through a miniature storm that would have engulfed a less able craft.[6]

Much to Scotty's pleasure, the three-year old *PT 9*, which had been built at Hythe in the heady days before the outbreak of war, had arrived in Montreal in August 1941. Along with some other PT Boats of the original Squadron 1, the boats had been transferred to Britain under lend lease and then lent to the Canadian Government to replace its boats that had been taken over by the Admiralty. The Rolls-Royce engines of *PT 9* had been transferred to the Royal Canadian Air Force and the boat had arrived under tow to have two Kermath engines installed. Re-designated *SO 9*, she was re-commissioned on September 25th, 1942 and set out for Halifax, before being sent to Toronto in May 1944 to serve as a firing range patrol vessel off Frenchman's Bay.[7]

The Montreal factory was rapidly running out of work, and most of the workforce had been laid off by June 1942. It was heart-breaking for Scotty, who had almost killed himself building the factory and training the staff. He employed George Sutton as a public relations advisor to 'revive the fact that the credit that is being given to a great many people for the design and construction of the Mosquito or PT boats belongs to me'. On July 20th, 1942, Scotty attended the launch of HCMS *Montreal III*, a re-fitted submarine-chaser of World War One, where he met the Minister of Marine, Angus MacDonald, whom he tried to interest in developing the role of motor torpedo boats. He also spoke to Vice-Admiral Percy Nelles, who was also at the launch, but was firmly told that there was no likelihood of a change of policy.

A few days later, he met Desmond Clark, Director of the Ministry of Shipbuilding who had received an enquiry from the United States about the availability of spare capacity to build MTBs at St Patrick Street. However, nothing came of this approach and, on July 22nd, Scotty went to see the Minister of Munitions and Supply, S. D. Howe, in his office in the Houses of Parliament, Ottawa. He told the Minister that the Canadian Power Boat Company had no work, and, in a lengthy discussion, he again stressed the role of fast motor boats in combating the U-Boat threat, and the fact that he was the sole inventor of all motor torpedo boats in action throughout the world.[8]

George Woods Humphery was lukewarm about

The final batch of boats nearing completion at Montreal on May 18th, 1942.

Scotty's attempts to change Canadian motor torpedo boat policy, as the month before he had obtained a contract from de Havilland Aircraft of Canada Ltd for the production of fuselages and wing-flaps for the all-wood Mosquito aircraft. Scotty accepted the inevitable and agreed to turn over the St Patrick Street plant to this new work. Although it involved a considerable amount of re-tooling for the factory, the construction of parts for the Mosquito aircraft was to keep a significant part of Scotty's workforce in employment at Montreal through- out the rest of the war.

Scotty wrote to Bill Sheaff in England that 'we are now producing the DH Mosquito instead of the SP Mosquito,' but work was also started on a new private venture motor torpedo boat, 'PV 73'. The boat was powered by two of the latest Packard 4M-2500 engines, and, with an overall length of 73 foot, was slightly larger than the 70 foot boats. The lines were redesigned, and Scotty introduced many improvements based on his experience with the American PT boats and the boats built at Montreal over the previous year and a half. It was designed to facilitate pre-fabrication of entire areas of the accommodation such as the officers' quarters and the engine room, for subsequent installation into the hull. During trials, *PV 73* achieved a speed of 45 knots in a light condition.[9]

The construction of *PV 73* in 1942 was to be Scotty's last major project, but, while the tide was running out for him in Canada and America, it was turning in favour of his old yard at Hythe, where

Barker had returned to work in February 1942. Searle's arrival in the yard had been greeted with mixed feelings. Bill Sheaff wrote that he 'is certainly bucking things up and since M.W. left us, things seem to be working much more smoothly . . . we shall soon be one happy family again, instead of always at loggerheads.' Others found the new Deputy Chairman difficult to get on with. He was later described by George Selman as 'a man who had a hell of a presence . . . you know he was a sort of a stage colonel, fresh complexion, white moustache, white hair, upright—big man with quite a bearing. It was all bluff.'[10]

Selman's work on the prototype motor gun boat was the subject of enthusiastic praise when it was formally handed over to the Royal Navy in February 14th, 1942. Lieutenant Commander Hichens wrote: 'Gun boats were on the map. They had acquired full status as one of the weapons for combatting the E-boat'. It was the start of a long association between Selman and Hichens which ended only when the

Hichens was killed in action on April 13th, 1943. Soon after the introduction of the new MGBs, Hichens came to Selman, complaining that enemy E-Boats could hear the engines of the motor gun boats miles away. He suggested that the engines could be silenced by taking the exhaust pipes through the bottom of the boat near the transom. Selman's response was that it could not be done, but such was the force of Hichen's personality that he persuaded the designer to try the idea, with startling results. Not only was an almost silent approach made possible, but the speed of the boats was increased by 3 knots. The underwater exhaust did, however, seriously affect the steering of the boats, and it took months of experimenting with different types of rudder before Selman found a simple solution; adding small fins to the rudders. Selman later said of Hichens: 'He was really a first class bloke'.[11]

As Scott-Paine's fortunes declined in Canada, the British Power Boat Company was developing new types of boat at Hythe. In February 1942, Selman

MTB 488, a Mark VI 71 foot 6 inch British Power Boat craft combining the role of motor gun boat and motor torpedo boat.

A British Power Boat Company 64 foot HSL
rescuing ditched airmen in the English Channel.

was asked by the Ministry of Aircraft Production to design an air/sea rescue boat to replace the earlier 63 foot, high speed launches. Scotty's design philosophy had always been the pursuit of speed, but the improvements that had been made in aircrew flotation gear and dingies now meant that it was more important to be able to get to ditched aircrews in all weathers rather than get to them very quickly in fair weather. The brief was to design a boat with good sea-keeping qualities with a minimum top speed of about 25 knots. The new boat was also to be designed so that it could proceed to a rendezvous position and remain there for some hours, keeping position with its head to the sea, or stemming the tide using one engine throttled back. The older 63 foot and 64 foot high speed launches had not been suitable for this type of operation.[12]

Selman informed the Board of the British Power Boat Company in February 1942 that he had been asked to design a new air/sea rescue boat. Within weeks, a preliminary order for eleven boats had been

received. Selman had been told that the boat was to have two or more engines of proved reliability and that: 'In this respect, no technical records are held by Air/Sea Rescue, but it is understood that Coastal Command, the users of marine craft do not consider the Napier Lion engine to be of proved reliability.' Despite this, the 68 foot High Speed Launch was designed with three Napier engines. The hull was designed with a high rise to the chine to reduce pounding and improve sea keeping qualities, and extensive hospital accommodation was designed for the comfort of rescued airmen. The height of wheelhouse, which provided easy access to the hospital accommodation for stretcher cases, gave the boats the nick-name of 'Hants and Dorset', after the double-decker buses that took many workers to Hythe from their homes in Southampton.

The design of the 68 foot HSL was completed in March 1942 when, before work on a prototype had even started, an urgent order for eight-two of the new boats was placed. There was no shortage of work at

A British Power Boat Company 63 foot HSL which had its bow destroyed by a shell off Cherbourg. Despite the damage it planed back at speed to its base on the south coast.

HSL 2688, a 68 foot air-sea rescue boat designed by George Selman to Air Ministry specifications.

Hythe: in April 1942, there were four 63 foot high speed launches under construction along with two of the new 71 foot 6 inch motor gun boats and three 41 foot 6 inch launches for the RAF. The yard was also constructing large numbers of the 'Queen Gulls' and had orders for 16 foot and 18 foot dingies, a number of 25 foot Fast Motor Boats and 24 foot launches. The total number of employees was about one thousand five hundred men, women and boys, and a further five hundred were employed at Poole where it was agreed, a number of the 68 foot HSLs were to be built for 'dispersal reasons.'[13]

The success of the 71 foot 6 inch gun boat led to Selman being asked to provide preliminary designs for a larger gun boat. Several designs, including one for a 115 foot boat, were produced, but nothing came of the idea. The need for a more heavily armed gun boat was argued by Hichens who, with George Selman and Marine Mountings Ltd, came up with a proposal for a light-weight mounting for a hand-operated Oerlikon so that an additional gun could be carried. It was the start of a long campaign to improve the gun boat in the face of what Hichens described as 'the extraordinarily intractible attitude taken up by the authorities immediately responsible for the development of our boats, who turned their faces deliberately and steadfastly against our pleadings'. Selman worked closely with Hichens and in November 1942, he reported that he was working on a proposal to improve the offensiveness of the 71 foot 6 inch boat by stripping out the interior in order to save weight so that additional armaments might be carried.[14]

On several occasions, Hichens and his gun boats had come up against larger enemy vessels that would have made ideal targets for a torpedo boat. The gun boat was unsuitable for attacking anything larger than an E-Boat. Hichens wrote that, 'except for the excessively risky chance of delivering a successful depth charge attack . . . the ultimate ideal for the small fast boat was obviously for the gun boats to carry torpedoes, and the torpedo boats to carry sufficient guns to enable them to tackle E-Boats. If this could be achieved,' Hichens asserted, 'there would be a vast saving of boats and personnel. Both type could tackle either job.' Selman's response was to submit five proposals, all based on the light-weight hand-operated Oerlikon mount which he had developed with Marine Mountings, for converting the 71

foot 6 inch boat into a combined gun and torpedo boat.

MGB 123 was selected for a mockup of a new gun arrangement which was viewed by a conference of Admiralty officials and naval officers on February 25th, 1943. Selman and Hichens were both infuriated when the gun arrangement they had mocked-up was rejected in favour of an inferior gun arrangement designed by the DNC. Selman handed Hitch a wooden mockup of a machine gun, saying, 'Here, take this and give it to your young boys'.

During the summer of 1943, *MGB 123* was developed as a prototype motor torpedo/motor gun boat, and later re-designated *MTB 446*. A further seventy-one of the highly successful MTBs were built during the war and, despite the addition of more and more armament, Selman managed to maintain the performance of the boat through the development of new propeller types. In March 1944, George Selman visited Bath with R. A. Manthei, then the Deputy General Manager of the yard, and was told by Holt, who had rejected the 71 foot 6 inch boat when it had first been designed in January 1941, that the type was 'absolutely second to none in service'.[15]

During 1943, Selman designed and built a 30 foot radio-controlled target boat, known as 'Queen Pelican'. It was powered by a single Napier Lion engine and was estimated to have a speed of 30 knots. The engine and radio control equipment was to be installed in an armoured box, designed to be placed as a unit into the hull which, like the 'Queen Gull', was sub-divided into a number of water-tight compartments, filled with Onazote to provide reserve bouyancy. The construction of the 'Queen Pelican' took several months, and considerable problems were experienced with the radio control equipment designed by Victor Bull in association with Rediffusion. Preliminary radio trials were held near Bournemouth and in December 1943, it was handed over for preliminary trials with HMS *Excellent* before being taken by Kenneth St John Beaumont to Scapa Flow for operational trials.[16]

The Hythe yard was busier than it had ever been and, further work came in June 1943 when the War Office ordered a number of target towing launches identical in most respects to the 68 foot high speed launch being built for air/sea rescue duties. Across the Atlantic, however, Scotty knew little of what was going on at Hythe as communication with England remained difficult and, apart from occasional visits from Wilson Hamill, he was out of contact with the factory that he had built up from nothing and which he had 'loved as a mother loves her child'. Notwithstanding, the fact that the yard was now the most complex and sophisticated boat building operations

MGB 123 undergoing trials as the prototype British Power Boat Company motor torpedo boat. It was later re-numbered *MTB 446*.

The launching of a motor gun boat at Hythe
during World War Two.

of World War Two, Scotty might have been forgiven
if he had got the impression from Bill Sheaff's letters
that the opposite was the case and that the management of the yard was out of control.

Scotty's 'little bodyguard of faithful fellows'
watched the management changes with some misgivings. 'I wish you would come back,' Sheaff wrote
in July 1941: 'I have been trying to tell some of the
people over here that if only some of them were to
work as hard and as well as you, we should have the
tide turning full flood.' Stuart Barker resigned his
position as Managing Director to become Technical
Director in October 1942, and an industrial
efficiency expert, R. A. Manthei, was appointed as
Deputy General Manager. Sheaff wrote that 'his
ideas are alright where about 25,000 hands are
employed but not for a factory of this size. In fact one
of the old hands remarked that the trial boat [*MGB
123*] which was built in record time is no record, as a
boat was built and finished in much less time when
you were here.'[17]

Sheaff often sent Scotty the best wishes from his old
gang. 'Best of luck to Bob Freemantle', he wrote,
'from old special shop hands such as G. Thomas,
Charlie Chiverton, Steve Biggs—Biggs is now a big
noise at Poole. The man at Southampton Station
asks after you and says he misses his little drop of
whisky.' To Scotty's dismay, Tommy Quelch, who
had worked with him on all his great triumphs,
including *Miss Britain III*, had been passed over for
promotion within George Selman's design office and
had left the company in October 1942. 'Poor old
Tommy Quelch in his heart did not want to leave the
old place,' Sheaff wrote to Scotty, 'although he has
stepped into a very good job . . . he has been
miserable for a long time.'

Colonel Searle's style of management at Hythe
caused a revolution in January 1943 and again
Admiral Tower had to visit the yard and 'read the
riot act'. Sheaff was in no doubt as to who was in the
wrong:

Struma, a British Power Boat 68 foot target towing launch built for the Royal Army Service Corp in 1944.

To begin with Colonel Searle has most definitely saved the place from going down any further. He has had a most difficult time of it. This being due to the fact that most of the executives would not receive him as they should have done. The way they have carried on amounts almost to sabotage. This is a very strong word to say, but it is the way I view it. I went to No 2 Factory on Friday last to see Bill Bradbury about some transport. He was telling me about the bust up and his views are now we have the Colonel they are getting better every day and now these rats have shown themselves in their true colours it may make things easier for the Colonel . . . You will no doubt see a vast difference in the place when you get here some day, the sooner the better as far as the old hands are concerned.[18]

CHAPTER 23
The End of an Era

Early in 1943, the Canadian motor torpedo boats that had been turned over to the Royal Navy in 1941, returned from service in the Caribbean, making the 3,200-mile trip back to New York under their own power. The boats were to be refitted for service with the Royal Air Force in India, but Scotty was again disappointed when he learnt that, although the Canadian Power Boat Company was to provide technical expertise, it had not been selected to carry out the work on the boats. The modifications were completed by the end of the year when Scotty was delighted to be taken out in his old *PV 70*. 'We were out in my old PV, five years and four months old', he wrote to William McComb of Packards:

Just as good as new and running as sweetly as a sewing machine—what an amazing career she's had, half way round the globe, reputed to have sunk a U-Boat, rescued 68 men from the deep ocean, trained the Dutch, Norwegians and Swedes, the British and Canadians, and with your engines, in Canada 1940 and at Trinidad, ran over 1,000 hours without any engine overhaul, attention or adjustment. Just filter treatment.[1]

Scott-Paine shared his disappointments about the shortage of work at Montreal and what he called 'the mutinous stupidities at Hythe', with his old colleague Sir Geoffrey Blake who had been appointed flag officer liaison with the United States naval forces in Europe in 1943. He complained,

The war has hit me very hard . . . I have not received the benefit of the Dutch, French or Baltic contracts. I have had to pay for and have had to bear the financial responsibilities with which, in my vainglorious haste to try and be of some use to the people at home, I loaded myself building

factories etc. which have been very heavy. On top of it all I am not weathering very grandly.[2]

Frank Searle crossed the Atlantic in March 1944 to bring Scotty up to date on the situation at Hythe and to discuss post-war plans. Despite the reports he had received about Searle's management problems, Scotty learnt that Hythe was still the most sophisticated mass production boat building yard in the country, and was producing the 71 foot 6 inch motor torpedo boats at the remarkable rate of about one every week. The first of the twenty-one 68 foot target towing launches for the War Office had successfully undergone official trials in January, 1944, and the last of the eighty-two 68 foot High Speed Launches ordered in May 1943 was almost ready for handing over. Fifty-five had been built at Hythe and twenty-six at Poole.[3]

Searle also took some pleasure in recounting the successes of the No 2 Factory at Poole, which was still fully engaged in the construction of 68 foot HSLs and repairs to MTBs. Scotty was intrigued to hear that his pre-war 64 foot and 60 foot boats were still in service and were being re-fitted at Poole as distant control boats or minesweeper attendant craft. Searle expressed the view that company policy should be to concentrate work at Hythe as the Poole contracts would soon be coming to an end. In January 1944, the Deputy Director of Dockyards, Mr Bassett, had visited Poole, and had told Bill Bradbury that the yard was unlikely to receive any new construction work. With the invasion of Europe in mind, his instructions were to turn the yard over to the repair of metal landing craft as soon as one could be made available for training purposes.

Searle also told Scotty about possible new work. Just before he had left for America, George Selman had again been asked to design an airborne rescue dingy. In February, complete designs and a brief

45 foot round bilge boat constructed at Hythe during 1945.

specification had been sent to the Ministry of Aircraft Production for a 30 foot dingy for dropping from a Warwick aircraft. The boat was designed to accommodate ten men and could be powered by an Austin 8 engine, sails or oars. The construction of the hull was both simple and light-weight, a double-chine structure, with straight frames covered with two skins of plywood. It was to be built in six longitudinal segments, each 'shaped like the quarter of an orange', that could be assembled into a complete boat with bolts.[4]

Another possibility of new work at Hythe was an enquiry for a 45 foot General Service Launch for the War Department. Selman had proposed a modified 41 foot 6 inch boat, but the War Department opted for an Admiralty design, and for the first time the Board at Hythe had agreed to take on the construction of round bilge boats.

Scotty was pleased that, in February 1944, the Board at Hythe had placed a memorandum on the work's notice board, asking employees for their ideas for postwar work. The electrical department came up with two suggestions; a 'midget' radio for use in motor cars and a washing machine that could be

manufactured for a cost of £21 11s. 0d. The most hopeful avenue appeared to be the construction of wooden temporary houses. George Selman had met with the Southampton Borough Architect to discuss the construction of timber temporary houses, designed to last ten years, but had come away feeling that a house could be designed using of high-quality ply that would last fifty to sixty years. A design based on stressed plywood panels, of the sort used in both the 71 foot 6 inch and 68 foot boats was soon completed and, in February, 1944, a building licence was obtained for a prototype 'Scottwood' house. A model was shown to the Board members and authority was given for the construction of a quarter scale model in the mould loft under the direction of Reg Holley.[5]

Searle concluded his report to Scotty with news that the training centre at Marchwood House had been closed down the previous September, when the Air Ministry had taken over the house as a rehabilitation centre for airmen who had undergone the new treatment of plastic surgery for extensive burns. British Power Boat employees arranged regular stag parties for the disfigured airmen, who produced small items of equipment for the boats at Hythe in the workshops that had been used by the women trainees.

The long standing rift between Scotty and Stuart Barker came to a head as soon as Frank Searle arrived back at Hythe in April 1944. Barker's relationship with his old friend and mentor had deteriorated despite Beauforte-Greenwood intervening on his behalf. 'I get along with S.P. well', he had written to Barker, 'he is always helpful and I am at a loss to understand what your differences with him really are. It was quite understood between us that our long friendship should never be broken whatever happened and I intend to keep to that agreement. I look upon it this way—he is the Chief and pays and therefore is up to me to meet his wishes.'[6]

Stuart Barker resigned from the company in April 1944, and in July a farewell dinner was given at which a presentation of a gold wrist-watch was made by the 'old hands all of whom have been at the factory for a good many years'. Bill Sheaff told Scotty about the presentation:

Amongst them there was Len Tilbury, Thomas Jeans, Jack and Harry Banks, Chiverton, Madgewick, Selman, Headland, Downing, Austin and Thomas and a good deal more. Of course speeches were made by a few, amongst them being poor old Leonard. He started off by saying that he would rather they asked him to adjust a carburettor or something as he was right out of place making speeches.

Stuart Barker responded with a nostalgic look back over the days at Hythe before the war, before proposing a toast to the absent Scott-Paine. A week later he wrote to his old friend and 'governor'.

I thought I would just write and tell you that all the old hands—and I mean the really old hands that we all knew gave me a wonderful reception a few nights ago and a most wonderful gold wrist watch which has gained only one second and a half per day, and I can guess it must have cost a packet in these days.

I am enclosing a cutting from the *Southern Daily Echo*. It doesn't really say enough, but I did pay you a lot of compliments which in many ways you deserve.

I nearly quoted you a verse from Kipling but refrained.[7]

The factory at Hythe was still fully occupied and orders for the round bilge boats were filling the gap left as the motor torpedo boats were completed. The Admiralty had ordered forty 45 foot 'Medium Speed Picket Boats' in July 1944, the War Department ordered ninety-eight 44 foot 6 inch hard-chine launches in September 1944, and were to order forty 50 foot general service launches on March 28th, 1945. The Ministry of Aircraft Production had ordered a further forty 68 foot High Speed Launches in July 1944 and thirty 24 foot marine tenders were ordered on March 24th, 1945.

Although some of these orders were to be reduced or cancelled after the end of hostilities in Europe, there was no evidence at the beginning of 1945 that there was going to be any shortage of work for Hythe as the war drew to a close. In addition, George Selman was designing and building a prototype long distance air sea rescue boat with an operating range of 2,000 miles, for use in the Pacific. During late 1944 Selman had put forward a number of schemes for boats ranging in length from 111 foot to 115 foot, and on February 20th, 1945 a contract was secured for the construction of a prototype 111 foot Long Range Rescue Craft, powered by four Napier Sabre engines. It was a red letter day for George Selman whose team started work on what was to be its masterpiece, and arguably the finest wooden boat of the entire war. Selman worked day and night, even taking a camp bed to the office, and the design work was finished in only six weeks. Reg Holley in the mould loft produced the tank test models in record time and in June, 1945, work started on the prefabrication of the main longitudinals in a large shed that had recently been completed on the mole at Hythe.[8]

As the war entered its final phases Scott-Paine spent most of his time at Greenwich, Connecticut, leaving George Woods Humphery and Beauforte-Greenwood to look after the Montreal factory and the de Havilland contract. With a view of postwar work at Montreal, Scotty encouraged his chief draughtsman, A.G. Hall to work on the design of a round-bilge 'marine station wagon', a 24 foot general service launch that emerged in 1946 as the *Sea Beaver*. A possibility of further work came in December 1944, when Hall was approached by the Scientific Advisor to the Chief of General Staff, to look at the manufacturing of plywood mudshoes, for use in the event of American troops getting bogged down in mud during the advance through France. A mudshoe could not be designed along the lines of a standard snow shoe so Hall came up with a design for a shoe very much like a miniature boat hull with three steps, to prevent back slip. Scotty came up to Montreal to inspect the prototypes which he took back to Greenwich where he and John Scott-Paine tested them on the mud of the harbour. An official demonstration was arranged at Greenwich during January 1945, following which further trials were held at McGill University, Montreal. The mudshoe was highly successful and allowed a man to walk over deep soft mud with little difficulty, but the army's operational requirement did not materialise and it never went into production.[9]

Scotty harboured a dream that there would be a postwar market for motor torpedo boats based on his PV 73 design. He made up his mind that he would return to England after the war to build a new yard at Marchwood, near Southampton. He wrote to his associates in America securing their continued co-operation in his plans, including Ted Meyer of the Federal Mogul Propeller Company of Detroit, whom he had first met during the Detroit International Trophy Race in 1930, and who had manufactured propellers for Scott-Paine boats throughout the war. Despite his bitterness at the Admiralty decision to buy Vosper boats built in America, he had been happy for Ted Meyer to make available to Vosper the propellers they had jointly developed. The propellers had increased the speed of the American-built Vosper boats from 33 knots to 40 knots, some *twenty* per cent, and Scotty wrote to Meyer:

> Ted, I do want you to give me some part of our arrangement in writing which will enable me when the war is over to show that despite the wastage, the eight months building time, the nine months overrunning of the contract time, making seventeen months in all that was wasted in placing the Vosper contract as against using our boats, it had to take part of the arrangements that I made to turn the whole thing from a first class fiasco into what is still the slowest war vessel of its type. I shall be very much obliged personally because in any event the matter should go on record between us.[10]

Scott-Paine was particularly anxious that his role as inventor of the American PT Boat should be recognised after the war. In December 1944, he received a final payment of $200,000 in recognition of his services to Elco and the Secretary of the Navy, James Forrestal wrote;

> I would like to take this occasion to express the Navy Department's appreciation for the contribution which you have made to the development of one of its new and most successful weapons of war.
> I refer to the motor torpedo boat, its original conception and basic design, in the pioneering

and development of which you have figured so prominently.

> We have come a long distance in this field since the day when motor torpedo boat [*PT-9*] was first demonstrated by you to the Navy's representatives some five years ago. The exploits of our motor torpedo boat squadrons in both the European and Pacific theatres of war constitute one of the most thrilling chapters in the story of our war accomplishments. From the very first days of the war, the PT's have been in the thick of the fight and we believe they will continue their good work without interruption up to the day of final Victory.

> It was fortunate that the United States Navy was enabled to take advantage of your years of research and experimentation in this field so as to permit it to enter into motor torpedo boat construction with the minimum of delay. The savings in time made possible by the acquisition of your design accomplishments, by the use of your patents and by the engineering services which you rendered to Electric Boat Company in connection with its motor torpedo boat building have paid dividends many times over.[11]

The end of hostilities brought a sudden end to new work at Montreal and at Hythe, where many of the existing contracts were reduced or cancelled. To Selman's bitter disappointment, the contract for the 111 foot Long Range Rescue Craft was cancelled on September 22nd, 1945, following the end of the war with Japan. By this time the hull was well advanced and although it was completed and launched, the marinised Sabre engines were never installed in Selman's creation which Scotty instructed should be sold. Selman walked the decks of his masterpiece, wishing that he could set it alight. In the event, the hull ended its days as a houseboat in Poole Harbour.[12]

However, the construction of round bilge boats for the War Department continued to provide enough work to keep a reduced work force together at Hythe well into 1946. Contracts were also received from housing authorities, including the London County Council, for Scottwood Houses, following the successful erection of the prototype in the grounds of the nearby Dibden Hospital in 1945. Scott-Paine actually came up with a scheme for the factories at Hythe and Montreal to co-operate on the production of up to two thousand Scottwood Houses a year, but the scheme was abandoned when the British government refused to allocate timber for the production of the houses.

In February 1946, Scott-Paine, after six years of

45 foot round-bilge Royal Navy Picket Boat.

The prototype Scottwood house being erected in the grounds of Hythe hospital.

living apart from his wife Brenda, obtained a legal separation with a divorce obtained in the State of Nevada. Margaret Dinkeldein wrote to Bill Sheaff:

> I am sure by now that you will have received Mr Scott-Paine's letter and know we are getting married next week. I think Mr John is getting more excitement out of this event than either of us, but naturally we are all very happy about it. I know Mr Scott-Paine had written to Col Searle and Miss Andrew, but I don't think he would mind if you told George Biddlecombe as well. No one else will know until the marriage notice is put in the papers about two weeks after the event.[13]

On February 21st, 1946, Hubert Scott-Paine was married to Margaret Dinkeldein in New York.

Scotty had been suffering from high blood pressure for many years and the happiness of the marriage was marred suddenly when, in April, 1946

174

he suffered a severe stroke while at a theatre in Montreal. The summer months were spent in a cottage on the Maine coast, where Scotty endured a prescription of complete rest and a strict diet, a combination which brought about bouts of severe depression.

Frank Searle retired early in 1946, and, with the slow-down of boat production at Hythe, a Southampton businessman, Percy Preen, was appointed General Manager to look after the factory on a care-and-maintenance basis. Preen visited Montreal and then travelled to Maine to meet Scotty at his holiday cottage during the summer of 1946, and advised him to close the yard at Hythe. He told Scotty that the yard had grown in size during the war to a point where it was uneconomical to run and that he could not see the business in front of it to justify continuing to spend the large amount of money necessary to keep it going in the meantime.

Scotty took the inevitable decision to close down Hythe and Preen returned to dismiss the employees as the existing contracts came to an end. The decision to close down the Hythe yard led to the breaking up of the design team that George Selman had developed into the best in the country, and the dismantling of a mass production facility of unparalleled sophistication and efficiency. Scotty had decided that if he were going to come home, it would be to start a new yard at Marchwood with his old and favourite 'little band of fellows'. The wartime reports of Colonel Searle had soured his view about the yard management, in spite of its evident success. 'I can just imagine the people you mention being disgruntled', the new Mrs Scott-Paine wrote to Bill Sheaff.

'There is no job for any of them any longer at Hythe and being as they are, of course, would not think it necessary to work out their time there—I am sure you will understand what I mean. In a way, if we do start another business at any time at Marchwood I think it would be a good thing to have fresh blood in the business.'[14]

Scotty held on to the hope that his Marchwood project might become a reality, and that his son, John, would help him run the new yard, but the decision to close down Hythe brought about a bout of depression and a further lapse in his health. Although, by November, his health was improving considerably, he then decided to go ahead with the sale of the Montreal factory and to develop a small experimental shop at Greenwich, where a *Sea Beaver* cruiser was produced with the help of Len Munn in

time for the New York Motor Boat Show in January 1947.

Scott-Paine returned to Connecticut where he mused over what he had achieved towards the defeat of Germany and Japan during the war. In stark contrast to the American government's unequivocal acceptance that he had made a significant contribution to the Allied war effort, Scotty's role in developing the motor torpedo boat and the air sea rescue boat, and his role in securing the Packard engine for the Allies in the dark days of 1940, received scant recognition during the postwar review of the role of Coastal Forces undertaken in Britain.

The fact that there had been an engine crisis in 1940 was finally acknowledged in March 1947, when a paper on Coastal Forces Design was presented to the Institution of Naval Architects by W.J. Holt, Chief Constructor of the Naval Construction Department. Admiral Tower admitted to the experts gathered to listen to the paper that the question of engine supply had been a critical problem:

In the early days, we were desperately short of engines. We ordered about thirty boats as soon as war was declared, and it was imagined that we had engines for them. A certain number of Rolls-Royce Merlin engines were to be made available by a pre-war arrangement with the Air Ministry, but, to my horror, I found that we could not have any at all, as all were wanted for aircraft. We had a certain number of Isotta-Fraschini with which we were equipping the 1938 flotilla. I tried to get a few more of these from Italy. We got about thirty per cent of the Isottas we ordered before Italy came into the war. No suitable engines for MTBs became available until the Americans produced the Packard. This was a very serious matter and undoubtedly our early MTBs got a bad name because they had to be equipped with engines of far too little HP, *viz* the Hall-Scott.

Only one of the distinguished gathering actually mentioned Scott-Paine's role in resolving the crisis. In a grudging acknowledgement, J.W. Thornycroft said:

The availability of the Packard was no doubt accelerated by Scott-Paine going to the USA with his 70-foot PV boat in 1939 and his association with Elco Co. This we have to thank him for, although he is not now contributing to the Chancellor of the Exchequer as a resident British citizen in the United Kingdom.[15]

The following month, in April 1947, Scotty took

another turn for the worse when a further stroke left him paralysed down the right side. By December, he had improved and was able to get about the house slowly. Scotty fought hard against his disability but continued to suffer from bouts of acute depression. Bill Sheaff travelled to America to see his old 'governor' during the summer of 1947 and was horrified to see the change that the years of toil and sickness has wrought. Scotty broke down and cried as he saw his old friend who sadly recalled the man who had thought nothing of working sixty or seventy hours without a break, and who had inspired such loyalty and dedication in so many employees over the years. Scotty begged his old employee to rejoin him as a personal assistant and mechanic/chauffeur, but Bill Sheaff had family commitments and went back to England in September.[16]

By Christmas 1947, Scotty was able to get up, shave and dress by himself and was able to walk to the boatyard with the aid of a stick, although he had to resort to his wheelchair to push himself around the yard buildings. The winter months of early 1948 saw a further relapse and Margaret wrote to Bill Sheaff: 'The great difficulty is not to let him get depressed, and of course as soon as we try to get him to stop in bed for a day or two he feels he is back for another six months—as he puts it.'

Despite a series of further relapses, Scotty still hoped to return to England and as Percy Preen sought new occupiers for the Hythe yard, Marchwood House and the Scottwood House were retained as stores for drawings and equipment that he thought might be useful if the Marchwood project ever came to anything. In May 1948, Scotty underwent an experimental operation involving the cutting of major nerves, which it was hoped, would control his high high blood pressure. He appeared to start a slow recovery, and by the summer he was able to walk up and down stairs at Smythe House with little ill effect. Scotty had lost a lot of weight, was looking younger and his perception was again improving. Despite the improvement, he at last acknowledged that his days of active business life were over and he made the final decision to dispose of all his assets in England including Marchwood House and the land where he had hoped to build his new yard. On June 29th, 1948, a special session of the Superior Court was convened at his bedside and, with Judge O'Sullivan presiding, Scotty was made a citizen of the United States of America.[17]

Scott-Paine spent the summer of 1948 in a cottage at Hyannis Port, Cape Cod and, in December, he and Margaret travelled to Barbados for Christmas and then to Florida early the following February. Whilst at Florida, Scotty purchased *Mimosa*, an 80 foot yacht which he intended to use for a leisurely cruise through the inland waterways back to Greenwich. En route he was taken ill in North Carolina where the yacht was laid up and where Scotty was subjected to a strict diet of rice and fruit, an experimental treatment intended to lower his abnormally high blood pressure. Scotty was back at Greenwich by December and, despite the bouts of depression brought on by the frustration of his condition and the strict diet, was delighted to supervise the arrival of crates of his old belongings from The Cliff that he had not seen for ten years.

Scotty spent most of the summer of 1950 cruising in *Mimosa*, and the following winter he was again at the cottage at Cape Cod. He was still an invalid although he was able to go out once or twice in a small sailing dinghy. John Scott-Paine and A. G. Hall continued to work on PV 73 and on January 3rd, 1951, Irwin Chase came up to Greenwich where he had a discussion with John over the future of his father's PV 73. The boat had been completed at Greenwich and an optimistic Scotty had invited officials from the Navy Department to attend trials of the torpedo boat. Chase told John and Margaret that he had been told about the approach but, as there was still a strong anti Scott-Paine feeling in the Department even though many of the officials had changed since the war years, there was little chance of the invitation being accepted.[18]

Scott-Paine fulfilled his wish to return to England when he made a brief visit in October 1951. He sailed to Southampton in the *Caronia*, and travelled to London formally to present *Miss Britain III* to the National Maritime Museum, Greenwich. The liner docked at the quayside in Southampton Docks and Scotty was wheeled in his chair to the top of the gangway. There was some discussion as to how the invalid was to be got down the steep slope, when a burly docker saw the sad figure of the man he remembered from before the war, and whose energy had been legendary. Striding up the gangway, he gathered Scotty in his arms, saying, 'You've been good to me in the past, Gov, now its my turn to do you a good turn!'

Following the presentation at the National Maritime Museum, Scotty and Margaret stayed at a hotel in Brighton, occupying the entire first floor, where they were introduced by Bill Sheaff to Ted Carmen, a Rolls-Royce trained mechanic whom he interviewed as a possible manservant and mechanic in charge of his boats and cars. The Chairman of Rolls-Royce gave a personal undertaking that should it not work out, Carmen would always find a job back with Rolls-Royce. Ted Carmen accompanied Scotty on a holiday to the South of France, then travelled to

Connecticut where he started work on getting the Rolls-Royce Phantom III back on the road. Scotty and Ted Carmen got on well and spent happy hours yarning about the old days and watching movie film of Scotty's many exploits. Scotty had regained his sense of humour and enjoyed conspiring with Ted Carmen to break his diet with illegal snacks, particularly at cocktail parties. The two men enjoyed several long drives in the Rolls, visiting places of interest such as Colonial Williamsburg.[19]

Scotty's love for his home country was intense and in 1953 he again undertook the trip back to Southampton on the *Queen Mary*. He told Ted Carmen that he wanted to come home to live, but upon his arrival, his health rapidly deteriorated and Margaret took the decision to make the journey back to America. A permanent nursing staff was employed to look after the bedridden invalid during the return voyage on the *Queen Elizabeth*. Several of the stewards were old employees from Hythe and gave Scotty a warm welcome. They visited him in his cabin where Carmen spent many hours reading out loud from *The Cruel Sea*, Scotty's favourite book.

Stuart Barker heard about Scotty's death on April 14th, 1954, when a reporter from a Southampton newspaper broke the news to him over the telephone. He was grieved to hear of the death of his old 'governor' whom he still regarded as a close and dear friend. He told the reporter:

He was a genius. He made an outstanding contribution to the motor boat industry. Every one copied him, but no-one has had the genius to produce anything really new since.[20]

Epilogue

On September 29th 1967, five hundred former employees of the British Power Boat Company met at the Top Rank Suite in Southampton. It was the fourth annual re-union of the men and women who had worked at the Hythe Yard and who, despite the fact that it had closed down twenty years earlier, retained a love for the old firm and an undiminished sense of com-radeship. They talked with fond recollection about the remarkable Hubert Scott-Paine who had played such an important part in their lives, and welcomed his son John who, enthused with the spirit of the occasion, had travelled to Southampton from Connecticut to take part in the celebration.[21]

Endnote References

Notes on Sources.
1. Ancramdale Archive: This refers to the collection of papers in the custody of Mrs Joyce Zissu (née Scott-Paine), at Ancramdale, Columbia County, New York State, United States of America. In 1980, John Scott-Paine transferred a portion of this archive to the National Maritime Museum, England. At the time of publication, it is intended that the remainder of this collection will be transferred to the Southampton Maritime Museum, by courtesy of the Scott-Paine family.

2. Barker Collection. This refers to the collection of papers belonging to the late Stuart Barker and donated to the Southampton Maritime Museum in 1989 by his son, Richard Barker.

1 How Many? How Much?
1. *At Close Quarters—PT Boats in the United States Navy*, Capt. R.J. Bulkley Jnr. Naval History Division, Washington (1962), 43.
   Letter from H. Scott-Paine to Stuart Barker, October 6th, 1939. Barker Collection Southampton Maritime Museum.
2. *Courier*, Summer 1939.
3. Interview with Bill Sheaff, January 16th, 1980.
4. Diary by H. Scott-Paine, Ancramdale Archive.
5. 'A Brevet Before Breakfast', Philip Jarrett. *Aeroplane Monthly*, December 1977.
6. *vide* n. 4.
7. *Flight*, March 7th, 1914.
8. *Bats in my Belfry*, unpublished manuscript by G.S. Grey.
9. *vide* n. 4.

2 A Question of Survival
1. 'Boats that Flew: Pemberton Billing Flying Boats 1914–1916', Philip Jarrett. *Air Britain Digest*, September/October 1979.
2. *P-B The Story of His Life*, Noel Pemberton Billing. The Imperialist Press, Hertford (1917).
3. Trophy now in Ancramdale Archive.
4. *The Solent Sky*, Eric New, Southampton (1976), 16.
5. Diary in Ancramdale Archive.
6. *ditto*.
7. 'Mr Billing's War Baby', Philip Jarrett. *Cross and Cockade (GB) Journal* (no date).
   'The Seven Day Baby', Philip Jarrett. *Aeroplane Monthly*, October 1981.
8. *Early Birds*, H.C. Millar. Angus and Robertson (1968).
   The subsequent history of PB 9 is detailed in *Supermarine Aircraft since 1914*, C.F. Andrews and E.B. Morgan. London (1981), 17.
9. 'The Incredible Pemberton Billing', Philip Jarrett. *Aircraft Sixty Nine*. Ian Allan, London (1969).
10. Diary in Ancramdale Archive.

3 A Personal Fortune
1. I am grateful to E.B. Morgan for details of the balance sheet.
   Pemberton Billing, *op. cit*, Chap. 2, n. 2.
2. Letter in Ancramdale Archive. Carol Vasilesco was probably the 'French Draughtsman' referred to by Scott-Paine in his diary entry of February 21st, 1914. The name is Rumanian, a country in which French was a second language at the time.
3. Andrews and Morgan, *op. cit*, Chap. 2, n. 8.
   Letter from Admiral Sueter to Supermarine, March 6th, 1916. Ancramdale Archive.
4. N. Pemberton Billing, *op. cit*, Chap. 2, n. 2.
5. *Air War and How to Win It*, N. Pemberton Billing (1916). This book publishes a retrospective redesignation of the PB designs that is often in conflict with the original designations.
   See also: *The Aeroplane of Tomorrow*, N. Pemberton Billing, London (1941).
6. 'Notes on Flying Boat Hulls', Major Linton Hope. *The Aeronautical Journal*, August 1920.
7. Interview with George Selman, January 1981.
8. Andrews and Morgan, *op. cit*, Chap. 2, n. 8.
9. 'As it was in the Beginning', H.C. Biard, in *Vapour Trails*, London (no date).
10. *British Aviation, The Pioneer Years*, Harald Penrose, London (1966).
11. *Thirty-Eight Years of Public Life in Southampton*, Sir Sydney Kimber. Southampton (1949).
12. *Wings*, H.C. Biard, London (no date), 78 ff.
13. Andrews and Morgan, *op. cit*, Chap. 2, n. 8, 56 ff.
14. *The Schneider Trophy Races*, R. Barker, Shrewsbury (1981), 45 ff.

4. In Pursuit of a Vision
1. 'The AD Flying Boat', J.M. Bruce, *Air Pictorial*, November 1963, 350–355.
   See also: Andrews and Morgan. *op. cit*, Chap. 2, n. 8.
2. H.C. Biard, *op. cit*, Chap. 3, n. 12.
3. *ditto*.
4. *ditto*, 115 ff.
5. *Hampshire Advertiser*, August 11th, 1923.
6. *Hampshire Advertiser*, August 18th, 1923.
7. *Hampshire Advertiser*, September 8, 1923.
8. Andrews and Morgan, *op. cit*, Chap. 2, no. 8, 64–68.
9. C.G. Grey, *op. cit*, Chap. 1, n. 8.
10. Diary in Ancramdale Archive.

5. A Second Career
1. *Wings Across the World*, Harald Penrose, London (1980), 33 ff.
   The inscribed model is in the Ancramdale Archive.
2. Interview with Len Parfitt, July 18th, 1981.
3. Interview with 'Nanny' White, April 28th, 1981.
4. There are various suggestions about the origin of *Tiddlywinks*. One is that the boat was the hull of PB 7, another is that it was the hull of a Supermarine Seagull. Supermarine also constructed speed boats and Lloyds Register of Yachts records it as built by Supermarine in 1919.
5. Interview with Len Parfitt. *vide* n. 2.
6. Prospectus for the Puma One-Class Hydroplane. Published by the Royal Motor Yachts Club, February 15th, 1927. Southampton Maritime Museum.
7. *Southern Daily Echo*. March 10th, 1927.
8. Dairy in Ancramdale Archive.
   Interview with Bill Sheaff, January 16th, 1980.
9. Interview with Len Parfitt. *vide*. n. 2.

6. The Hire'em and Fire'em Yard
1. *Yachting World and Marine Motor Journal*, April 15th, 1922.
2. Interview with Reg Holley, December 4th, 1980.
3. 'For H S-P'. Typescript of history of British Power Boat Company *c.* 1941. K. St John Beaumont Collection. Southampton City Museum.
4. Cutting from *Illustrated London News* (no date), in Southampton Maritime Museum, on the Puppy Dog Class. Photocopy of British Power Boat Catalogue *c.* 1929. Southampton Maritime Museum.
5. Pat. No 325, 839. Date of application, November 29th, 1929, by Hubert Scott-Paine and Fred Cooper.
6. 'The Design and Construction of High-Speed Motor Boats', David Nicolson, *Engineering*, April 19th 1927, 527–530.
7. Letter from British Power Boat Company to Reg Holley. Photocopy in Southampton Maritime Museum.
8. *Yachting World*, March 23rd, 1929.
   Hampshire Advertiser and Southampton Times, March 23rd, 1929.
9. 'Speed Boats and Racing', by H. Scott-Paine, in *The Book of Speed*, Batsford, London (1934).
10. Catalogue of the Science Museum, London (no date).
11. Interview with Len Parfitt. *vide* Chap. 5, n. 2.
12. *The Times*, April 18th, 1929.
13. *Yachting World*, February 2nd and February 9th, 1929.
14. *Hampshire Advertiser and Southampton Times*, March 9th, 1929.
15. *The Times*, April 18th, 1929.

7. The Crest of a Wave
1. *Yachting World*, July 31st, 1931.
2. Interview between Scott-Paine and George Sutton, May 1943. Photocopy in Southampton Maritime Museum.
3. *The Motor Boat*, March 7th, 1930.
4. *Southern Daily Echo*, February 18th, 1930.
5. *Canadian Power Boating*, September, 1930.
   The Motor Boat, August 15th, 1930.
6. *Canadian Power Boating*, September, 1930.
7. Diary in Ancramdale Archive.
8. 'Lawrence and Motor Boats', Sqd Ldr R. Manson. Unpublished typescript *c.* 1978.
9. *Yachting Monthly*, Vol. XLIX (1930), 1440.
   Yachting Monthly, Vol. LI (1930), 208.
10. *The Letters of T. E. Lawrence*, ed. D. Garnett, London (1938), 720–1.
    Letters from T. E. Shaw to Flt Lt. Jinman, April 21st 1931 and April 27th, 1931. Lent to author by Mrs Brazier, daughter of Flt Lt. Jinman.
11. R. Manson, *op. cit*, n. 8.
    The Golden Reign, Clare Sydney Smith (3rd ed 1978).
12. *The Bystander*, July 29th, 1931.
13. *Southern Daily Echo*, various dates in July 1931.
    Yachting World, July 24th, 1931.

8. The Phoenix Rises
1. Interview with John Scott-Paine, September 1980.
2. Although *Miss Britain II* was lost in the fire, the almost identical *Whyteleaf III* survived. In 1936, she was renamed *White Lady II* and taken to Lake Windermere. She sank in the lake on June 20th, 1937, and was recovered forty-five years later. The boat was restored to original working condition and took the waters of the lake with her original engine on July 18th, 1984.
3. Interview with Harry Banks, July 24th, 1980.
4. 'The Progress of the Reconstruction of the British Power Boat Company's Premises following the Disastrous Fire on August 3rd last', typescript dated October 10th, 1931. Ancramdale Archive.
5. *Yachting Monthly*, Vol. LIII (1932), 122.
   The Times, March 30th, 1932.
6. *Motor Boat*, May 6th, 1938.
   Interview between Scott-Paine and George Sutton, May 1943. *vide* Chap. 7, n. 2.
7. *A Prince of our Disorder*, John E. Mack, London (1976), 519, n. 33.
8. *The Times*, Saturday, April 16th, 1932.
   Although Shaw's name is not mentioned in the newspaper reports, his role in the Donibristle run is made clear from a manuscript notebook kept by Shaw containing technical details of trials carried out between November 1931 and July 1932. Personal communication from Prof. Wm Brice, Manchester University.
9. Manson, *op. cit*, Chap. 7, n. 8.
   Letter from Shaw to Flt Lt Jinman June 25th, 1932. *vide* Chap. 7, n. 10.
10. Clare Sydney Smith, *op. cit*, Chap. 7, n. 11.
    See also, Mack, *op. cit*, n. 7, 393.
11. Manson, *op. cit*, Chap. 7, n. 8.
12. D. Garnett, *op. cit*, Chap. 7, n. 10, 742.
13. Interview between Bill Sheaff and Kevin Desmond.
14. *Yachting World and Motor Boating Journal*, April 7th, 1933.

9. The Red Fox of Hythe
1. H. Scott-Paine. Lecture to the Society of Automotive Engineers, Detroit, February 7th, 1944. Transcript in Southampton Maritime Museum.
2. *Yachting World*, March 3rd, 1933.
   The Motor Boat, August 11th, 1933.
3. Interview with George Selman, January, 1981.
4. Interview with Reg Holley, December 4th, 1980.
5. *The Motor Boat*, September 8th, 1933.
   The World Speed Record, Leo Villa and Kevin Desmond, Batsford, London (1976).
6. *The Motor Boat*, September 1933.
   Interview with Len Cox, September 8th, 1981.
7. *The Motor Boat*, November 24th, 1933.
8. *The Daily Telegraph*, December 15th, 1933.
9. 'For S-P', typescript history of British Power Boat Company. St John Beaumont Collection, Southampton Maritime Museum.
10. *Fast Attack Craft*, Kieren Phelan and Martin H. Brice, London (1977), 81 ff.
11. *An Engineer of Sorts*, Peter Du Cane, Lymington (1971).
12. Garnett, *op. cit*, Chap. 7, n. 10, 792–4.
13. 'The Builders of MTB's', A. J. G. Coleborn, *Journal of Naval Engineering*, Vol. 13, No 1 (June 1961), 101–129.
14. See, for instance, Sutton, *op. cit*, Chap. 8, n. 6.

10. A Visit to Devonport
1. *Yachting World and Motor Boating Journal*, March 3rd, 1933.
2. *Yachting World and Motor Boating Journal*, April 20th, 1934.
3. *The Motor Boat*, April 20th, 1934.
   Yachting Monthly, Vol. LVII, (1934), 134.
   Catalogue of British Power Boat Company craft *c*. 1934. Southampton Maritime Museum.
   Shipping World, August 1934 and December 1934.
4. Interview with Vic Stride, 1980.
   The Times, May 15th, 1935.
5. Interview with George Selman January 1981.
6. *The Motor Boat*, September 21st, 1934.
7. *The Aeroplane*, December 12th, 1934.
8. The Estonian incident is referred to in several summary chronologies of the British Power Boat Company. See, for instance, St John Beaumont Collection, Southampton Maritime Museum.
9. *The Motor Boat*, March 8th, 1935.
10. Clare Sydney Smith, *op. cit*, Chap. 7, n. 11, 179.
11. *A Record of a Talk at Devonport*, H. Scott-Paine, privately published, Southampton (1934).
12. Interview with George Selman, January 1981.
13. *The Times*, July 9th, 1935.
    The Motor Boat, August 9th, 1935.
14. *The Motor Boat*, January 31st, 1936.
    Flight, January 30th, 1936.
15. 'High Speed Rescue', R. Bicknell, typescript history of the British Power Boat Company contribution to Air Sea Rescue. Dated: Hythe May 1st, 1946. St John Beaumont Collection. Southampton Maritime Museum.
16. H. Scott-Paine. Lecture to Society of Automotive Engineers of Detroit, *vide* Chap. 9, n. 1.
17. *vide* Chap. 9, n. 9.
18. *Yachting World*, August 9th, 1935.
    The Motor Boat, August 9th, 1935.
19. *Daily Mail*, Monday, September 9th, 1935.
20. Garnett, *op. cit*, Chap. 7, n. 10, 852–3.

11. The Motor Torpedo Boat
1. Correspondence with Graham Cooksey.
   I am grateful to Geoffrey Hudson for details of the building dates.
2. Interview with Graham Cooksey.
3. License in Ancramdale Archive.
4. 'MTB 102', Geoffrey Hudson, typescript history produced on 50th Anniversary of *MTB 102* (1986).
5. Scott-Paine. *vide* Chap. 7, n. 2.
6. Public Record Office ADM 1/9497.
7. Public Record Office ADM 1/9497. Memo dated May 14th, 1937.
8. *The Aeroplane*, June 19th, 1936.
9. *The Motor Boat*, July 3rd, 1936.
10. *The Motor Boat*, July 24th, 1936.
11. Public Record Office ADM 116/4043. Memo from Director of Tactical Division, June 19th, 1936.
    The DTD instructed that the first MTB of the second batch would join the first flotilla so that *MTB 1* could be retained for training and experimental purposes. *MTB 7* was completed within three weeks of official receipt of the order and was accepted on April 5th 1937. This boat was then renumbered *MTB 1*, while the original *MTB 1* became *MTB 7*. The order for the target vessels was placed on August 27th, 1937; one of these, *DCMB 1* was to be radio-controlled, while the other was to be a raft rather than the target hull discussed during the previous August. See: PRO ADM 1/9731. Letter from Director of Naval Contracts to British Power Boat Company, March 4th, 1937. The eighth boat of the 1938 Programme was to be an experimental craft capable of carrying twenty-one inch torpedoes.
12. Public Record Office. ADM 116/4043. Memo from Director of Tactical Division, August 14th, 1936.
    The General Arrangement drawing of the proposed 66 ft boat is in the Ancramdale Archive.
13. Coleborn, *op. cit*, Chap. 9, n. 14.
14. *Southern Daily Echo*, November 13th, 1936.

12. Competition with Vospers
1. Hudson, *op. cit*, Chap. 11, n. 4.
2. Interview with George Selman, January 1981.
3. *The Times*, August 27th, 1937 and August 28th, 1937.
4. Public Record Office ADM 116/4043. Press Acquaint October 9th, 1936.
5. 'Coastal Forces Design', W. J. Holt, *Transactions of the Institute of Naval Architects*, (1947), 186–194. Holt accompanied the flotilla on this voyage.
6. Public Record Office ADM 116/4043. Signal in Cypher A from C-in-C Mediterranean, November 9th, 1937.

7. Public Record Office ADM 116/4043. Minute of November 16th, 1937.
8. Coleborn, *op. cit*, Chap. 9, n. 13.
9. Public Record Office ADM 1/9497. Notes of a meeting between Scott-Paine and Director of Torpedoes and Mining July 9th, 1937.
10. Public Record Office ADM 1/9731. Letter from Scott-Paine to Secretary of the Admiralty October 20th, 1937.
    The land referred to by Scott-Paine was probably portions of Bathurst Farm and the foreshore at Marchwood Magazine on Southampton Water which was sold at Auction at the Dolphin Hotel on Tuesday October 12, 1937.
11. Public Record Office ADM 1/9731. Memo from Director of Naval Equipment October 29th, 1937.
12. Public Record Office ADM 116/4458 Signal to C-in-C Portsmouth January 6th, 1938.
    In the event, the purchase of further anti-submarine boats was included in the 1938 programme.
13. Public Record Office ADM 116/4043. Notes of a meeting held by Chief of Naval Staff, November 26th, 1937.
14. Hudson, *op. cit*, Chap. 11, n. 4.
    A General Arrangement drawing, dated April 10th, 1937, by Tommy Quelch of a proposed 75 foot boat, is in the Ancramdale Archive.
15. J. W. Thornycroft in Holt, *op. cit*, n. 5.
16. *Hansard*, March 17th, 1938, 695 ff.
17. Sheaff Collection, Southampton Maritime Museum.

13. Private Ventures
1. The 1937 Programme included nine 60 foot MTBs (*MTBs 10–18*). Three were to complete the Second Flotilla destined for Hong Kong while six were to form a Third Flotilla at Singapore.
2. *The Times*, January 28th, 1938.
3. Interview with John Scott-Paine, 1980.
4. *Southern Daily Echo*, March 21st, 1938.
5. *Hansard*, April 13th, 1938, 1102 ff.
6. Interview with George Selman, January 1981.
7. *ditto*. See also: 'The Durability of Aerolite 300', Technical Notes 205 from CIBA (ARL) Ltd, (January 1960).
8. 'Report on structural failures in 70 ft and 63 ft boats built by British Power Boat Company', January 22nd, 1944. Barker Collection, Southampton City Museums.
9. Agreement between Rolls-Royce and British Power Boat Company, December 1938. Barker Collection.
    'Some of the Aspects and Problems of the Development of High Speed Craft and its Machinery', H. Scott-Paine. *Thomas Lowe Gray Lecture to the Institution of Mechanical Engineers*, Friday January 6th, 1939.
10. Typescript history of British Power Boat Company in St John Beaumont Collection, Southampton City Museums.
    The engine situation at the beginning of the war is referred to in Holt, *op. cit*, Chap. 12, n. 5.
11. Selman, *vide* n. 6.
12. Patent Specification 515,051. Application dated April 22nd, 1938. Complete Specification accepted November 24th, 1938 in names of Hubert Scott-Paine and James Wrann.
13. Brochure describing PV 70. Sheaff Collection, Southampton Maritime Museum.

14. 'PV 70'
1. *Southern Daily Echo* June 1938.
    Memorandum and Articles of Association of British Power Boat Company. Copy in Southampton Maritime Museum.
2. *Yachting World*, July 8th, 1939.
3. *The Times*, January 2nd, 1939.
    In the event, only two Scott-Paine MTBs were built by Werf Gusto, *TM 52* and *TM 53*. These boats were completed after the German invasion of Holland and eventually became Bulgarian *MTBs 3* and *4*. The remainder of the MTBs ordered by the Royal Netherlands Navy in 1939 and built by Werf Gusto (*TM 54–61*) were an early German E-Boat type. (Information from Geoffrey Hudson). The intention to build Scott-Paine type boats is clear from wartime correspondence between Scott-Paine and Barker concerning the supply of Rolls-Royce engines for the Dutch contract.
4. Interview with George Selman, January 1981.
5. The business arrangement in which Werf Gusto was to build further boats for the Swedish Navy under licence is set out in a letter from Scott-Paine to Packards dated December 1939. Ancramdale Archive.
6. *Shipping World*, January 18th, 1939.
    Selman, *vide* n. 4.
7. *Shipbuilder and Marine Engine Builder*, February 1939.
    Journal of Commerce and Shipping Telegraph, Liverpool, January 12th, 1939.
    Shipping World, January 18th, 1939.
    Glasgow Herald, January 19th, 1939.
    Motor Boat and Yachting, January 20th, 1939.
    Yachting World, January 13th, 1939.
8. 'The Development of the PT', W. C. Specht Cmd USN, and W. S. Humphrey Lt USNR, typescript in Ancramdale Archive.
9. Bulkley, *op. cit*, Chap. 1, n. 1, 29–47.
10. 'The Story Behind the Expendables', Irwin Chase. Typescript in Ancramdale Archive.
    George Woods Humphery had resigned as General Manager of Imperial Airways upon the appointment of Sir John Reith as Chairman in June 1938, and had been recruited by Scott-Paine to represent his interests in America. Scott-Paine had lost his seat on the Board of Imperial Airways at the same time.
11. Copy of the agreement, Barker Collection.
12. Coleborn, *op. cit*, Chap. 9, n. 14.
    Selman, *vide* n. 4.
13. Letter from Barker to Scott-Paine, with covering letter from Admiral F. T. B. Tower, May 30th, 1941. Barker Collection.
14. *The Aeroplane*, May 31st, 1939.
    Reading Evening Gazette, May 27th, 1939.
    Motor Boat and Yachting, May 26th, 1939.
15. Geoffrey Hudson, personal communication.
    The British Power Boat Company developed its own torpedo tubes for the French boats. Torpedo firing experiments were carried out during 1938 in a field near Hythe, using cordite charges developed in association with ICI.
16. Correspondence with Packards. Ancramdale Archive.
17. Minute Book of Marine Design and Engineering Development Corporation in Ancramdale Archive.

18. *Yachting World*, August 12th, 1939.
   Sporting craft such as the 20 foot Sea Arrow continued to be built at this time and a fire-fighting tender was built for use on the River Thames. In June, 1939, a 37 foot 6 inch luxury cruiser was launched for a private owner. cf *Motor Boat and Yachting*, June 16th, 1939.
19. *Hants Advertiser and Southampton Times*, July 8th, 1939.

15. The Outbreak of War
1. Letter from Scott-Paine to W. W. Wright, Company Secretary to British Power Boat Company, September 8th, 1939. Ancramdale Archive.
2. Typescript history of British Power Boat Company. K. St John Beaumont Collection, Southampton Maritime Museum. The extent of establishment resistance to Scott-Paine's training proposals was such that he was not permitted to donate a 37 foot 6 inch tender to Dartmouth College for Training purposes.
3. Barker Collection.
4. Letters from Scott-Paine to Miss Gibbons of British Power Boat Company, sent from the Mohican Hotel, New London. September 27th and October 9th, 1939. Barker Collection.
5. Bulkley, *op. cit*, Chap. 1, n. 1, and interview with John Scott-Paine.
6. *vide* n. 4.
7. Letter from Scott-Paine to Air Marshal Sir C. S. Courtney. 17th October, 1939. Barker Collection.
8. Notes of meeting at the Mohican Hotel, New London, September 28th, 1939. Ancramdale Archive.
9. Recollections of this visit and other aspects of work with Elco have been recorded by Leonard Munn, Technical Assistant from the British Power Boat Company who accompanied Scott-Paine at this time. Manuscript in Southampton Maritime Museum.
10. Details of the modifications to the Packard engine suggested by Scott-Paine are from 'Draft Statement of Claim under the Compensation (Defence) Act 1939—General Claims Tribunal in respect of Packard Marine Engine. Mr Scott-Paine and the British Power Boat Company'. Prepared by R. A. Ball, Company Secretary to BPB Co May 1946. Ancramdale Archive.
11. *vide* n. 4.
12. Letter from Margaret Dinkelein to Barker, October 9th, 1939. Barker Collection.

16. Elco and Packard
1. The Norwegian MTB had been temporarily fitted with the Rolls-Royce engines from PV 70 immediately prior to Scott-Paine's departure for America.
2. Letter from Barker to Scott-Paine, September 19th, 1939 and letter from Scott-Paine to Barker October 18th. Barker Collection.
3. *ditto*.
4. Letter from Maurice Wright to Scott-Paine, November 14th, 1939. Barker Collection.
5. Letter from Scott-Paine to Mr Wardell of Canadian Vickers, October 26th, 1939. Barker Collection.
6. Bulkley, *op. cit*, Chap. 1, n. 1, 47.
7. Letter from L. Y. Spear to Henry Sutphen. Ancramdale Archive.
   Scott-Paine to Barker, November 17th, 1939. Barker Collection.
8. Letter from Scott-Paine to Gilman. October 9th, 1939. Ancramdale Archive.
9. Cables in Ancramdale Archive.
10. Correspondence between Gilman and Scott-Paine. Ancramdale Archive.
11. A letter from Brodie to Scott-Paine on January 11th, 1941, notes that 149 engines were produced during 1940; the first eighty-one going to Elco with the remainder divided between Britain and Canada. Commission payments were made to the Marine Design and Engineering Development Corporation which, for instance, received $90,535.50 commission for technical services in respect of 224 engines between August 1940 and November 1941.
   By the end of the war 4,686 Packard marine engines had either been purchased by the British Purchasing Commission or had been made available to Britain under Lease-Lend. *vide* Chap. 15. n. 10.
12. Copy of agreement with Elco in Barker Collection. It was subsequently recorded by Henry Sutphen that Elco lost $600,000 on the first contract to build boats for the US Navy.
13. Letter from Scott-Paine to Geoffrey Blake, December 1939. Ancramdale Archive.
14. *New York Times*, December 31st, 1939.
15. Barker Collection and Bulkley, *op. cit*, Chap. 1, n. 1.
16. Sheaff Collection, Southampton Maritime Museum.

17. 1940—The Storm Breaks
1. Cable in Ancramdale Archive.
2. Letter from Scott-Paine to Admiral Blake November 28th, 1939. Ancramdale Archive.
3. Lt Walter ('Fish') Rowe of the US Navy was appointed as Superintendent of the Elco construction programme. In order to bypass the Bureau of Ships, Rowe's orders had been signed by President Roosevelt personally and had been passed to him by Secretary of the Navy Edison. (Interview with Walter Rowe, 1984).
4. Letter from Scott-Paine to Admiral Blake. Ancramdale Archive.
5. Correspondence in Barker Collection.
6. Letters between Scott-Paine and Admiral Blake. Ancramdale Archive.
7. Letter from Scott-Paine to Barker April 10th, 1940. Barker Collection.
8. The exploits of the First Flotilla are recorded in '1st MTB Flotilla' by Cdr Charles (Monzie) Donner and 'First-Flot Early Days' by Cdr H. L. (Harpy) Lloyd. See also: *Coastal Forces in the War and Historical Survey part 1: State of Coastal Craft on the Outbreak of War* (no date).
9. Barker Collection and correspondence between Scott-Paine and Admiral Blake. Ancramdale Archive.
10. Public Record Office ADM 116/4458. Minutes of D of L 29/8/39 and 13/9/39.
   ADM 116/4458 memo from Capt. A/S HMS *Osprey*, September 1939.
   Policy for Coastal Forces was established at a meeting held by the Deputy Chief Naval Staff on Monday October 30th. PRO ADM 116/4458.
11. Notes of a meeting held at the War Office, May 20th, 1940. Ancramdale Archive.
12. Cable dated May 17th, 1940. Ancramdale Archive.
13. Letter from Scott-Paine to Frank Bishop. May 18th, 1940. Ancramdale Archive.
14. Letter from Scott-Paine to Winston Churchill. May 22nd, 1940. Ancramdale Archive.

18. The Canadian Power Boat Company
1. Letter from M. Wright to Scott-Paine at 1, East Putnam Avenue, Greenwich, Connecticut, June 7th, 1940. Ancramdale Archive.
2. Letter from Scott-Paine to Admiral Blake April 12th, 1940. Ancramdale Archive.
3. 'Scott-Paine's Canadian MTBs', George W. Sutton *Motor Boating* (Canada), September 1942, 2-6.
4. Correspondence between Brodie and Scott-Paine. Ancramdale Archive.
5. Letter from M. Wright to Scott-Paine, May 23rd, 1940. Ancramdale Archive.

6. Letter from M. Wright to Scott-Paine, June 15th, 1940. Ancramdale Archive.
7. Letter from Scott-Paine to Barker, July 1st, 1940. Barker Collection.
8. 'He Who Thinks He Can. Adventures in Canada of the Private Venture Boat Designed and Built by Mr Hubert Scott-Paine', typescript. Ancramdale Archive.
   'CMTB 1—Adventures in Canada of the Private Venture Boat Designed and Built by Hubert Scott-Paine', *The Marine Engineer*, June 1941, 134–5.
9. 'The Canadian Power Boat Co. Ltd. History of the Firm from its Inception', typescript. Ancramdale Archive.
   'Canadian Power Boat Company Limited. Diary of Events', typescript. Ancramdale Archive.
10. Letter from Scott-Paine to Barker, August 26th, 1940. Barker Collection.
11. Letter from Scott-Paine to his brother Victor, February 17th, 1941. Ancramdale Archive.
12. Memo, April 3rd, 1941. Ancramdale Archive.
13. *vide* n. 11.
14. *The Aeroplane*, May 9th, 1941, 523.
15. Letter from Scott-Paine to his brother Victor, March 8th, 1941. Ancramdale Archive.
16. Letter from Scott-Paine to Barker, November 27th, 1940. Barker Collection.
17. 'Log of journey of *CMTB 1* from Montreal to Halifax, November 25th to December 21st, 1940', typescript signed James A Yeaman. Ancramdale Archive.

19. The Boats go to War
1. Letter from Maurice Wright to Scott-Paine, June 7th, 1940. Ancramdale Archive.
2. *The Battle of the Narrow Seas*, Lt Cdr Peter Scott, Country Life Books, London (1945), 7–8.
   De Schepen van de Koninklijke en die den Governementsmarine 1918–1942, A. J. Vermeulen.
3. Letter from Frank Bishop to Barker in America, May 24th, 1940. Ancramdale Archive.
4. Daily Reports from Cherbourg by K. St John Beaumont and *Cherbourg Intermission*, handwritten account of personal experiences. St John Beaumont Collection, Southampton Maritime Museum.
5. Details of the British Power Boats craft at Dunkirk from Geoffrey Hudson. See also *Finest Hour: Winston S. Churchill 1939–1941*, Martin Gilbert, London (1983), 432.
6. Notes of meeting held on May 23rd, 1940. Ancramdale Archive.
7. Public Record Office ADM 116/4458. Letter from M. Wright, July 6th, 1940, and report on trial of experimental 63 foot boat, June 25th, 1940.
   Also George Selman, personal communication.
   The South African boats were ordered as 64 foot boats in 1939 but, following the trials of the prototype boat (No 1447) in June 1940, the order was completed as 63 foot boats. Analysis of ''brought on charge'' dates and yard numbers has established that the nine South African boats were taken over by the Royal Air Force as HSL 141–149. See Appendix 3.
   In 1940, *MA/SBs 6–30* were allocated to Air Sea Rescue Duties at Milford Haven, Portsmouth and Harwich. The Directorate of Air Sea Rescue was formed within the Air Ministry on February 1st, 1941, to co-ordinate all air-sea rescue work which until then had been carried out by the Royal National Lifeboat Institution, Trinity House, the Royal Navy and the Royal Air Force.
8. Letter from M. Wright to Scott-Paine, June 15th, 1940. Ancramdale Archive.
9. *New York Herald Tribune*, June 19th, 1940.
10. Letter from Scott-Paine to Barker, July 1st, 1940. Ancramdale Archive.
    New York Times, June 20th, 1940.
    New York Herald Tribune, June 25th, 1940.
11. Gilbert *op. cit*, n. 5, 605.
12. Letter from Blake to Scott-Paine October 22nd, 1940. Ancramdale Archive.
13. Public Record Office ADM 116/4458. Memo from Director of Anti-Submarine Warfare August 12th, 1940.
14. 'Design Office Report on 71 ft 6 in Motor Gun Boat', George Selman, January 1944. Barker Collection.
15. *vide* Chap. 18, ns 8 and 17.
    'Spite Wind and Weather', *Yachting Monthly*, July 1941, 196–8.

20. Reports from Hythe
1. Letter from Scott-Paine to V. Scott-Paine, February 17th, 1941. Ancramdale Archive.
2. Letter from Scott-Paine to Barker, February 21st, 1941. Barker Collection.
3. 'Extracts from My American Diary', Rt Hon. Sir Walter Citrine KBE, typescript. Ancramdale Archive.
4. Letters from Stuart Barker. Barker Collection.
5. Details of the agreement between the Admiralty and the British Power Boat Company are in the Barker Collection.
6. Letter from Barker to Scott-Paine, June 25th, 1941. Barker Collection.
   The first boat to be re-engined was *MA/SB 13* (Yard No 1552). Information from Len Cox.
7. Letter from Scott-Paine to Barker. Barker Collection.
   Interview with George Selman, January 1941.
8. *We Fought them in Gunboats*, Lt Cdr Robert Peverell Hichens, London (1944).
9. *vide* Chap. 19, n. 14.
   Interview with George Selman, January 1981.
   For confirmation of the outstanding success of the type see, for instance, Holt, *op. cit*, Chap. 12, n. 5.
   'Notes by G. Selman on British Power Boat Company Craft', typescript of lecture given *c*. 1944 to Marine Mountings Ltd. St John Beaumont Collection, Southampton Maritime Museum.
   Detailed description of proposed MGB and 'Specification of 24 Motor Gun Boats', typescript. Ancramdale Archive.
10. Twenty-four motor gun boats were ordered in late 1940, but sixteen were cancelled in early 1941, leaving eight boats, *MGB 74–81*, to be completed. The first boat was completed on February 14th, 1942.
11. Scott-Paine to Barker, 25th March, 1941. Barker Collection.

21. Lend Lease and the Plywood Derbies
1. Bulkley, *op. cit*, Chap. 1, n. 1, 51–2.
2. Barker Collection.
3. Interview with John Scott-Paine, September 1980.
4. Letter from Scott-Paine to Barker, July 31st, 1941. Barker Collection.
5. Bulkley, *op. cit*, Chap. 1, n. 1, 52.
6. 'Scott-Paine and Elco Motor Torpedo Boats', Leonard Munn (September 1983), typescript. Southampton Maritime Museum.
7. Bulkley, *op. cit*, n. 5, 57.
8. Letter from Scott-Paine to Barker, May 27th, 1941. Barker Collection.
9. Letter from Barker to Scott-Paine, May 30th, 1941. Barker Collection.

10. Letter from Admiral F. T. B. Tower to Scott-Paine June 5th, 1941. Barker Collection.
11. Memo on alterations to the design of 70 foot boats at Montreal. Ancramdale Archive.
12. Letter from Scott-Paine to Barker, June 1st, 1941. Barker Collection.
13. *The Naval Services of Canada Vol. II*, G. N. Tucker, Ministry of National Defence, Ottawa (1952), 48.
14. *Greenwich Times*, October 19th, 1941.
15. 'Account of the movement of Scott-Paine High-Speed Surface Craft from Montreal to Greenwich, Connecticut 1941', typescript. Ancramdale Archive.

22. Turning of the Tide
 1. Letter from Scott-Paine to Barker, October 5th, 1941. Barker Collection.
 2. Letter from Barker to Scott-Paine, November 15th, 1941. Barker Collection.
 3. Bulkley, *op. cit*, Chap. 1, n. 1.
 4. *They were Expendable*, W. L. White New York (1942).
 5. Memo by H. Scott-Paine on attempts to influence Canadian motor torpedo boat policy, dated July 24th, 1942. Ancramdale Archive.
    Interview with John Scott-Paine September 1980.
 6. 'Scott-Paine's Canadian MTBs', George W. Sutton, *Motor Boating* (Canada), September 1942, 2–6.
 7. *Ships of Canada's Naval Forces 1910–1981*, Collins, Toronto (1981), 141.
 8. *vide* n. 5.
 9. 'Aide Memoire on Features of PV-73 with Particular Reference to Differences and Improvements on 70 ft Boat', typescript, dated February 7th, 1951, by A. G. Hall. Information from A. G. Hall.
10. Sheaff Collection. Southampton Maritime Museum.
    Interview with George Selman, January 1981.
11. A long memo from Hichens on possible improvements to gun boats is incorporated in the design office report, *vide* Chap. 19, n. 14.
12. 'Staff Requirements for Air/Sea Rescue Marine Craft', signed G. Barnard A/SR 1. Barker Collection.
13. Details from reports prepared by Departmental Heads for monthly Board Meetings at Hythe. Barker Collection.
14. *vide* n. 11.
15. Design Office Report March 1944. Barker Collection.
16. Design Office Reports, various dates 1943/44. Barker Collection.
    Interview with Kenneth St John Beaumont.
17. Correspondence in Sheaff Collection.
18. Letter from Bill Sheaff to Scott-Paine, January 24th, 1943. Sheaff Collection.

23. The End of an Era
 1. Letter from Scott-Paine to William McComb of Packard, December 30th, 1943. Ancramdale Archive.
 2. Letter from Scott-Paine to Admiral Blake. Ancramdale Archive.
 3. Details of production at Hythe and Poole is contained in the Board Meeting Reports. Barker Collection.
 4. Design Office Report February 1944.
 5. 'The Scottwood House Designed by the British Power Boat Company', *The Architect and Building News*, April 26th, 1946.
    The prototype Scottwood House was constructed in the grounds of Hythe Hospital and is still in use as a private residence in Noads Way, Dibden Purlieu, near Hythe.
 6. Letter from Beauforte-Greenwood to Stuart Barker, no date—summer 1942. Barker Collection.
 7. Letter from Barker to Scott-Paine 6th August 1944. Barker Collection.
 8. Design Office reports to Board Meeting, Barker Collection.
    Interview with George Selman, January 1981.
 9. 'Report on Special Type of Mudshoes Designed for Use on Impassable Mud Terrain', A. G. Hall, typescript per A. G. Hall. Southampton Maritime Museum.
10. Letter from Scott-Paine to Ted Meyer. Ancramdale Archive.
11. Ancramdale Archive.
12. George Selman, *vide* n. 8.
13. Letter from Margaret Dinkeldein to Bill Sheaff, February 12th, 1946. Sheaff Collection.
14. The British Power Boat Company went into voluntary liquidation on October 31st, 1952. The assets at the commencement of liquidation were valued at £410,000. In December 1953, the shipyard at Hythe was sold to the Commercial Union Ltd for £110,000.
15. Holt, *op. cit*, Chap. 12, n. 5.
16. Interview with Bill Sheaff.
17. Details from letters to Bill Sheaff from Mrs Scott-Paine. Sheaff Collection.
18. Record of a conversation with Mr Chase on Wednesday, January 3rd, 1951. Ancramdale Archive.
19. Ted Carmen, personal communication.
20. *Southern Evening Echo*, Thursday, April 15th, 1954.
21. *Southern Evening Echo*, Tuesday, November 10th, 1964 and, September 30th, 1967.
    The re-unions were organised by Mr Bill (Hoppy) Wilson of Hythe.

Appendices

Compiled in collaboration with Geoffrey Hudson

Appendix 1

Summary of Contracts with Supermarine Aviation 1914–1917

As listed by Hubert Scott-Paine in a personal notebook
in the Scott-Paine family papers.

Date	Contract No	Details
1914	CP 65552/14/ × 29591	Repair to Sopwith 137 Seaplane
1914	CP 63375/14/ × 23258	Repair to B.E.2 C and B
1914	CP 70706/14/ × 32810	Repair to R.E.5, No 26

1915	CP 49282/15/P.5244	Repair to Sopwith Type 806
1915	CP 37655/15/P.52475	Repair to Avro Type 504B No 1017
1915	CP 76972/15/P.53943	Repair to Bristol Type TB.8 No 1226
1915	CP 53265/15/P.53578	Repair to Sopwith 806 No 802
1915	CP 79936/15/P.56836	Repair to Avro Type 504B No 1032
1916	CP 171720/R.14/2322	Repair to Avro Type 504B No 1002
1915	CP 62042/15	Construction of PB 23E, Push-Proj 236 No 8487
1916	CP 172285/R.31.2992	Modifications to Sopwith Schneider Cup Machine 3726
1916	CP 173688/P.69/4419	Repair to Sopwith Schneider Cup Machine 3719
1916	CP 173771/R.71/4474	Repair to Avro Type 510 seaplanes Nos 130, 134
1916	CP 202219/R858a	Repair to B.E.2C No 1170
	CP 202443/R/148/937a	Repair to Bristol Scout Type 'C' No 3050
28. 5.16	CP 109611/16/ × 15846	Construction of AD Flying Boats Nos 1412 and 1413
	CP 105865/16/ × 15939	Shorts' Packing Cases
25. 6.15	CP 50249/15/ × 33846	Construction of Shorts Aircraft Nos 1580–1591 (twelve)
5.11.15	CP 146767/15/ × 48642	Construction of PB 23 Pusher Scouts Nos 9001–9020 (twenty). Delivery twenty-four weeks from date.
28. 3.16	CP 109444/16/	Construction of Nighthawk Experimental PB 31E Nos 1388–1389
24. 5.16	CP 113726/16/	Construction of Admiralty Navyplanes 9095–9096
25.10.16	CP 131157/16/ × CP 133372/16/ ×	Construction of AD Navyplanes N1070–1074 (five)
7.10.16	CP 129957/16/ × 29432	AD 1412 Spare wings
8.11.16	CP 131623/16/ × 34363	Pusher Scout Spares
21. 1.17	CP 100428/17/ ×	AD 1412 Experimental wings
16. 2.17	CP 105013/17	Supermarine Patrol Machines N24 and N25. Cancelled 1917
12. 5.17	AS 5388/17/C.A.2.	AD Flying Boats N 1520–1529 and 1710–1719 (twenty)
28. 6.17	AS 17278/17	N.1.B Single Seater seaplane N59–N61 (three)
16. 7.17	AS 18936/17	AD Flying Boats N2450–2499 (fifty). Only N2450–2455 (six) built.

Appendix 2

Pre-War Motor Torpedo Boat Development by British Power Boat Company

60 foot Type Programme	Admiralty No	Date Accepted	Renumbered
1935	MTB 1	17. 5.36	MTB 7₂, MTB 13₂, MTB 19
	MTB 2	13. 8.36	
	MTB 3	24. 8.36	
	MTB 4	22. 9.36	
	MTB 5	12.10.36	
	MTB 6	17.11.36	
1936	MTB 7	5. 4.37	MTB 1₂
	MTB 8	3. 9.37	
	MTB 9	8.10.37	
	MA/SB 1	13. 4.38	
	MMS 51	29. 4.38	MTB 100
	DCMB 1	23. 5.38	
Private Motor Yacht (Yard No 1326)	Kalan	1938	Hired as Anti-Submarine Yacht October 1939. Purchased by Admiralty October 1941. Anti-submarine training May 1941. Target Service 1944–1946.
1937	MTB 10	11. 7.38	
	MTB 11	26. 7.38	
	MTB 12	3. 8.38	
	MTB 13	31. 8.38	MTB 7₃
	MTB 14	25.10.38	
	MTB 15	17. 2.39	
	MTB 16	3. 3.39	
	MTB 17	17. 3.39	
	MTB 18	24. 3.39	
1938	MA/SB 2	15. 5.39	
	MA/SB 3	13. 6.39	
	MA/SB 4	30. 7.39	
	MA/SB 5	21. 7.39	
	MA/SB 6	21.12.39	Built as Prototype 70 foot Motor Anti-Submarine Boat.

70 foot Type

PV 70	Launched 6.11.38	Shipped without engines to Canada in 1940. Became Canadian *MTB 1*, then Royal Navy *MTB 332* and finally Royal Air Force *HSL 332* serving in India.
TM 51	Ordered for Dutch Government December 1938 and delivered 1939	Taken over by Admiralty as *MA/SB 46* 13. 7.40 Shipped to America
PT 9	Ordered March 1939	September 1939 as prototype of Elco 70 foot PT boats. Scheduled to transfer to Royal Navy as *MTB 258* under Lend-Lease, but became Royal Canadian Navy *MA/SB 09*.
MA/SB 6	Accepted 21.12.39	Prototype 70 foot MA/SB with three Napier Lion engines. Followed by order for *MA/SB 7–39* (thirty-three boats) in September 1939 as part of Emergency War Programme.
VTB 23–40	Ordered by French Government during Summer 1939	Taken over by Admiralty as *MA/SB 50–67*

63 foot Type

T 1–2	Designed by January 1939 Ordered by Swedish Government, 1939	Requisitioned by Admiralty as *MA/SB 40* and *41*
MTB 1–4	Ordered by Norwegian Government, 1939	Requisitioned by Admiralty as *MA/SB 42–45*

Notes on re-numbering of 60 foot MTBs

1. The original *MTB 1* was returned to the builders after a successful demonstration with *MTB 2* with King Edward VIII on board on June 30th, 1936. In April 1937, in order to bring the 1st MTB flotilla up to strength of six boats to sail to the Mediterranean on June 22nd, 1937, *MTB 7* was renumbered *MTB 1₂*, *MTB 1₁* was renumbered *MTB 7₂* and remained with the builders at Hythe.

2. In 1938, *MTB 13* was renumbered *MTB 7₃* to enable the 2nd MTB Flotilla to be shipped to Hong Kong in September 1938 as *MTB 7–12*, *MTB 7₂*, the original MTB 1 was renumbered *MTB 13₂*.

3. The new *MTB 13₂*, had its number changed again in order to avert the superstition attaching to the number 13. In June 1938, it was renumbered *MTB 19*.

Pre-war development of High Speed Launches for the Royal Air Force
64 foot Type

Year	Service No	Delivered	Comments
1935	HSL 100	1936	Prototype. Yard No 884 Tender date 24.7.35. Contract CP Branch 8/10328/35
1936	HSL 101–105	1937–1938	Three ordered July 1936
	HSL 106	1938	Contract date not recorded
1936	HSL 107–114	1937–1939	Contract in late 1936
1938	HSL 115–116	1939–1940	Contract date 1938
1939	HSL 117–132	1940	Contract 931160/39, 1939. Only HSL 117–121 were completed as 64 foot boats

Appendix 3

Summary of wartime production of the British Power Boat Company at
Hythe and Poole

Part A: Production at Hythe

Type	Hull	Yard No	Service/ Service No	Comments	Quantity
September 1939–September 1940					
Fast Motor Dingy	16ft		Royal Navy		25
Fast Motor Dingy	16ft		Royal Air Force		9
Bomb Dingy	18ft		Royal Air Force		1
Fuel Dingy	20ft		Royal Air Force		8
Sea Rover	23ft				2

Fast Motor Boat	25ft		Royal Navy		15
Fast Motor Boat	30ft				3
Seaplane Tender	35ft		Royal Air Force		4
Fast Motor Boat	35ft		Royal Air Force		6
Seaplane Tender	37ft 6in		Includes *ST 292–303* and *323*, and possibly 287–291	Earlier boats *ST 265–291* had Yard Nos 1289–1315	18
Armoured Target Boat	40ft			Probably includes *A 559–561* and *556* Two boats for South Africa (Yard Nos 1516 trials 23.10.39 and 1628 trials 21.12.39) and Yard No 1535 shipped to Canada 1940	7
Picket Boat	45ft		Royal Navy		3
Motor Torpedo Boat	63ft	includes 1374 (Swedish boat)	*MA/SB 40–45*	Sweden *T 1–2* Norway *MTB 1–4*	6
High Speed Launch	64ft		*HSL 114–121*		9
		1371	*Malmock*	For South Africa Prototype	1
Motor Anti-Submarine Boat	70ft	1546–1553	*MA/SB 6*		1
			MA/SB 7–14		8
			MA/SB 46	Dutch *TM 51*	1
			MA/SB 50–59	French *VTB 23–32*	10
				Total for Year	**136**
October 1940–September 1941					
Fast Motor Dingy	16ft		Royal Navy		23
Fast Motor Dingy	16ft		Royal Air Force		1
Bomb Dingy	18ft		Royal Air Force		40
Fast Motor Dingy	25ft		Royal Navy		18
High Speed Launch	32ft				1
Seaplane Tender	37ft 6in		Possibly *ST 324*		1
Armoured Target Boat	40ft		Includes *A 597–600* and two unknown		6
Seaplane Tender	41ft 6in	1846–1849	ST 357–366 ST 436–439		14
High Speed Launch	63ft	Includes 1499	*HSL 122–133*	122–124 ordered as 64 foot boats in 1939 Nine South African Air Force boats completed as HSL's for Royal Air Force	21
		Includes 1477 (Prototype South African boat), and 1632	*HSL 141–149* (*HSL 143*)		
Motor Anti-Submarine Boat	63ft	1561–1571	*MA/SB 22–32*	Ordered as 70 foot boats with *MA/SB 7–21*	11
Motor Anti-Submarine Boat	70ft	1554–1555	*MA/SB 15–16*		2
Motor Gun Boat	70ft	1556–1559	*MGB 17–20*	Ordered *MA/SB 17–20*	4
			MGB 60–67	French *VTB 33–40*	8
				Total for Year	**150**
October 1941–September 1942					
Queen Gull	12ft 6in		War Dept.		18
Fast Motor Dingy	16ft		Royal Navy		3
Bomb Dingy	18ft		Royal Air Force		8
Fast Motor Boat	25ft		Royal Navy		4
Seaplane Tender	41ft 6in	1850–1855 1886–1903	*ST 440–445* *ST 1500–1517*		24
High Speed Launch	63ft	1827–1831 1856–1885 1951–1953	*HSL 134–140* *HSL 156–160* *HSL 161–190* *HSL 2546–2548*	See Note 1	36
Motor Anti-Submarine Boat	63ft	1572–1578	*MA/SB 33–39*		7
Motor Gun Boat	70ft	1560	*MGB 21*		1
Motor Gun Boat	71ft 6in	1800–1807	*MGB 74–81*	Five survivors became *MTB 412–416*	8
		1808–1809	*MGB 107–109*	Two survivors became *MTB 417* and *418*	3
				Total for year	**112**
October 1942–September 1943					
Queen Gull	12ft 6in	Includes 1662/3, 1673, 1675–1678, 1681, 1684, 1686–1704, 1706, 1726–1741 (forty-five known)	Royal Navy and War Office	Includes at least nine to Royal Navy 1662/3, 1676–1678, 1681, 1684, 1687, 1690	59
Fast Motor Dingy	16ft	1933–1949	RN *41701–41717*		17
Salvage Dingy	18ft	2215	Royal Air Force		1
Fast Motor Boat	25ft	includes twenty boats 1910–1929	RN *41722–41741*		32
Seaplane Tender	41ft 6in	1904–1905 2152–2180	*ST 1518–1519* *ST 1592–1620*		31
High Speed Launch	63ft	1954–1956	*HSL 2549–2551*		3

High Speed Launch	68ft	1999–2001	*HSL 2552–2554*		46
		2003–2009	*HSL 2556–2562*		
		2010–2013	*HSL 2579–2582*		
		2053–2066	*HSL 2593–2606*		
		not known	*HSL 2619–2631*		
		2185–2189	*HSL 2677–2681*		
Motor Gun Boat	71ft 6in	1811–1823	*MGB 110–122*	Twelve survivors became *MTB 430–441*	21
		2014–2021	*MGB 123–130*	Later *MTB 442–449* (*MGB 123* was the prototype *MTB 446*)	
				Total for Year	**210**

October 1943–September 1944

Queen Gull	12ft 6in	Includes 1716, 1718, 1720, 1721, 1745, 1753, 2023	War Dept.		33
Queen Pelican	30ft		War Dept.		1
Seaplane Tender	41ft 6in	2181–2184	*ST 1621–1624*		4
High Speed Launch	68ft	2190–2199	*HSL 2682–2691*		10
Motor Gun Boat	71ft 6in	2226–2233	*MGB 131–138*	Later *MTB 450–457*	8
Motor Torpedo Boat	71ft 6in	2235	*MTB 458*	First Mark VI Boat	1
		2236–2266	*MTB 459–489*		31
				Total Eight months	**88**

October 1944–end June 1945

Queen Gull	12ft 6in		War Dept.		21
Fast Motor Dingy	16ft		Royal Navy		10
Bomb Dingy	18ft		Royal Air Force		1
Seaplane Tender	41ft 6in		*ST 1634–1636* and five unknown		8
Fast Launch	44ft 6in		War Dept.	'River' Class	3
Medium Speed Picket Boat	45ft		Royal Navy	Round Bilge	6
Motor Torpedo Boat	71ft 6in		MTB *490–497* and *MTB 499–506*		16
				Total for year	**65**

Boats completed 30.6.45–30.9.45

Fast Motor Boat	16ft		Royal Navy		17
Fast Launch	44ft 6in		War Dept.	'River' Class	14
Medium Speed Picket Boat	45ft		Royal Navy	Round bilge	6
High Speed Launch	68ft		*HSL 2739*		1
Motor Torpedo Boat	71ft 6in		*MTB 498*	delivery delayed for extra trials	1
				Total for 3 months	**39**

Orders outstanding 30.9.45

Fast Motor Boat	16ft		Royal Navy	ten further boats were cancelled 26. 9.45	13
Marine Tender	25ft		Royal Air Force probably *3184–3186*	twenty-seven further boats were cancelled 2/26. 9.45	3
Fast Launch	44ft 6in		War Dept.	Last 'River Class' boat delivered March 1946 fifty-eight further boats cancelled 3. 9.45	23
Medium Speed Picket Boat	45ft		Royal Navy	Round bilge twenty-one further boats were cancelled 26. 9.45	7
General Service	50ft		War Dept.	Round Bilge 'Dickens' Class Last boat delivered Feb 1947 twenty-one further boats cancelled 25. 9.45	19
High Speed Launch	68ft	2321–2359	*HSL 2740–2746*	thirty-two further boats *HSL 2747–2778* (2328–2359) were cancelled 21.11.44	7
Motor Torpedo Boat	71ft 6in		*MTB 507–509* *MTB 519–522*		7
Long Range Rescue Craft	111ft		Royal Air Force	Hull only completed Cancelled 22. 9.45	
				Total	**79**

Part B: Production at No 2 Factory, Poole

As well as repairs to coastal craft, the replacement of Napier Lion engines with Packard engines and conversion of pre-war craft for target towing service, production at Poole included the following:

Type	Hull	Yard No	Service/ Service No	Comments	Quantity
Marine Tender	24ft		Royal Air Force	Contract MC308/C42A 1942/43	84
High Speed Launch	63ft	including 1861, 1863, 1872, 1874, 1878, 1879	including *RAF HSL, 166, 168, 177, 179, 183, 184*		9
High Speed Launch	68ft	2002 2200–2214 2216–2225	*HSL 2555* *HSL 2692–2706* *HSL 2707–2716*		26
Target Towing Launch	68ft	2273–2293	Royal Army Service Corps	'Battlefield' Class. Last boat delivered January 1945	21

Note

1. Thirty-six 63ft High Speed Launches are recorded as having been built at Hythe in 1941/1942. The thirty numbers recorded here (*HSL 161–190*) include the nine boats built at Poole, of which two, at least, (1878/9 *HSL 183* and *184*) were not completed until 1942–43.

Appendix 4

Summary of production by the Canadian Power Boat Company of Montreal and by Elco

The Canadian Power Boat Company

Boat No	Service/Service No	Planned launch date	Comments
1000	RCN: V 250 (*CMTB 1*)	12.40	Ex PV 70 built at Hythe. Became *MTB 332* then *HSL 332*.
1001	RCN: *V 254*	7. 6.41	Became *MTB 333* then *HSL 333*
1002	RCN: *V 252*	17. 5.41	Became *MTB 334* then *HSL 334*
1003	RCAF: *M 208*	16. 6.41	
1004	RCAF: *M 231*	23. 6.41	
1005	RCN: *V 253*	31. 5.41	*MTB 335* then *HSL 335*
1006	RCAF: *M 232*	28. 7.41	
1007	RCAF: *M 233*	21. 7.41	
1008	RCN: *V 251*	30. 6.41	Became *MTB 336* then *HSL 336*
1009	RCAF: *M 234*	4. 8.41	
1010	RCAF: *M 235*	11. 8.41	
1011	RNN: *TM 22*	14. 7.41	
1012	RCN: *V 255*	18. 8.41	*MTB 337* then *HSL 337*
1013	RNN: *TM 23*	25. 8.41	
1014	RCN: *V 256*	1. 9.41	*MTB 338*
1015	RNN: *TM 24*	8. 9.41	
1016	RCN: *V 257*	15. 9.41	*MTB 339*
1017	RNN: *TM 25*	22. 9.41	
1018	RCN: *V 258*	29. 9.41	*MTB 340* then *HSL 340*
1019	RNN: *TM 26*	6.10.41	
1020	RNN: *TM 27*	13.10.41	
1021	RCN: *V 259*	20.10.41	*MTB 341* then *HSL 341*
1022	RNN: *TM 28*	27.10.41	
1023	RCN: *V 260*	3.11.41	*MTB 342* then *HSL 342*
1024	RNN: *TM 29*	10.11.41	
1025	RCN: *V 261*	17.11.41	*MTB 343* then *HSL 343*
1026	RNN: *TM 30*	24.11.41	The boats of the second order of eight MTBs for the Royal Netherlands Navy (TM 30–37) were not completed until Summer 1942.
1027	RNN: *TM 31*	1.12.41	
1028	RNN: *TM 32*	8.12.41	
1029	RNN: *TM 33*	15.12.41	
1030	RNN: *TM 34*	22.12.41	Became USN *PT 368*
1031	RNN: *TM 35*	29.12.41	Became USN *PT 369*
1032	RNN: *TM 36*	5. 1.42	Became USN *PT 370*
1033	RNN: *TM 37*	12. 1.42	Became USN *PT 371*

40ft Boats

Boat No	Service/Service No	Planned launch date	Comments
1535	RCAF	24. 2.41 (completion, not launch date)	The hull of the first ATB was shipped from Hythe in 1940 and subsequent yard numbers may be a continuation of a Hythe number sequence. All the boats laid down as armoured target boats were completed as target towing launches.

1536	RCAF	6. 3.41
1537	RCAF	16. 3.41
1538	RCAF	21. 3.41
1539	RCAF	25. 3.41
1540	RCAF	29. 3.41

Summary of Production at Montreal

Royal Canadian Air Force (RCAF)	6 boats	
Royal Canadian Navy (RCN)	11 boats	plus PV 70 from Hythe
Royal Netherlands Navy (RNN)	16 boats	
Armoured Target Boats (RCAF)	5 boats	plus one hull from Hythe
Experimental PV 73 MTB	1 boat	not completed
Total	**39 boats**	

Elco production for the United States Navy

70 ft Elco/Scott-Paine Boats	*PT 10–19*	Became *MTB 259–268*
	PTC 1–12	Became *MGB 82–93*
77 ft Elco Boats	*PT 20–68*	*PT 49–68* became *MTB 307–326*
80 ft Elco Boats	*PT 103–138*	
	PT 139–196	
	PT 314–361	
	PT 362–367	
	PT 372–383, 546–563	Originally Russian PT boat order *RPT 1–30*
	PT 486–545	
	PT 565–624	
	PT 731–790	Thirty-two were cancelled 1945

A total of 358 Elco 80 foot boats were ordered and 326 were completed.

Photographic acknowledgements

All photographs are in the collections of the Southampton City Museums other than the following. Numbers refer to page numbers.

Ancramdale Archive: 11, 14, 17, 19, 21, 57, 96, 97
Mrs Elizabeth Ridgway: 39, 92
Kieren Phelan: 46, 106
Mrs R. Woodgate: 85
Wright and Logan: 88
G. Hudson: 113, 161
L. Munn: 120, 128, 146, 148, 150, 156, 157, 158, 160
Public Archives (Canada): 129, 139, 162
D.E.J. Hunt: 145, 154
A.D.G. Gordon: 165 (upper)

Index